About the Authors

Mette Bryld is associate professor at the Department of Russian and East European Studies at Odense University, Denmark. She has published a number of books within the field of cultural studies with a focus on Soviet civilization, Russian culture, and feminism.

Nina Lykke is professor in gender and culture at the Department of Gender Studies, Linkoeping University, Sweden, and director of research of a project on gender, cyborgs and cyberspace at the University of Southern Denmark. She is the author of a number of books on feminist theory and feminist cultural studies, and together with Rosi Braidotti, she has edited *Between Monsters, Goddesses and Cyborgs* (Zed Books 1996). She is also member of the editorial board of several international feminist journals. Both authors travel widely and have given lectures at many feminist conferences in both Europe, USA and the South.

Cosmodolphins: Feminist Cultural Studies of Technology, Animals and the Sacred

Mette Bryld and Nina Lykke

Zed Books
LONDON • NEW YORK

Cosmodolphins: Feminist Cultural Studies of Technology, Animals and the Sacred was first published by Zed Books Ltd, 7 Cynthia Street, London N1 9JF, UK and Room 400, 175 Fifth Avenue, New York, NY 10010, USA in 1999.

Distributed exclusively in the USA by St Martin's Press, Inc., 175 Fifth Avenue, New York, NY 10010, USA.

Cover designed by Andrew Corbett
Set in Monotype Ehrhardt and Franklin Gothic by Ewan Smith
Printed and bound in the United Kingdom by Biddles Ltd, Guildford and King's Lynn

A catalogue record for this book is available from the British Library

Library of Congress Cataloging-in-Publication Data
Bryld, Mette.
    Cosmodolphins: feminist cultural studies of technology, animals, and the sacred/Mette Marie Bryld and Nina Lykke.
        p. cm
    Includes bibliographical references and index.
     ISBN 1-85649-815-8 (hb) – ISBN 1-85649-816-6 (pb)
      1. Feminist theory. 2. Nature—Effect of human beings on. 3. Human–animal relationships. 4. Outer space—Exploration—Social aspects. 5. Dolphins—Research—Social aspects. 6. Astrology—Social aspects. 7. Science—Social aspects. I. Lykke, Nina. II. Title.
    HQ1190.B78 2000
    306.4'5—dc21
                                        99-052387

ISBN 1 85649 815 8 cased
ISBN 1 85649 816 6 limp

Contents

List of Tables and Plates   viii

Acknowledgements   ix

Prelude   **1**

From 'Earth Dolphins' to this book ... /7

Introduction   **9**

To rewrite the master narratives of space flight /12
Inappropriate contiguities: the spaceship, the horoscope
and the dolphin /14   Cosmos and ocean: the extraterrestrial
'commons' /19   To cannibalize and worship the wild: in
early modernity and today /21   Amazing stories /23

1   Map of Matrices   **25**

Methods and materials /26   To speak as implicated
strangers /27   On the inclusion of 'nature' in feminist
cultural studies /28   Human, non-human, posthuman /30
Are animals a feminist issue? /32   Do feminists need a
cosmology? /34   Feminism, science and spirituality /36
Philosophy's shadows and the female divine /37
Feminism, story-telling and extraterrestrialism /39
To widen the geographical map of cultural studies /40

**Amazing Stories I–III: The Spaceship, the Horoscope
and the Dolphin**   **44**

Touch the moon! /44   A coincidental meeting /46
This is a trick! /48

2   Between Amazement and Estrangement   **50**

The space age adventure: to leave human marks in outer
space /53   'The Space Mural – a Cosmic View' /54
'To the conquerors of space ... ' /55   The masculine
adventure story /56   The New Age pilgrimage: to be
pervaded with macrocosmic meaning /58   Celestine

messages and meaningful coincidences /59 A world of
reversals /61 Dolphin fables of New Age and Space Age:
between pastoral and science fiction /63 The dolphin as
noble savage /63 To be imprinted with cetacean wisdom /64
Pastoral precursors /66 The dolphin as cyborg /67
'Uplift' and 'education in humanity' /68 To read out of
context /69

3 The Big Mission   **72**

To devote one's life to the Big Mission /73 The adventurous
journey /76 The high frontier /78 The enigma /81 To will,
to know, and to know-how /84 The masculine hero /87

4 Terraforming: Farmers in the Sky   **92**

Bio-power: from human to planetary bodies /93 Civilizing the
deserts of Earth and space /96 Human and divine will to cosmic
bio-power /99 Panspermia or the New Genesis /103 Out of
the cradle /106 The bodyscapes of men of steel and of their
mock mirrors /109 From superman to post(hu)man cyborg /113
Conclusion: bio-power and the sacred /115

Amazing Story IV: The Dark Side of the Moon   **118**

5 As Above, So Below   **122**

To devote your life to cosmic guidance /123 To be imprinted
with cosmic meaning /126 Astrology and gender /130
The dyadic relationship /136

6 One Does not Stir without the Other   **139**

Astrology – a cosmic *écriture féminine*? /140 An outline of
the approach /141 Cosmos as living body – the rebirth of an
ancient episteme /143 To be guided by fate /144 How to
think in the image of the body /145 The universe as mother
body /148 The universal mother body in New Age guise /149
The Great Cosmic Mother – as phallogocentric or feminist
construction /151 To speak the cosmic or the female body /153
A divine of one's own /155

**7 Voices from Inner and Outer Space: Refiguring
   Mother Sea and Father Sky**   **159**

The message of the cosmodolphins /159 Voices from the global
commons /161 Refigured Mother Sea /164 The sea as pastoral
source /166 The noble dolphin-speak /168 Refiguring Father
Sky /171 The broadcasting universe /172 An era of space
messages /175

Amazing Story V: Dolphin Versatility – from Living Missiles to Healers   **180**

8   Rocket State and Dolphin State   **183**

Dolphin ambiguities /184   A modern rebirth of dolphin lore /186   The 'father' of the post–Second World War dolphin script /189   Lilly's talking cyborg dolphins /191 Elite scientists on a cyborg dolphin: cosmic encounters /194 Cohabitation in a flooded house /197   From cyborg to noble savage /202   Socialism with a dolphin face /202   The noble savage of the New Age /206   The dolphin in a *perpetuum mobile* of circulating meanings /209

9   Conclusion: Inappropriate Contiguities Revisited   **215**

Conquerors of space in the underground /216   To posit a Fathergod through an illusory Genesis /218   To posit a female divine, a carnival may be necessary /220   Ocean and cosmos revisited: a feminist reconfiguration /222

Bibliography   **227**

Index   **239**

Tables and Plates

Tables

2.1 Main features of the master narratives of the spaceship, the horoscope and the dolphin icons   52

7.1 'Voices' from inner and outer space. Scientists picking up noises from the ocean and the cosmos via high-tech equipment = secondary orality   163

Plates

1   'Earth Dolphins'   x

4.1 The right place for the 'wrong stuff'? Valentina Tereshkova, the first woman in space, depicted in a New Age astrology book   112

IV.1 'Do you see what I see?'   119

8.1 'Can Man and Dolphin communicate? Dr. Lilly "talks" with a flippered student in a sound-proof room at his Communication Research Institute in Florida.'   192

8.2 The Soviet Russian vision of socialism with a dolphin face: a civilization of caring grandmothers   204

8.3 Cyborg-dolphins! Advertisement for computer software   212

8.4 One more cyborg-dolphin. Advertisement for telecommunication   213

Acknowledgements

We feel a deep sense of gratitude towards all the humans and non-humans who have so generously helped us with this book. In particular, we want to thank Elizabeth Sourbut, whose clever advice, brilliant suggestions and linguistic revision kept the manuscript afloat. The Institute of Cosmic Research in Moscow, NASA's Kennedy Space Center, Space Camp, Dolphin Plus, and the Dolphin Research Center in Florida all received and assisted us with great hospitality and patience, as did the California Institute of Integral Studies in San Francisco and astrological organizations such as Omega, the Academy of Astrology, and the astrological club in Ulitsa Baumanskaya in Moscow. We also cherish the time we spent with our wilderness guide, Captain Victoria Impallomeni from the Florida Keys.

We would like to thank Eigil Bryld for his terrific photos of the US space visions, Trisha Lamb Feuerstein for graciously sharing her fantastic bibliographic knowledge of the cetacean world with us, and Susan Squier from Penn State University for her unfailing encouragement and support. Financial support for the linguistic revision was provided by Møllerens Fond and the University of Southern Denmark. Special thanks to Professor Mogens Brøndsted.

We also thank Stanley, the spotted dolphin 'rocketman', and the black and white cat, Bandini, who both taught us about the trickster souls of animals.

Finally, we dedicate this book to the human dolphins of the future – Asker and Sofus.

Parts of Chapter 8 have been published in slightly different versions in Lykke and Braidotti (1996: 47–71) and Bryld (1998).

PLATE 1 'Earth Dolphins' Image @'95, Daniel McCulloch
DESIGN SYNERGY, U.S.A.
369 Montezuma Ave, Suite # 110,
Santa Fe, NM 87501, USA
Tel: 505 986 1215
Fax: 505 986 1207
synergy@dolphinsynergy.com
URL: www.dolphinsynergy.com
(Reproduced by permission of Daniel McCulloch)

Prelude

Two Earth dolphins, launched as Cosmodolphins in the cyberspace or dream-machine of the computer:

- leaping innocently in the cosmic ocean around our unique Blue Island;
- forming with the S-shape of their bodies a yin/yang symbol in the mandala of Gaia, the Holy Earth Mother, our sacred home;
- happily unaware of the distant camera-eye, observing them and the Blue Planet from the high-tech panopticon of outer space.

Two boundary-creatures:

- confronting us with mammalian life in the strange border zone between water and air;
- signalling with bodies that offer no decisive visual clues as to their individual sex, a sex that is not one;
- but evoking by etymology the Greek word for womb and vagina = *delphys*, closely akin to the word *delphis* = dolphin.

Are the two leaping dolphins, as noble extraterrestrial savages, trying to convey to us an ancient wisdom about harmony between macro- and microcosmos?

- Or do their spaceship-bodies and artificial environment indicate that they are cyborgs, simulations created in the galactic high-tech laboratory of a distant super-civilization?
- Or are they rather jesters who ironically expose ambivalent late twentieth-century attitudes of 'civilized' selves *vis-à-vis* 'wild' others?

The picture, 'Earth Dolphins', was produced by the photographer Daniel McCulloch in 1995 to support a 'Save the Dolphins' campaign organized by the eco-NGO Earth Island Institute in San Francisco. We have chosen this picture to provide the keynote to our book because, as one in a plethora of related examples, it presents a cluster of late twentieth-century icons that are central to the themes we shall explore. McCulloch's picture is a computer amalgamation. It merges the famous NASA photo of the Earth, seen from outer space, with dolphins as evocative icons of interfaces between feminine and masculine, water and air, Earth-bound and extra-terrestrial spheres of existence. Popular culture of today is obsessed with the two icons. It explores them separately, or combined into one. In merging the two icons, McCulloch's picture stirs up an evocative network of circulating meanings, which in different ways will be in our spotlight: gender, race, animal and cosmic nature, spirituality, extraterrestrialism and technoscience are all negotiated by the picture.

In terms of iconography, the picture allows the Holy Earth Mother, Animals (enigmatic sea mammals) and Sacred Nature to displace one another in apparently innocent and idyllic ways. At first sight we seem to be confronted with a New Age pastoral, a dream of a prelapsarian and paradisic state of existence, where wholeness and harmony, joy and natural pleasure reign.

In the late twentieth century, the Blue Planet, Gaia, the Holy Earth Mother, plays a similar role to the nineteenth-century Romantic image of the white cottage with a thatched roof, an idyllic garden and a good wife and mother who tends the sacred hearth for children and husband. The Blue Planet Earth is presented as a unique 'pearl of space' (Borisenko and Romanov 1982: 21), a 'sacred blue' planet (Sagan 1995: 156). Floating in the infinite wilderness of black space without visible national borders, the Blue Earth appears as a perfect image of sacred domesticity, intertwined with contemporary origin fantasies of wild and unspoiled nature. NASA's Blue Planet photo presents us with a modern version of the story of the Garden of Eden, mingled with a radically updated narrative of the 'sacred home' of nineteenth-century Romantic evangelism, which depicted it as

> A little spot enclosed by grace
> Out of the world's wide wilderness.
>
> (from the 'Puritan Poet' by Isaac Watts)[1]

When two dolphins are positioned leaping in front of the Blue Planet, using the S-shape of their bodies to transform it into a yin/yang symbol of wholeness, the original, paradisic harmony becomes even more conspicuous. Since the 1960s, dolphins have occupied the cultural imaginary[2] as bearers of alternative values such as collectivity, compassion, friendliness, creativity, joyful sexuality, androgyny, spiritual wisdom and intuitive intelligence. With their huge brains and legendary helpfulness towards humans, the enigmatic sea mammals have been cast by popular culture as well as by scientific discourse as our extraterrestrial *doppelgänger*. Like another double, the 'noble savage' of early modernity, the dolphin and the whale will allegedly guide us to insight into the 'true and sacred' pleasures of a simple life in harmony with the natural environment.

Taken at its innocent face value, the picture reflects the nostalgic imaginary of postindustrial culture, longing for an alternative world where the wounds inflicted by the destructive logic of present-day social relations between humans, technoscience and nature are healed; a world in which humans no longer seek to profit from the technoscientific control and domestication of nature; and where instead we may use the two dolphins as role models and abandon ourselves to nature and its cosmic rhythms; a world in which a primordial mother–child dyad between human and nature, between micro- and macrocosmos has been restored as a stable reference for our lives.

However, the pastoral idyll of the holy Earth Mother, the noble dolphin savage, and a primordial world without technology is not the only story conveyed by McCulloch's picture. An important excess of meanings surfaces when we include what film theory calls a space-off perspective – that is, when we ask questions about the invisible framing of the picture, the apparatus behind its production, the visualization technologies, the construction of the spectator's position. If we take into account the space-off position, a complex set of intersections emerges that reveals a world quite different from the primordial one that first catches the eye. Seen from the oblique angle of the space-off perspective, the picture becomes pervaded by meanings that link it to high-tech science and the epistemologies of the modern scientific world view.

First of all, space flight technology and advanced photographic techniques are, of course, a *sine qua non* for 'Earth Dolphins'. Although NASA, following Hollywood rather than postmodern film making, has done its best to keep the high-tech enterprise needed to position photographer and camera in outer space away from the Blue Planet photo, this is an unavoidable part of its apparatus of production. And when we come to McCulloch's recycling of the NASA photo, computer amalgamation techniques also play a vital role in its creation.

Secondly, the lofty panopticon view of Earth, created by space flight, is definitely not an innocent one. This was emphasized in an insightful analysis of the NASA photo by Garb (Diamond and Orenstein 1990: 264–78), and in somewhat different ways by Bordo (Berry and Wernick 1992: 165–78) and Haraway (1992). The spectator position invited by NASA's

Blue Planet picture demonstrates perfectly the vantage point of the scientific world view in general, and positivist epistemology in particular: the dissociated gaze, which can command and keep everything under control. The hidden camera-eye, looking at Earth from far away, is obviously placed in the most favourable position for playing the 'god-trick' of modern science (Haraway 1991: 189). The 'God's eye view' (Diamond and Orenstein 1990: 264) of the camera lens sustains the illusion that it is possible to act from an allegedly omniscient and omnipotent epistemological position.

A study of the space-off of the NASA photo also offers an appropriate illustration of the thesis formulated by Heidegger, on the modern creation of the world as picture. According to him, 'the conquest of the world as picture' (Heidegger 1979: 13), as representation, which the subject can stand back and perceive in its totality, is a specifically modern phenomenon. The total condensation of the world into one visual representation constitutes, the German philosopher argues, nothing less than the founding act of modern epistemology. It is the act through which the modern subject 'fights for the position in which he can be that existent which sets the standard for all existence and forms the directive for it' (Heidegger 1979: 13). The synonymy of the totalizing, the dominating and the phallogocentric gaze could hardly be articulated in a clearer way.

Seen from the dissociated extraterrestrial position of the camera's eye, representing humans who have left the 'cradle'[3] of Earth's gravitational field, the innocent idyll of McCulloch's picture becomes thoroughly disturbed. The space-off perspective transforms Earth into a small, and apparently easily manageable, visual object, which can be taken in at one glance – or contained within the circumference of the thumb, as *Apollo 8* astronaut Jim Lovell (a member of the first crew to orbit the Moon) evocatively describes his most amazing experience in space.[4] Simultaneously with the transformation of Earth, the meanings of the two dolphins also begin to change. If their background, Earth, appears as the dominated object of a distant, totalizing gaze, it may well be that we are hoodwinking ourselves when we insist on seeing nothing but wild and free dolphins as referents of the picture. Instead, it seems appropriate to include the staged performances of captive dolphins – kept for show or research – in our network of references. Following this line of interpretation, we may acknowledge that the picture's presentation of Earth Mother, noble savage dolphin and wild, 'untouched' nature matches the trinity Woman–Native–Nature that we find in colonialist and patriarchal discourses of early modernity.

Thus it obviously makes an important difference whether we include the space-off perspective in our reading of the picture or not. By alternately including and excluding it, we can switch between an innocent picture of the holy Earth Mother, with her happily leaping animal–human offspring, and a non-innocent view of Nature performing as domesticated object, seen through the distant gaze of an enterprising human manager enacting the god-trick of modern scientific epistemology. McCulloch's picture is in this way comparable to those puzzle pictures where immediate observation shows us, for example, a tree, while closer scrutiny discloses a human face: 'now you see it, now you don't'. As puzzle picture, 'Earth Dolphins' presents us with a significant narrative of deeply ambivalent trends in high-tech culture. It tells the story of a simultaneous cannibalizing and resacralizing of 'Wild Nature', which we consider typical of postindustrial culture, constructing it now as resource for technoscientific, military or commercial projects and now as a site for the inscription of nostalgic desires for a sacred, motherly Eden.

By suggesting a reading of 'Earth Dolphins' as puzzle picture, full of changing meanings and patterns of ambivalence, we wish to avoid one-dimensional interpretations. It would, of course, be naïve just to take the picture at its innocent and idyllic face value. But it would be just as reductive to read it exclusively as yet another homage to the technoscientific conquest of Nature and a celebration of the omniscient and omnipotent subject of positivist epistemology.

Garb is well aware of the excess meanings that still remain after the second kind of reading. Having interpreted NASA's Blue Planet picture as 'magnum opus of patriarchal consciousness' (Diamond and Orenstein 1990: 275), he does wonder why the Whole Earth image, despite the very problematic spectator position, has attracted 'peace activists, environmentalists, and proponents of a new Earth-based spirituality' (Diamond and Orenstein 1990: 275). How can the picture appeal to many of those who rebel against, rather than celebrate, the dissociated and objectifying gaze of the knower of modern science?

We shall suggest an answer by taking our interpretation of 'Earth Dolphins' as a multi-layered puzzle picture one step further, displaying an array of ambivalences present in contemporary culture. We have mentioned some of the contradictions between the immediate message of the picture and its space–off perspective. However, it should be acknowledged that the latter itself is affected by puzzles and ambivalences. To reduce the position of the camera-eye exclusively to the totalizing, objectifying and god-like gaze of the omniscient and omnipotent subject of science is in a sense to confirm the epistemological illusions of positivism. It would be more appropriate to displace them along lines suggested by Heidegger, who tells us how the shadow of 'the incalculable' (Heidegger 1979: 14) intrudes on the quantifying processes that are activated in order to define the world as picture. Moreover, a matching act of displacement can be initiated by reference to social constructivist critiques of modern scientific epistemologies. When pointing out that the technoscientific gaze in total control of its object is an *imaginary* construction, a conjuring *trick* (cf. Haraway's term 'god-trick'), these critiques also emphasize that the controlling eye may indeed produce uncontrolled, unintended and subjective side-effects and excess meanings.

We therefore suggest that the spaceman's 'God's eye' position, which NASA's Blue Planet photo has made vicariously accessible to billions of people, is fraught with ambivalences. As noted by Garb, it represents an instrumentalizing act of technoscientific visualization that reduces Nature to manageable object. Clearly, however, the NASA camera is doing more than just repeating the classic act of mechanistic science and its reduction of Nature to material resource for capitalist cannibalism. A high-tech resacralization process seems involved as well, which inscribes Wild Nature in quite different kinds of cannibalistic images than those of industrial society and classic mechanistic science. With the help of highly sophisticated visualization technologies, Nature is being reinterpreted and transformed from object of material consumption to virtual-reality object of worship, awe and aesthetic-spiritual consumption. The multi-billion-dollar photo of the Blue Planet, born out of advanced technological apparatus, undoubtedly performs as such a virtual-reality icon, displaying the Sublime Beauty of Sacred Nature and Sacred Mother, welcoming her cyborg-sons back to their 'natural' home after their dangerous voyage in the extraterrestrial wilderness of (cyber)space. In all its Technicolor beauty, the NASA photo aligns itself with the current plethora of highly aestheticized photos of endangered species and wilderness areas. Like them, it is circulated as a sacred icon of a mythical Garden of Eden, a lost origin, which, like the flesh and blood of Jesus, may reappear endlessly, transubstantiated through the 'miraculous' intervention of the virtual reality of high-tech images – through a politics of simulation that pretends to be a politics of 'true' representation.[5]

When McCulloch adds the two dolphins to the Blue Planet photo, these cyber-sacral dimensions of the puzzle picture become even more distinct than on the original NASA image. The two dolphins, leaping in beautiful synchrony in the Cosmic cyber-ocean, without any trace of the real-life sea from which they were originally jumping when the camera shot them, set off the virtual-reality character of the picture. These literally dislocated dolphins, circling like spaceships around the Blue Planet, make it plain that they inhabit a virtual world without any real-life referents. Furthermore, they effectively draw our attention to the links between the original NASA photo and the numerous techno-images of Wild Nature in general, and dolphin or whale pictures in particular. They emphasize its connection with this plethora of images, which, like the NASA picture itself, have had enormous commercial success. These images seem to appeal to strong contemporary desires to worship and sacralize icons which claim to convey the double message that a 'truly' transcendent, Sublime and Sacred Nature exists, and that a happy and carefree high-tech future is on its way.

As a vehicle for this kind of wishful thinking, 'Earth Dolphins' inscribes itself in the new religious Utopianism, which since the 1960s has invoked in varying forms the coming of a new era of human history, simply called 'the New Age' or named along the lines of the ancient astrological calendar as the 'Age of Aquarius'. It is an age that is expected to call forward a higher human consciousness, which, sustained by feelings of global oneness and empathic communication across the borders of space and time, will bring salvation and heal the spiritual relations between human beings, technoscience and Earth Mother.

From 'Earth Dolphins' to this Book ...

As multi-layered puzzle picture, 'Earth Dolphins' causes the spectator to waver between nostalgic longings for an original bliss, the triumphant gaze of the distant technoscientist and conqueror, and awe-struck worship of new cyber-sacral miracles of transubstantiation. In so doing, it both re-enacts and displaces classic colonialist and patriarchal self–other images. It is a high-tech reconfiguration of early modern constructions of the trinity of others: Woman–Native–Nature. Not a mere repetition. There are continuities at play, but also transformation and excess meanings.

The colonial quest for an elsewhere in the European Renaissance and early modernity gave rise to constructions of the wild and the savage with the trinity Woman, Native and Nature as central icons. They were cast as wild others: good or evil, challenging or threatening, inherently inferior and lacking, but also capable of producing sublime experiences in the observer. Their opposite emerged as Universal Man, the 'civilized', enlightened self. In contrast to Woman, Native and Nature, he was supposed to carry the 'white man's burden'.

One of these 'burdens' was that the projects and endeavours of the white man seemed to link up in an ambivalent picture. The overall project could be unambiguously defined: to civilize and modernize the world, and to pursue freedom and happiness by seeking control and mastery over wild others through technoscience, and colonial and capitalist power. An intrinsic goal lay, moreover, in secularization: the liberation of knowledge-seeking and political institutions from the obscure twilight zones of occultism and superstition, identified, for example, with the 'childish' and 'irrational' attitudes of Woman and Native. However, the fact that civilization, secularization and Enlightenment reason obviously failed in any simple or unambiguous way to bring about the Utopian goal of paradise on earth engendered cultural ambivalences and contrasting trends. Rebuking the civilized world for having alienated itself from the true and sacred pleasures of the natural life, embodied by the trinity of others, became itself an integral part of early modern philosophy.

Our book is a feminist cultural study of contemporary transformations or re-enactments of these classic constructions of ambivalent self–other images. We shall focus on the entangled stories of space flight, New Age spirituality and dolphin mythology, which are all evoked by McCulloch's picture. We shall read them as significant post-Second World War narratives of quests for a wild elsewhere. With this perspective, we will analyse how they reproduce or displace the classic colonialist, patriarchal and 'naturist'[6] oppositions between 'civilized' selves and 'wild' others, as well as Enlightenment constructions of occult and spiritual thought systems as the reverse of 'masculine' *ratio*.

Notes

1. Quoted in Dawson (1994: 65).

2. 'The imaginary' is a concept originating in Lacanian psychoanalysis; here it refers to the self-images of the child in its mirror stage (6–18 months of age). In a broader sense, the concept is used within cultural studies to characterize the fantasy images in which a culture mirrors itself, and which thereby come to act as points of reference for its identity-production.

3. With genealogies in a quote from the writings of the Russian 'father' of modern space flight, Konstantin Tsiolkovsky, American as well as Russian space flight discourses often depict man's future in space with the metaphor 'out of the cradle', cf. e.g. the title of a popular US book on this theme *Out of the Cradle. Exploring the Frontiers Beyond Earth* (Hartmann et al. 1984). Cf. also Chapter 4 of this book.

4. Cf. Jim Lovell's comments on the NASA tape that was played during the sight-seeing tours on the premises of Kennedy Space Center in 1998.

5. For an interesting discussion of the ways in which a politics of simulation can be used critically to go beyond a politics of representation instead of uncritically simulating it, see the analysis of Kim Stanley Robinson's Martian trilogy in Markley (1997).

6. The term 'naturism' was coined by ecofeminists in analogy to sexism and racism (Warren 1990: 132–3). It refers to abusive and violent treatment of non-human Nature.

Introduction

The first inspiration for this book grew out of an alien encounter. In 1987 we participated in the Third International Interdisciplinary Congress on Women, which took place in Dublin. The congress was attended by well over a thousand Women's Studies researchers from all over the world. They discussed their work in about 250 different workshops on topics covering a broad spectrum from 'Feminization of Poverty in a Global Perspective' to 'Experiences of Women on Test Tube Baby Programmes'; from 'War and Patriarchy' to 'Goddesses and Feminist Spirituality'.

The alien encounter took place in a workshop on 'New Technologies as a Challenge to Women's Work Roles'. One of the papers was given by a high-ranking NASA employee, JoAnn Morgan, who had taken on the amazing mission 'to inform the community of international women about one aspect of the depth and variety of responsibility women have in the United States civilian space program' (Cullen et al. 1987: 433). The congress had attracted a diversity of women in terms of different disciplines, approaches and cultural backgrounds. Nevertheless, the majority of participants shared political commitments, inspired by feminist and left-wing orientations, and in this context Morgan appeared to be alien and politically out of touch. Nobody was inclined to celebrate the statistics on which her paper was based, nobody seemed impressed by her figures that showed a small increase in women's participation in academic work at NASA's Kennedy Space Center from only a few to around 9 per cent. Her presentation was questioned from quite different angles from the liberal affirmative action politics for which it argued. Her undisguised and proud promotion of American nationalist goals created a great deal of hostility in the audience. Feminist peace activists asked about NASA's concealed involvement with the military. African feminists, engaged in programmes for poor rural women, angrily pointed out that the billions of dollars spent on man's space adventures should have been transferred to initiatives that sought to counter the feminization of poverty, especially in Third World countries. All in all, the workshop session was transformed into a veritable confrontation between liberal and left-wing feminism.

In itself, this confrontation did not stir our imaginations. Having been committed ourselves to left-wing feminist activism for many years, we were thoroughly familiar with the differences between the two sides. This was not new. But what did catch our attention was the extraordinary and amazing topic of the discussion. Should feminists embrace or repudiate space flight – not as a theme in science fiction, but as a real-life issue? Although we had worked within the field of feminist cultural studies of technology for several years at that time, it had never occurred to us that space flight might be a feminist issue. Peace feminists had for some time, of course, been bringing a critical focus to bear on war technologies, including rockets and missiles, which obviously played important roles in the development of space flight technologies, and vice versa. But space exploration in general appeared to be a totally 'dark continent' in the otherwise extremely diverse and multi-faceted landscape of feminist concerns.

The heated debate on space flight was evoked, like a bolt from the blue, by JoAnn Morgan's unlikely presence in this left-wing and radical feminist setting. While listening, it suddenly struck us as somewhat conspicuous that the otherwise mistrustful and vigilant feminist cultural critics had turned a deaf ear to what was happening in this highly political and sociotechnically powerful field. The more we considered the forceful historical marks left on post-Second World War culture by the space race between the USA and the Soviet Union, and also its technological consequences, the more we asked ourselves why a critical feminist gaze was lacking in this field. The same questions raised themselves when we looked at Morgan's statistics, which, contrary to what she had been trying to argue, showed space flight to be not the next step in women's liberation, but rather an extreme residuum of the unfolding of classic, national-romantic and phallocentric myths of masculine superheroes.

Besides wondering about the conspicuous lack of critical feminist eyes in the no-woman's land of space flight, a different train of thoughts and feelings caught our imagination as well. We had to admit that we were attracted by the adventure tale that performed as a hidden layer in Morgan's very matter-of-fact and down-to-earth presentation. The extraordinary point of reference for the speech made by this nice, white North American middle-class woman was the amazing and fascinating story of real-life travel to distant and alien worlds. Our childhood fascinations with Jules Verne's novels of thrilling voyages to exotic places beyond the dull, mundane world of everyday life and with Tarzan's adventures among the apes in jungles far away from the conventions of European upper-class life were re-awakened. Morgan had actually spent most of her adult life sending people and human-made things into 'the unknown', the vast world beyond the limits of Earth's gravitational field. She appeared alien not only because her patent nationalism and her liberal feminism clashed with the left-wing and radical feminist audience. She also carried a touch of a much more thrilling kind of alienness – that of the world beyond. Seen in retrospect, this was obviously one of the reasons why her appearance in Dublin remained intriguing to us and prompted us to write to her three years later when we were due to visit the USA for another interdisciplinary world congress on women. This time, Morgan did not attend, but she kindly invited us to visit her at NASA's Kennedy Space Center in Florida. This visit became the actual starting point of this book. It was impressive in two respects.

On the one hand, we felt much more amazed and awe-struck than we had expected. Everything smelled of adventure. We interviewed people for whom preparations for the cosmic exodus of humankind was not science fiction, but the way they earned their living. On the sightseeing tour for special guests, we were allowed to touch the tiles of the space shuttle *Discovery* and inhale the cathedral-like atmosphere of the building, which during the days of the Apollo project had been used to assemble the gigantic *Saturn V* rocket – the one that launched the moonships. Although we do not normally consider ourselves to be gadget-fetishistic techno-freaks, we were, nevertheless, caught by the spirit of adventure.

On the other hand, the visit confirmed us strongly in the belief that the story of space flight is not only amazing and fascinating, but also very much in need of critical inquiries. The more so as the military's reliance on space grew in the 1990s in both the old spacefaring nations, the USA and Russia. A recent analysis of the space politics of the two nations notes that 'U.S. Department of Defense space spending exceeded NASA's budget every year from 1982 to 1995' and points to the remarkable integration of space in the military operations in the Persian Gulf War (Von Bencke 1997: 190). Moreover, Ronald Reagan's Star Wars project has not been buried, only redesigned (*Newsweek*, 22 February 1999). And Russia, whose government is unable regularly to pay salaries to coalminers, teachers and medical doctors, not to mention old-age pensioners, has managed not only to 'maintain its military space constellations at Cold War levels', but actually to improve and expand certain aspects (Von Bencke 1997: 190–1). So, whether seen through the lens of post-Second World War high politics and post-Cold War military strategies or from the perspective of the adventure story, it is a tale in need of feminist deconstructions and critique far beyond the limits of Morgan's liberal affirmative action politics.

To Rewrite the Master Narratives of Space Flight

In her book *NASA/TREK*, Constance Penley (1997) rewrites the NASA story from the point of view of feminist cultural studies. She provokes sceptical European readers like us by declaring herself a fan of NASA, and surprises us by cleverly emphasizing the critical potentials of the reading strategies of fans. In her opinion, critical fans transgress the impasse of standpoint criticisms and Enlightenment critiques of ideology. In particular, she underlines the subversive potential of the many female slash-writers,[1] who for years have been rewriting the Star Trek series as a pornographic and Utopian romance of male homosexual love. Her intention is to view the NASA story from the oblique angle of the Star Trek adventures, which in their turn she re-reads from the consciously improper and inappropriate perspective of the slash-writers. NASA's high-flown rhetoric of masculine superheroes, national symbols of the USA, is by contiguity associated with the slash fans' lustful constructions of a homosexual love affair between Star Trek's Kirk and Spock. In this way, Penley builds herself a platform for a critical discussion of NASA's extremely repressive attitude towards the taboo subject of sexuality, and also of 'its inability to manage the meanings of women in space' (Penley 1997: 3).

Like Penley, we want to engage in a cultural critique without excluding our fascination with the space adventure. We also feel a feminist urge to rewrite the master narratives of space flight in a Bakhtinian way, that is, to subvert their national-romantic and phallocentric rhetoric via reading strategies that put improper and carnivalesque contiguities on display.

Our book is, however, different from Penley's. First of all, we are too sceptical to write as critical fans and, unlike her, we did not grow up in the neighbourhood of the Kennedy Space Center launch site. We are, on the contrary, offspring of a small North European nation that constructs its national identity around an unheroic, pragmatic, down-to-earth attitude that makes the high-flown, national-romantic NASA rhetoric sound very alien and pompous to our ears. Rather than writing as fans, we write as implicated but sceptical strangers since, due to the cultural hegemony of the USA in the post-Second World War period, we are both a part of American culture and outside it. But although we do not share the enthusiasm of American NASA fans, we bluntly admit that the adventurous quest stirred our imagination.

Second, our focus is not only on the USA. We have expanded our perspective to include Soviet Russian versions of the master narrative of space flight. We take into consideration the space race and the competition between the political superpowers over global hegemony, both of which have left their historical marks on the master narrative of space flight. The early space race was, among other things, a discursive battle over entitlement to represent Universal Man in the biggest story told in modern times. Who was going to be the script-writer and the protagonist of the master narrative of humankind's cosmic exodus? This was and is a question that matters a great deal when the official story of space flight is retold in the two countries. The Russian Yuri Gagarin is inscribed in world history as the unmarked representative of universal man by being 'the first man in space'. In return, the authors of the American version of the master narrative have had to construct a marked category: John Glenn is celebrated as 'the first American in orbit'. To appropriate the prestigious unmarked position is, of course, not only a matter of linguistics, but a serious question of national pride. By drawing on both American and Russian materials, we can follow such constructions with a cross-cultural perspective.

Third, we share Penley's desire to subvert by putting improper contiguities on display, but we link the space narrative with other kinds of mock images, carnivalesque representations and inappropriate others. In our story, the spaceship icon of the heroic master narrative of the American and Russian space adventure will be confronted with the horoscope and the dolphin, two popular contemporary icons that, like the spaceship, have significant genealogical roots in the 1960s. Invoking the eagerly awaited New Age as the Age of Aquarius, countercultural movements of the time initiated a revival of astrology and other ancient occult practices. Also coinciding with the space race, the scientific discovery of the 'intelligence' and outstanding communicative skills of dolphins made its first and much debated headlines around 1960. In this way, our three icons touch one another in terms of historical emergence on the cultural scene of post-Second World War society, while the stories they generate put strange and inappropriate interference patterns and reversals on display.

We stumbled upon the dolphin icon as a mock image of spaceman and his *alter ego*, cosmic high-tech aliens, because in a literal sense it interfered with the space narrative and the scientific search for extraterrestrial intelligence in the early 1960s. The horoscope icon came forward as the other improper mirror, because, to our rationalistic and matter-of-fact minds, it appeared to match the space narrative in weirdness, while reversing the way gender was discursively invested in the story.

Inappropriate Contiguities: The Spaceship, the Horoscope and the Dolphin

Our Prelude presented a first description of some inappropriate contiguities between Space Age and New Age narratives. In the analysis of McCulloch's picture, we pointed out how New Age stories of unity with a 'pure', 'authentic' nature clashed with the master narrative of techno-scientific power and control in the shaping of the ultimate story of the world as picture and manageable object. What came to the fore seemed to be a mixture of attraction and repulsion, embrace and collision. We shall define this as inappropriate contiguity, while drawing inspiration from the notion of 'the carnivalesque' of the Russian cultural historian Mikhail Bakhtin (1984).[2]

'Earth Dolphins' negotiates the proximity between two opposing kinds of discourses that the adoption of NASA's Blue Planet photo by New Agers, deep ecologists, etc., has engendered. The picture bonds together stories of a mystical unity with 'nature', Earth Mother Gaia[3] and her dolphin-human offspring, and narratives of the controlling gaze of the distant scientist-engineer. But the discursive bonding is clearly not based on mere harmonious attraction. Indirectly, the picture also reveals the repulsion such a misalliance is bound to evoke. In order to mediate between the discourses on unity and detachment, of merging and control, of mystery and technoscientific rationality, the picture has to repress and police the surfacing of certain obvious links. Thus the technological apparatus of production – the spaceship, the camera of the astronaut-photographer, etc. – were kept away from the eyes of the spectator. To sustain the illusion of unity, merging and sacred mystery, the emblems of detachment, control and rationality had to be hidden and repressed, relegated to the invisible space-off. To show the contiguity openly would be inappropriate and make the picture ambiguous.

The specific mixture of attraction and repulsion, which apparently ensures the New Age career of NASA's Blue Planet photos (with or without dolphins) as spiritual symbol of holism and healing, is, however, not the only way of working out the complex relationship between the Space Age and New Age narratives. A kind of reversed version of the repressions of the Whole Earth image also seems to be operative. When we shift the focus to the national-romantic American and Russian narratives of the spaceship and the rocket as vehicles of the heroic 'conquest of space', we see a high-tech aesthetics and a gadget-fetishism brought into full play that show how the 'technological sublime' (Nye 1994) is celebrated intensively in both countries. The USA and Russia have both sustained their space narratives by celebrations of the powerful hardware and the super-brave steel men who made the 'conquest' possible. This has been done through innumerable pictures, videos, books, exhibitions, official events (parades, etc.), that run counter to the conspicuous erasure of any trace of technology from the surface of the Whole Earth image, but at the same time maintain their own set of repressions. Whereas the Blue Planet picture keeps the question of technology, power and control out of sight, it is precisely these issues that the fiercely nationalistic American and Russian demonstrations of space-ships, rockets, launch-pads, astro- and cosmonaut equipment, mission control centres, etc., put on display. Conspicuously absent from these gadget-fetishistic representations is, in return, any shadow of the in-calculable and any trace of the uncontrollable, even though these are an inescapable part of any story of interactions between human and nature. Both the USA and Russia like to demonstrate their technopower and indulge in narratives of technological infallibility and the highest potency of human power, control, cool detachment and rationality. In its own way, the traumatic shock evoked by the *Challenger* catastrophe in 1986 shows how forceful and persistent the myth of infallible technopower and complete human control is. The disaster clashed too discordantly with the narrative of total calculability and controllability to which NASA had contributed heavily, underplaying risks and safety problems when promoting the 'teacher in space program' that the 'ordinary school teacher' astronaut, Christa McAuliffe, should have conducted on board the space shuttle.

We shall explore the attractions and repulsions between Space Age and New Age discourses through analyses of a range of stories clustering around our three icons: the spaceship, the horoscope and the dolphin. After a contextualization of our epistemological position and theoretical approaches (Chapter 1), we present the patterns of similarities and differences, opposi-tions and reversals, binding together the three icons (Chapter 2). In the following chapters (3 to 8), we analyse them further one by one. The concluding Chapter 9 returns to the general question: whether or not this contemporary configuration of stories reinvents and recirculates the classic trinity of others, Woman–Native–Nature, in new versions. Through a brief analysis of three subversive novels, Victor Pelevin's *Omon Ra* (1992/1996), Jeanette Winterson's *Boating for Beginners* (1990) and Vonda McIntyre's *Superluminal* (1983), we also summarize the acts of destabilization and denaturalization at which the book has aimed.

The spaceship icon, which is the focus of Chapters 3 and 4, will serve as a signifier of the gadget-fetishistic dream of unbounded power and control that is articulated by the American and Russian space narratives. We unravel some of the stories in the spectacular quest for an extra-terrestrial elsewhere, for a place never before visited by earthlings. We discuss how the spacecraft refers to a web of myth, politics, reinvention of nature and technoscientific desires to domesticate as yet untamed wilderness areas, and how intermingling stories of steel men and heavenly powers sustain the illusion that the god-trick of modern science, the vanquishing of incalculable and uncontrollable coincidences, is possible.

As part of the discussion, we look at the consequences of the cultural historic semantics that lends significance to the spaceship icon as a vehicle designed to bring humans to the sphere that, for centuries, has been associated with the divine realm of the white Christian Fathergod. In addition, we analyse how space exploration, in both an American and a Russian context, invokes a discursive field in which classic, national-romantic myths of the masculine hero seem able to survive in immaculate form. True to tradition, this hero is totally dedicated to performing sacred deeds for the benefit of the nation and all mankind (Dawson 1994). Just a brief glimpse of the tough, serene and determined faces of the astronauts in Hollywood's blockbusting film from 1995 about the *Apollo 13* disaster (*Apollo 13*) is enough to convince that the myth of the Man made of the 'right stuff' (Wolfe 1988) has not yet become extinct. In his screen incarnation, he appears to be as absorbed as ever in the effort to carry out his national-heroic duties. He may be threatened by Fate – the film plays on the ominous number 13 – but the will of the genius Godfather of technoscientific controllability and calculability, the modern Cyber-Apollo, is definitely on the side of our heroes. Therefore, they survive the near-fatal attacks of the hostile wilderness 'out there'.

In order to analyse the reverse side of the inappropriate contiguities between Space Age and New Age discourses, to which recyclings of the Blue Planet picture as Earth Mother, Gaia, call attention, Chapters 5 and 6 zoom in on New Age astrology. In contrast to the high-tech gadget-fetishism, which sticks to the spaceship, the horoscope icon mediates the same kind of nostalgic longings for holism, healing, home-coming, that have also been projected onto the Whole Earth image. New Age astrology reinvents ancient, occult symbols of spiritual and bodily unity between micro- and macrocosmos, human and universe, and promises salvation through a 'pure' and sacred bond to Cosmic Nature.

Other popular New Age revivals of ancient forms of occultism – tarot, I Ching, channelling, etc. – might just as well have sustained our discussion. But we chose the horoscope, because it provides a particularly good match for the spaceship in its explicit reference to cosmic themes. In addition, the horoscope has a special iconographic value since the upcoming astrological Age of Aquarius has served as a powerful explanatory metaphor for the fundamental shift of mentalities that the New Age is supposed to bring about. A third reason for taking the horoscope as our direction-finder is that astrology, more than other kinds of New Age occultism, makes visible an obsession with calculability and predictability that matches the techno-scientific rationality of space flight as a mock-image. Like modern science, the practice of astrology is based on complex computations and calculations that, at the same time, are inscribed in a totally 'unscientific' context of intuitive feelings and a mystic interconnectedness between human and cosmos.

We will interpret New Age astrology as a paradoxical counter-image to the spaceship. As an icon of the Space Age, the spacecraft embodies modern scientific epistemology and the will to technoscientific power, knowledge and control. In significant contrast to this, the horoscope icon of New Age astrology signifies a will to give up the cult of *ratio*, command and control and instead to accept the guidance of occult messages created by the rhythmic movements of Earth and cosmos, which, nevertheless, has to be decoded by means of a 'quasi-scientific' grammar of calculable astronomical constellations.

As a kind of reversal of each other, the spaceship and the horoscope can illustrate a lability that may be characteristic of high-tech societies. For many people, the semantics of cosmos seem able to change as easily as a puzzle picture, now displaying a 'frontier to be conquered' by techno-scientific power and reason, and now a screen full of occult messages of holism and healing. Such lability may be an expression of widespread present-day oscillations between belief in the explanatory frameworks of science and a *bricolage* of alternative world views (Eastern mysticism, ancient occultism, etc.). The latter seems to be evoked in order to explain existential excess meanings, for which science, obsessed with total rational control, command and calculability, cannot account.

When exploring the inappropriate contiguities between the master narratives of Space Age and New Age, we will also consider how gender reversals is at stake. The configuration of the spaceship and the horoscope thus refers to a certain division of labour by gender. On the one hand, the victorious mission of the spacecraft is discursively linked with the sacred image of the masculine national hero, whose voyage shall bring us closer to the omnipotent Cyber-Godfather. On the other hand, both popular New Age and spiritual feminist stories of astrology and horoscope casting evoke the feminine: they tell of salvation via (re)constructions of ancient world views, based on the celebration of a mother–child symbiosis of macro- and microcosmos. This may remind us once more of the lability of the present-day disourses on cosmology, gendering the universe now masculine, now feminine.

While the configuration of spaceship and horoscope will give us the opportunity to highlight patterns of repulsion, opposition and reversal, our third icon, the dolphin, is by contrast fitted to stress the contiguity and proximity of Space Age and New Age discourses. Chapters 7 and 8 present a wide spectrum of cetacean stories that unfolds an extreme polysemy. Included are both dolphin and whale narratives, for, in spite of some differences in lifestyle and iconography,[4] there are so many parallels between contemporary constructions of these two marine mammals that we use them interchangeably. As generic term we prefer the evocative word 'dolphin' instead of the – strictly speaking – more precise 'cetacean'. It will be evident from the context whether we refer to dolphins or to whales.

As a multi-layered image, the dolphin can link up with the opposing themes evoked by the other two icons in our configuration. Adapted to be one with their oceanic element as well as to perform as 'mind in the waters' (McIntyre 1974) and 'intellectuals of the sea' (Belkovich et al. 1965, 1967), dolphins leap smoothly into the role of boundary figures. With the same effortless ease, they relate to narratives of a wet and symbiotic, motherly past and a future enlightened by consciousness, communication and brain activity, to New Age spirituality and to the master narrative of space flight, to ancient beliefs and to high-tech science, to a feminization and to a masculinization of the universe. Therefore, they can also perform in the carnivalesque role of the jester and the mock-hero, who expose the improper proximity and deconstruct the opposing spheres of meaning of the other two icons. In this way, they function analogously to the 'undecidable' signifier 'Woman', which Jacques Derrida (1979, 1987) promoted as the perfect expression of *différance*, the unending chain of displacements characteristic of signifying processes.

One part of the dolphin stories allows the enigmatic marine mammals to perform as noble savage in a pastoral, pre-technological environment, or as spiritual messenger from an other-worldly site, endowed with alternative, feminine values similar to those evoked by New Age astrology. But the flexible animal can equally well take up a role as emblem of high-tech communication. We encounter them, for instance, in computer and telecom ads, signifying global communication, speed, nomadism and a carefree future in cyberspace; in the 1960s they even popped up as stand-ins for the cosmic Cyber-Godfather. The second part of the paradoxical post-Second World War dolphin script thus connected this animal icon with space flight and its new science project: the search for extraterrestrial intelligence in the vast cosmic ocean. All of a sudden, these sea creatures jumped smilingly out of the blue as stand-ins for the citizens of the cosmic super-civilizations that possessed techno-godfatherly wisdom, and with whom it was believed the Space Age would bring us into contact.

Cosmos and Ocean: The Extraterrestrial 'Commons'

Besides the inappropriate contiguities displayed in the patterns of repulsion and attraction between the spaceship, the horoscope and the dolphin, another shared, but much more streamlined, framework of meanings links the three icons. In different ways, they all refer to twentieth-century stories of two rather special kinds of wilderness areas: the cosmos, and the world beneath the ocean surface. This joint framework of reference is analysed in Chapter 7, which marks the transition between the chapters on the cosmos (3 to 6) and the dolphin (8); the latter features the animal icon leaping energetically up and down between the cosmic and the oceanic world.

There are several reasons for choosing to study the role of the cosmos and the ocean in the search for answers to the question we posed in the Prelude, as to how the classic trinity Woman–Native–Nature is re-enacted or displaced in present-day quests for a wild elsewhere.

One reason is the difference of both spaces from the current terrestrial abodes of 'civilized selves' that makes them a perfect match for contemporary desires for a 'truly' wild and vast elsewhere. For they present us with images of alien sites that today are very difficult to conjure up on the dry land of Earth. Domesticated land and cities have extended their space at an ever-accelerating pace throughout the last few centuries. The remaining wilderness areas on Earth's continents have been more or less transformed into the opposite of wilderness, being now predominantly well-ordered nature reserves and wildlife sanctuaries with paths, picnic areas and tagged animals, or else vast eroded and polluted wastelands. However, this terraforming[5] or domestication process has so far only begun to touch upon the cosmos and the ocean. Underwater national parks have indeed emerged; industrial fishing, off-shore oil drilling, sewage discharges etc. are placing increasing pressure on marine environments; and the pollution of orbital space is beginning to create problems. But, unlike the continental areas of Earth, the cosmos and the ocean can still represent vast spaces, different and distinct from the domesticated environments of everyday life in postindustrial societies.

As vast wilderness spaces, the cosmos and the extraterrestrial world beneath the ocean surface constitute a joint frame of reference for our three icons. A shared semantics can be found in the fact that the images these extraterrestrial spaces evoke have obvious points of resemblance to one another.

One resemblance is that outer space and the oceans are both regarded as 'global commons', to use the official language of the United Nations (UN). This concept was espoused by the organization in the early 1970s, and applied to outer space, the oceans and Antarctica in a later, much debated report from the UN's World Commission on Environment and Development (WCED 1987). In an ambivalent act of revitalizing and transforming the classic discussion of the 'tragedy of the commons' that occurred in seventeenth-century England, the 'global commons' of today are depicted as reservoirs of rich resources waiting for a human manager. Guided by a rather ill-concealed wish to exploit these resources, the Brundtland Report refers suggestively to 'managing the commons' (1987: 261). At the same time distancing itself from the worst excesses of capitalist greed, the report constructs the 'development' of the global commons as a 'common', international project. In this way Brundtland indirectly claims to promote a different attitude from the one that governed the classic transformation of the English commons into private property.

A further affinity concerns the way in which the two spaces, the cosmos and the ocean, are cast as settings for human experience of the unbounded, vast and natural sublime. Both represent borders between 'human civiliza-tion' and 'wild nature' that cannot easily be transgressed. In this sense, they resemble the terrestrial landscapes that two hundred years ago sustained the creation of classic theories of sublimity in nature (Burke 1756/1990). However, unlike those once-powerful terrestrial wilderness sites, both the cosmos and the ocean depths, so-called 'inner space',[6] can still perform as vast and sublime areas beyond human control. Both continue to be apparently unfathomable and therefore terrifying and awe-inspiring in a classic sense. The 'insurmountable' mountains, 'impenetrable' forests and deserts of early modernity have long since been 'conquered', as have the 'dark' continents and 'virgin lands' of the classic colonialist period. But outer and inner space are still unchanged in embodying powerful natural barriers to human enterprise.

Consequently, in the USA, outer space is often referred to as 'the high frontier'. The expression echoes the conquest of the American West, but it also signals the enormous obstacles confronting anybody who attempts to travel even a short distance beyond the atmosphere of Earth. The dark side of the Moon is still the most exotic place humans have ever visited. Compared to the nearest star, the Moon is, however, very close to home.

Just as the imaginary world maps of contemporary culture are marked by a 'high frontier', so they are also demarcated by a 'deep frontier', an expression used by marine explorers. It is true that electronic listening devices, scuba-diving technology and bathyscaphes (deep sea exploration vessels) have changed our relations to the world beneath the ocean surface. However, like the cosmos, this world still remains a wilderness outside of human control. Indeed, many more humans have been to the Moon than to the deepest part of the ocean. Thirty-three astronauts took part in the American Apollo project, of whom twelve set foot on the Moon; so far only two human beings have descended the 37,800 feet down to the bottom of the Marianas Trench (Jacques Piccard and Don Walsh in 1960).

As our 'high' and 'deep' frontiers, the two extraterrestrial commons fit perfectly into the role of objects to satisfy the desire for vast and sublime wilderness areas. Challenging and awe-inspiring, they fill our mindscape with new imaginary sites, whose significance we will attempt to decode with the spaceship, the horoscope and the dolphin icons as prism.

To Cannibalize and Worship the Wild: In Early Modernity and Today

Last, but not least, we shall emphasize the joint frame of reference of our three icons that lies in their shared relationship with the concept of wilderness in both its cultural historical and current meanings.

We consider the classic dichotomy between 'civilized' masculine selves and the trinity of 'wild' others to be an invention of so-called civilized society. Just as madness, according to Foucault (1989), emerged forcefully in the Age of Enlightenment and Reason, so are the *topos*, the wilderness, and the tropes, such as 'wild' and 'savage', used to characterize features of a site and its inhabitants, constructed by the 'civilized' self. Madness became an important object of cultural interest when the modern subject began to define itself as governed by the light of reason. Likewise, the wild and the savage caught the attention of white Europeans of the Renaissance and early modernity as they began to engage in the technoscientific and colonial enterprise aimed at the control of nature and the opening up of a globally unrestrained access to raw materials and slave labour. The wild and the savage were the human and non-human others who inhabited the wildernesses beyond the frontiers of civilization.

A high priority of the early modern age was to 'civilize', i.e. tame, domesticate, control and enslave the 'wild' other in order to transform her/him/it into a docile object and a resource for the greedy colonizer and the enterprising frontiersman. But, as earlier suggested, the civilized self of the Enlightenment and Romanticism sometimes characterized the wilderness in other ways as well, defining the wild other as noble savage or sublime nature, both of which might guide a civilization gone astray back to 'authentic' values. The powerful resonances of Rousseau's philosophy and the call for a 'return to nature' may be seen as the early beginnings of a modern sacralization process and a wilderness cult (Nash 1982), in which the securely positioned civilized self could indulge.

Thus, from the beginning, modern constructions of a civilized self versus a wild other were criss-crossed by intersecting approaches, and linked together in a pattern of ambivalence. We will discuss what has happened to these ambivalences, and explore the thesis that the simultaneous act of cannibalizing and worshipping the wild, which shaped early modern patterns of ambivalence, is being replayed today. Powerful new versions of deeply ambivalent and contradictory self–other images are surfacing. They appear in discourses on the extraterrestrial commons in general, and in stories of our three icons in particular.

At the end of the twentieth century, the colonial quest for new territories on the continents of Earth, which in early modernity engendered the problems of civilized selves versus wild others, has in a way become obsolete. The goal of 'modern man', limitless growth and unrestrained cannibalizing of terrestrial territories, has proved itself to be dangerous to our survival on Earth. Nevertheless, it seems difficult for ease-loving citizens of the postmodern world to deconstruct this particular part of modern Utopianism. The deceased utopias of European and American modernity, and the languishing belief in their 'civilizing' techno-political world-mission, persevere, as it were posthumously, in lending legitimacy to cannibalistic acts and new quests for resource-abundant areas of wilderness. This is one of the important factors behind the interest in the extraterrestrial commons, and partly the reason why they caught the imaginations of post-Second World War politicians and technoscientists. The resources and riches of outer space and the ocean depths, it is argued, might compensate for the lost terrestrial ones.

At the same time, however, a deep fascination with the wild and a desire to worship it are sweeping millennium minds. The more rapidly our 'civilized' ways of living devour the wild, the more we middle-class people of postindustrial cultures become obsessed with a radical nostalgia for healing the broken bonds between human and wild nature. Vanishing terrestrial wildernesses are reinvented in the shape of 'wilderness parks', or reconstructed as 'virtual reality' images, and new extraterrestrial ones, the cosmos and the ocean, brought into focus. We suggest that an important driving force behind this trend is the longing for a spiritual and metaphysical guarantee of the continued existence of a 'truly' wild and wise beyond-ness. This may also be one of the reasons why astrology and other kinds of ancient beliefs in cosmic messengers experience a renaissance in secularized countries. And explain why selected and ennobled icons of the wild, such as the enigmatically brainy and helpful dolphins, have been turned into cult figures and inscribed in new religious mythologies. There seems to be a strong desire today to merge with the presumed wise and wild extraterrestrial other, be it an astrological constellation of the Zodiac, perhaps conveying messages from the goddess of fate, or a Sibylline marine mammal.

Amazing Stories

Scattered between the chapters are five amazing stories. Some of them we took part in ourselves, others simply sent a current of high-voltage amazement through our bodies as we stumbled upon them in various texts. The stories act as prisms for the discussions of the spaceship, the horoscope and the dolphin in the regular chapters. But aside from brief comments, we retell the amazing stories *in medias res*, leaving it largely to the reader to trace links and draw conclusions about the connections. In this way we hope that others may spontaneously tune in on the amazement we felt ourselves, and which we consider a vital element of analyses. As we shall show in Chapter 2, we favour a balancing act between critical distance and amazement. Hence cultural critique and cultural amazement are both cues to a reading of this book.

Notes

1. 'Slash' refers to fiction writing of fan-cultures who rewrite popular television series, inventing homo-erotic relationships, most often male/male, between the characters. Specifically, the term refers to the use of a grammatical 'slash' to signify the relationship, for example Kirk/Spock from the Star Trek series, which is very popular with slash writers. Women produce most of the slash writings.

2. According to Bakhtin, the carnival in the Middle Ages was a forum for celebration

of inappropriate and improper contiguities between the official ideologies of Church and King and the 'inferior' world of ordinary people – that is, between 'high' and 'low'. The jester, who ridicules the King, and the *Testament of the Ass* (a popular text in the Middle Ages) that makes fun of the Holy Scripture are examples of how 'the carnival-esque' works on the basis of contiguities that are both inappropriate and improper when seen from the perspective of the official ideology. The role of the jester plays on a pattern of contiguity or attraction: he acts as if he were the King, but in doing so he produces mock-images of the royal performance. Since everybody knows that the jester is not the King, the contiguity or attraction is countered by a pattern of difference and repulsion. The laughter, evoked by the jester, is based on the interference of the two patterns.

3. The theory of Earth as Gaia, i.e. as one organism, which has become a popular part of New Age thought, was developed by the British scientist James Lovelock (1987). His first inspiration for the theory came during his work for NASA in the 1960s. It had two important sources: his engagement in the search for life on Mars and the idea of looking at Earth from outside (the Blue Planet picture). His own story and the popularity of his Gaia hypothesis illustrate the intertwinement between the Space Age and New Age stories from another angle than McCulloch's picture.

4. Dolphins can be classified as small whales. Since dolphins are much more easily studied – and captured – than the large whales, they were the first to enter the oceanaria and laboratories, and to draw public attention to the species (see Chapter 8). The main iconic difference lies in the serene distance and majestic monstrosity of the whales as opposed to the lively dolphins that often live closer to land.

5. The concept 'terraforming', to which we return in Chapter 4, is frequently used in futuristic space flight discourses. Normally, it describes the processes by which other celestial bodies may be made habitable with Earth, Terra, as the model. See also Fogg (1995: 9).

6. The expression 'inner space' was deliberately coined in the USA in the late 1950s in order to reinforce the parallel between deep sea exploration and space flight; cf. the expectations that 'the rush into outer space will be matched by an international invasion of inner space' (Piccard and Dietz 1961: 182–3); see also *Science* (1960: 1592) on ocean-ography as 'the exploration of "inner space"'. For a more recent example, see Earle (1995: 13).

1

Map of Matrices

In our analysis of contemporary relationships between 'civilized selves' and 'wild others', we intend to display and deconstruct the traps of the former, which oscillate between two problematic alternatives. They tend either to behave as if they could control the wild other, or, conversely, to reinvent themselves as mere receptacles and channels for its enigmatic messages. The former position is common in some scientific communities, whereas the latter is typical of trends within the New Age movement.

While exposing these traps, we want, of course, to avoid them ourselves. What strategy do we use to steer clear of these rocks? Epistemologically, we share with many researchers within feminist cultural studies a disbelief in the traditional dichotomies between theory and empirical objects of study, between knowing subjects and objects of knowledge. We believe in accountable story-telling and theoretically informed articulations by embodied and localized subjects in dialogue with other human and non-human subjects – a dialogue that should not, however, amount to a simple fusion (cf. Haraway 1991: 188ff.; 1992: 309). In this way, it seems possible to avoid the pitfalls not only of the command–control paradigm of some 'civilized selves', but also of its reversal to New Age romanticism and attempts to merge with 'wild others'.

Our epistemological position demands self-reflection, and in order to situate ourselves we shall, first of all, emphasize that the object for which we want to account is the set of narrations of the 'we' who engage in late twentieth-century quests for a wild elsewhere. The book is an analysis of the positions of 'civilized selves' in this period, and not of an essentialized wild and savage other. But, second, we will make it abundantly clear that we ourselves are part of the questing 'we' that is the focus of the analysis. In collecting materials for the book, we have undertaken many journeys, both real and imaginary, to alien and exotic places and spaces and enjoyed the spirit of adventure. This book is a situated reflection upon those journeys.

In this chapter we shall contextualize ourselves in more detail, outlining the map of matrices from which the book emerged: our methods and materials, our location and our theoretical inspirations – in order to make the point of departure for our reflections transparent.

Methods and Materials

The methodological pivots about which the book turns are discourse analysis, narratology, and semiotic and deconstructive readings of various kinds of textual and non-textual materials. Intertwined with these approaches, we make use of qualitative research interviews and inspirations from anthropology.

Like anthropologists, we have travelled a great deal in real life – and, as literary theorists, also in fantasy. We have visited worlds that were foreign to us and to each other. We crossed real and imaginary borders between Russia and the USA; between the cosmos and the ocean; between the apparently rational world of high-tech science and the occult world of New Age astrology; between worlds heroized as masculine or mystified as feminine; and we confronted the Mona Lisa smiles of dolphins and the beautifully serene monstrosity of whales.

Through textual and visual media, we followed astronauts to the 'high frontier' as well as aquanauts to the 'deep frontier'; we lent our ears to the voices of the cosmos as interpreted by New Age astrologers; and we shared the peepholes of researchers and dolphin lovers who were trying to catch a glimpse of the enigmatic world of these intelligent marine mammals or to construct interspecies encounters.

Consuming a lot of fuel in long-distance flights, we tried to meet in person with informants from both Russia and the USA. Our journeys made it possible for us to conduct 26 qualitative interviews with women and men belonging to the academic staff of space research centres in the two countries, and 15 interviews with female and male astrologers in Moscow and San Francisco. We also interviewed six women and men involved in dolphin studies in the USA, some of them affiliated with dolphin research centres, and others freelancers. The interviews took place during the period 1990–98. While the words of the space researchers and astrologers are considered separately in two different chapters, the perspectives of the dolphin-people mingle with our general depiction of cetacean iconography.

Our travels also gave us the opportunity to do field work and make observations at space flight facilities, space flight museums, Sea Worlds and dolphinaria, dolphin research and education centres, ocean areas with wild dolphins, eco-organizations and New Age fairs. We stroked Gagarin's spaceship *Vostok*, the tiles of the space shuttle *Discovery* and the smooth rubbery skins of dolphins. We swam close to wild dolphins and felt the splash-down of huge killer whales performing in the sad surroundings of the simulated ocean of Sea Worlds. We touched stones brought down from the Moon, we were invited into astrological mysteries and were even perceived as cosmic messengers ourselves. We could not have written this book if it had not been for these alien encounters. We are grateful to all the human and non-human inhabitants of the – to us – exotic and alien worlds we visited. They made the encounters possible and gave us the opportunity to try out the role of questing selves in search of adventure.

To Speak as Implicated Strangers

As we criticize the position of the questing selves that we scrutinize in the book, we are perfectly well aware that, on the one hand, it includes ourselves. On the other hand, we are on the margins in several respects, when, as female, feminist intellectuals with a background in the humanities and citizens of a small and densely populated Scandinavian country, we approach the worlds of space flight, astrology and dolphins.

First and foremost, we are different from people who grew up in big countries such as Russia and the USA, because 'wilderness' in our imaginary connotes exoticism and places far away. Our permanent location is in Denmark, whose main territory has, for centuries, been more or less devoid of anything that might live up to the name of 'vast untouched wilderness areas'. Contrary to the situation in countries such as the USA and Russia, our national identity includes neither the *topos* 'wilderness' that is such a popular component of the 'American mind' (Nash 1982), nor the 'immense space' that Russian literature back to Pushkin has celebrated as part of the special features of Russia (Edmonds 1994: 201).

Educated in the humanities, we are, moreover, only tourists in the world of high-tech science that makes up the context of space flight and of much dolphin research as well. As citizens of a small and unheroic nation, we are gazing from the margins at the web of major politics and national romantic mythologies, such as the ones constructed by the two superpowers around the first heroic deeds in space. As women, we are also confronting a very different world when peeping into the masculine subculture of space flight and inhaling the odour of brotherhood that unites the space heroes and their many fans. As individuals brought up in a rationalist tradition and rooted in an atheistic world view, a belief in astrology strikes us as extremely exotic as well. The same is true of the New Age sacralization of whales and dolphins.

Thus situated, we look upon the worlds of the spaceship, the horoscope and the dolphin as might anthropologists when they are interpreting foreign cultures. Nevertheless, we are analysing modern and postmodern cultures that, seen from a global perspective, are also our own. We are implicated in the global web that produced the twentieth-century configuration of these three icons. Hence we find it appropriate to define ourselves as implicated strangers.

On the Inclusion of 'Nature' in Feminist Cultural Studies

In theoretical terms, the book maps out a field of innovative approaches to feminist cultural studies of technoscience, animals and spirituality. Feminist studies in their intersections with poststructuralism, semiotics and cultural studies make up an important foundation. In particular, we found major sources of inspiration in Western feminist science studies, and we shall, therefore, begin with a survey of these. As of yet a feminist approach to this huge field has not emerged in Russia.

Feminist science studies constitute a hybrid in the sense coined by Latour (1993). They address the natural sciences and hence 'nature', but at the same time they intersect with another hybrid: feminist cultural studies that deal with 'culture'. When we join Haraway in defining 'science studies as cultural studies' (Haraway 1992: 296), we end up with a field that deals purely neither with 'nature', nor with 'culture' – i.e. a monstrous construct that lurks subversively in between the humanities and the natural sciences in their classical sense (Lykke and Braidotti 1996).

Feminist science studies as cultural studies expose the ways in which modern science has contributed to the othering of Woman, Native and Nature. Therefore, they became important critical matrices for our research on gendered and racialized constructions of 'wild nature' (dolphins and outer space). Especially influential were the works of Merchant (1980), Haraway (1989, 1991, 1997), Schiebinger (1993) and Birke (1994) who, in different ways, made the gender/nature nexus a central theme of their science critiques. Haraway and Schiebinger explore its intersections with race; together with Birke they also discuss constructions of animals, while Merchant for her part analyses cultural images of macrocosmic nature, the Earth and the Universe.

When we, working along similar lines, emphasize the network of meanings that circulate around gender/race/nature, we implicitly argue for a more systematic inclusion of 'nature' (on both a micro- and macro-level) in the intersecting aspects of otherness on which feminist cultural studies focus. Widespread consensus exists within the field as to the importance of scrutinizing the intersections of gender and race. But as the philosopher Val Plumwood argues (1993: 2), the human domination of nature is still a 'missing piece' in feminist cultural theory.

It is true that various kinds of ecofeminists have insisted on the parallels between sexism, racism and 'naturism'. When social ecofeminist Karen Warren coined the term 'naturism' (Warren 1990), she intended to make visible the analogies between sexism, racism and degrading and violent treatment of non-human nature, or 'earth others' as Plumwood poetically names the worlds of animals, plants and minerals (Plumwood 1993: 137). From angles different from that of ecofeminism, researchers within feminist science studies have likewise encouraged a more extensive interest in non-human others and nature.

Nevertheless, Plumwood has a point. Earth others are marginal in the overall framework of feminist cultural theory. Considering the obvious proximity between constructions of gender/race, on the one hand, and gender/earth others, on the other, this is problematic. As discussed in Lykke and Braidotti (1996), the nexus of gender/race/nature generates a whole chain of signifiers between which modern culture, sustained by science, establishes a plenitude of links that allow for rich and diverse displacements and metonymical substitutions. In our opinion this speaks for an integration of the human/nature axis into the framework of inter-secting othering processes that are scrutinized by feminist cultural studies.

A related reason for an inclusion of nature lies in the rapidly changing meanings of the concept. We agree with the editors of the collection *FutureNatural* (Robertson et al. 1996), when they argue that cultural studies cannot avoid the political question of the future of non-human nature, given 'the fragility of the concept "nature" and the instability of its referent'. Due to large-scale technoscientific transformations and reinventions of the once apparently secure 'ground of being' and 'stable otherness to the human condition', nature has, today, more or less lost its meaning as a 'foundational concept' (ibid.: 1). 'Nature' is currently being intensely renegotiated by technoscientists, politicians, etc., and considering the traditional proximity between the semantics of Woman and Nature, it is important that feminist cultural theorists interfere critically in these negotiations.

Together with different kinds of ecofeminism (social or spiritual), feminist science studies have laid the foundations for an inclusion of the human/nature axis in the feminist cultural studies matrix of othering processes in need of critical scrutiny. We chose to base our work primarily on inspirations from the latter, because we think that ecofeminism often discusses 'nature' in ways that are too naïve. Many ecofeminists write of nature as if they were dealing with an innocent concept that referred mimetically to an essentially given and stable referent. Feminist science studies, in contrast, have paid much attention to 'nature' as a construct in a textual as well as a material sense. They have developed sophisticated analyses of the non-innocent and constructed dimensions inherent in any view of nature, without evading the fact that science is also a dialogue with a material, not exclusively discursive, reality.

As important as it is to include 'nature' in the discussion of othering processes, it is crucial to do so without essentializing the category. To insist on multi-layeredness and hybridity is in our opinion decisive in order to avoid the cul-de-sacs of both romantic naïvety and the reduction-ism of positivist beliefs in 'nature' as a phenomenon supposedly 'out there', waiting to be discovered by 'pure', natural science. 'Nature' should be understood from at least a triple perspective: as 'ethno-specific' category (Haraway 1992: 296), as reinvention or 'co-construction' among human and non-human (machine, organic, non-organic) actors (ibid.: 297) and, finally, as something that, as Keller points out, cannot be 'named out of existence' (Keller 1989: 43).

Human, Non-human, Posthuman

When feminist science studies renegotiate the meanings of 'nature', the traditional antipode 'human' starts changing as well. This becomes very clear in the work of Haraway and her recycling of the cyborg metaphor (Haraway 1991, 1997; Gray et al. 1995) as a critical posthuman figure articulating subversive stories that deconstruct the privileged positions of humans, whiteness, and the masculine mind. In order to clarify how changes in the category 'nature' engender displacements along the whole of the human/nature axis of domination, we will briefly explain the concept.

The cyborg concept demonstrates that 'nature' today is normally neither 'pure' nor 'innocent', but 'reinvented' or 'co-constructed', as Haraway phrases it – mediated by sociotechnical interventions. A cyborg is an organism whose physiological functions are modified/transformed/simu-lated by technical control systems: a human-machine or an animal-machine. Not coincidentally, it was early space research that originally gave birth to the cyborg. If earthlings were to adapt to life in the hostile environment of outer space, their bodies would have to change radically. A fish that wanted to live on land would either have to bring along an aquarium or to learn to breathe air, wrote the fathers of the cyborg concept, the American biomedical researchers Manfred Clynes and Nathan Kline, in 1960. Likewise, the human who ventured into outer space would either have to carry huge oxygen tanks or to 'stop breathing':

> [T]here may be much more efficient ways of carrying out the functions of the respiratory system than by breathing, which becomes cumbersome in space. One proposed solution for the not too distant future is relatively simple: Don't breathe! (Clynes and Kline 1960: 30)

Hence the 'simple' idea behind the scheme of Clynes and Kline maintains that the best solution to the problem is technologically to redesign the human body – i.e. to integrate the necessary life-support system directly into the organism. The word that the two researchers proposed for such a new, 'non-natural' creature was not 'man' or 'human', but 'cyborg': a cybernetic organism.

Since the days of early space research, cyborgs have proliferated rapidly within many other fields of technoscience. This has made the perspective transparent: in the cyborg world 'nature' certainly is not what it used to be. But neither is Universal Man. When cyborgs start multiplying in his world, Man changes too. According to Haraway, cyborgs have to be viewed from several angles, negative as well as positive. On the one hand, they tell horror-stories of manipulations and power demonstrations that sustain the dominance of Universal Man, but, on the other hand, they may also challenge and deconstruct his superior position. As a boundary-figure that does not fit into such dichotomies as 'man versus nature', 'man versus machine' etc., the cyborg acts as a deconstructive device in a discursive as well as material sense.[1] In the post(hu)man world of cyborgs, 'man' is so fused with machines and reinvented natures, and nature so intertwined with culture, that the dichotomies become unstable and eventually break down. 'Man' is therefore not what he used to be, nor is the humanism of the 'civilized selves'. Cyborgs threaten the essential core of their identity, founded as it is on the Cartesian split between the superior, thinking subject (alias Universal Man) and the inferior world of non-human matter (alias earth others, machine others, etc.), which, through metonymically circulating meanings, is also linked up with 'Woman' and 'Native'.

When we focus our spotlight on 'civilized selves' and their constructions of the cosmic and oceanic worlds of wild others, and argue for the integration of the human/nature axis into feminist cultural theory, therefore, we do not speak of human versus natural essences. Seen from the post(hu)man position of cyborgs, all such essences need to be deconstructed. This is an important perspective for our analyses of some significant, contemporary master narratives of 'human' selves and 'wild others'.

By turning to the issue of 'wild others', however, we also aim to explore some analytical limits of the cyborg concept. What happens when we want to confront aspects of 'nature', which, as Keller says, cannot be 'named out of existence', and which in the shapes of wild animals and cosmos meet us as a 'beyondness' whose emergence seems in more ways than one to transgress human intervention? As we shall discuss later, this question has directed us towards poststructuralist analyses of spirituality and the divine as a supplement to feminist science studies.

Are Animals a Feminist Issue?

Ask a Feminist for Animal Rights activist this question, and you will hear an immediate 'Yes'. But if we go beyond this particular branch of feminism it seems that, until not so long ago, animals have been avoided, as though they were taboo, or a non-issue. It is true that certain authors (Haraway 1989; Birke 1994), have indeed contributed towards making animals an issue for feminism. The same goes for ecofeminist works such as Adams (1990), Gaard (1993) and Adams and Donovan (1995). But both groups deplore the general feminist neglect of animal perspectives. Gaard notes that the issue is conspicuously absent in major collections of eco-feminist thought (Gaard 1993: 4). In a somewhat parallel vein, Birke observes that animals are missing from feminist science studies as well:

> Yet despite the fact that much of the feminist literature on science focuses on biology, and despite the fact that much biological knowledge inevitably depends on information gained from animals, animals are scarce in that writing. (Birke 1994: 10)

Birke, Haraway, Gaard and others muster impressive arguments supporting the need for a feminist spotlight on animals. Animals play a prominent role in the definition of what is human in science as well as in the broader culture, and as 'human' is definitely not a neutral and innocent category, but a highly gendered and racialized one, discourses on animals, gender and race are deeply intertwined. 'We', the humans, construct animals as our mirrors whether we use them as substitutes for ourselves in pain-inflicting scientific experiments, degrade them as mindless, machinelike, brutish others in opposition to our own 'superior' human subjectivity (free will, intelligence, language), anthropomorphize them and educate them in humanity, or sacralize them as bearers of a transcendent wisdom that 'we', citizens of high-tech urban cultures, have lost. This mirroring business is a widespread activity in modern culture, and when 'we' engage in it, 'we' are rarely displaying either gender or race neutrality. 'She does not look Jewish at all', the diabolic entertainer in the well-known musical of the 1970s, *Cabaret*, sings of his wife in the song 'If You Could See Her with my Eyes', where he poses as a Nazi married to a monkey in women's clothing. The satirical scene is a striking reminder of how discourses on animals, gender and race intersect: in this playing of joint mirror games, racism and sexism blend with 'naturism', degradation of animals.

The clear discursive links between animals, gender and race provide excellent reasons for embracing animals as a feminist issue. Paradoxically enough, they can also explain the taboo. Easily activated substitutions and metonymical contiguities have been used so heavily throughout the modern period to sustain biological determinism and to legitimize social exclusions and hierarchies, that feminists reacted by denying any kind of connection between the free-willed, gendered subject and sexual biology. As Birke has suggested (1994: 11), this denial, promoted in the name of social constructionism, may account for the common feminist unease about and outright tabooing of animal issues, because behind the sex/gender dichotomy there lurks yet another. This is the dichotomy between static animal nature and dynamic human culture: when sexual biology is relegated to the status of a non-issue, so are animals and biology in general. However, we now find a growing recognition among feminists that the dichotomous detachment of the gendered subject from sex and biology had too many costs in the long run. It led to a loss of 'the body itself as anything but a blank page for social inscriptions' (Haraway 1991: 197). Therefore, it is time both to rethink the role of biology and to zoom in on the closely allied animal issue.

This book is inspired by a conviction that animal issues are of crucial importance. Our decision to centre on dolphins stems from an interest in the displacements between gender, race and animal discourses. In an even more radical sense than the terrestrial primates, which, as Haraway pointed out, perform in Eden, our imaginary origin, as well as in future-oriented space (Haraway 1989: 133ff.), cetacean iconographies mirror the contradictions of contemporary culture. The incredible polysemic bodies of dolphins and whales seem to be perfect screens for projections of ambivalent desires to reinvent nature as cyborg or, conversely, to reconstruct it as divine other beyond human intervention.

Do Feminists Need a Cosmology?

Ask a feminist astrologer if feminists need to think about cosmos, and she will answer 'Yes' just as promptly as the animal rights activist confirmed the importance of animal issues. Beyond this particular corner of the feminist landscape, interest in cosmos has also been cultivated by some social and spiritual ecofeminists, who emphasize planetary and cosmic perspectives as part of their holistic world view; by feminist science fiction writers and theorists, since outer space is often the stage where their stories are enacted; and by French sexual difference theorists who touch on cosmic themes as part of their evocations of the feminine in writing and philosophy.

In feminist science studies, a majority of texts have focused on biology and biomedicine; hence outer space has remained on the margins, albeit not totally absent. We have already mentioned that macro-cosmic nature plays an important part in Merchant's feminist science history (1980); she analyses the transition from an organically to a mechanically conceptualized cosmos in the European Renaissance and early modernity. In scattered comments, Haraway, too, refers to outer space, discussing primate performances in space flight and generally designating the space beyond the 'bounded globe' as a fertile place for the proliferation of science fiction cyborgs as well as those of science fact (Haraway 1989: 136ff., 1992: 315ff.). It is, however, significant that Penley's book (1997) is the first one to take up American space flight from a feminist cultural studies perspective. Aside from this study, two sociologists have published an interesting report on their interviews with NASA employees on gender, sex and reproduction in outer space (Casper and More 1995).

Although outer space has been thematized in different ways in feminist cultural studies, its position is still marginal, and the parallel with the sidelining of animal issues conspicuous. However, this marginalization needs an explanation different from that of the taboo on animals. Clearly, cosmos does not resonate with discourses sustaining biological determinism as those on animals do. Instead, we suggest that cosmological issues have escaped the critical eyes of many feminists for the following two reasons.

First of all, it is likely that the metonymic contiguity between cosmos and another taboo triggers an immediate stop-light: namely, its closeness to the sacred and the spiritual. Emerging out of a secular materialist modernity, major trends in feminism have for a long time denied such themes any relevance whatsoever.

But this is probably only part of the reason for the avoidance of cosmic issues in feminism. Another stop-light may be triggered by the extreme versions of the Law of the Father and phallogocentrism that, in mutually reinforcing ways, permeate dominant scientific, technopolitical and religious discourses on cosmos. The modern scientific world view has engendered an apparently empty vastness beyond Earth's atmosphere (discursively identified as cosmos, the universe, outer space, or simply space)[2], but at the same time it has set up an immense screen for projections of a masculine imaginary.

In a classic definition, the science fiction genre is described as speculative fabulation about man's place within the system of the universe, as it is reconceived by twentieth-century science (Scholes 1976: 54–5). Building upon several studies of the gendered world of physics, which acts as the science of cosmology *par excellence* (Easlea 1983; Traweek 1988; Keller 1985, 1992), it seems appropriate to recycle a slightly twisted version of this definition. We may thus assert that cosmological science fact discourses, too, address Universal Man's place in the Universe, and construct powerful master narratives about it. As feminist physicist Renée Heller points out, it is, for example, not a coincidence that the European Particle Physics Laboratory, CERN (Conseil Européen pour la Recherche Nucléaire) popularizes the origin story of the universe in pictures that position Auguste Rodin's *Thinker* as the central human icon (Lykke and Braidotti 1996: 72ff.). The white Christian fathergod may be 'crossed out' (Latour 1993: 32ff.) in the modern scientific world view, but the myth of the numinous and awe-inspiring thinking male genius, whose mind and words generate the order of the Universe, is nevertheless thriving. He can appear as dedicated to the pure exploration of the fundamental laws of astrophysics, or he can be obsessed with more mundane affairs, such as applying his basic knowledge to space missions. But whatever his special task is, it seems as if this universally thinking male mind has pervaded the imaginary cosmic void as thoroughly as his iconographic precursor, the Christian fathergod. In so doing, he has contributed to the historical construction of cosmos as a black hole of condensed masculine fantasies, collapsing into one another in such an intense way that critical feminist energies have so far apparently only had space enough to unfold outside; they are, in other words, left with the limited alternatives of either reinventing premodern cosmologies (as feminist astrology does), or conjuring up new poetic or science fictional ones.

In undertaking a feminist cultural study of the cosmic issue with a focus on both space flight and astrology, we attempt to assist in the deconstruction of the boundary between them that has protected the cosmos of high-tech science from feminist critique. We attempt to engage this masculine cosmos on two fronts. We shall deconstruct and carnivalize it from within, i.e. from a feminist science studies-inspired analysis of the phallogocentric master narratives of space flight that reconstruct the universe as a high-tech laboratory for cyborg activities. But we will also confront it from without, by a critical cultural study of New Age and feminist reinventions of premodern cosmologies, which, as if in a negation or reversal of the masculine cyborg-cosmos, celebrate the natural rhythms of a cosmic body conceived as female. With this pincer movement, we aim to expose and de-naturalize a perfect gender stereotype inherent in modern cosmological thought: high-tech science/masculinity versus occultism/femininity – a stereotype that remains unchallenged as long as both space flight and astrology are more or less shunned by critical, feminist cultural studies.

Feminism, Science and Spirituality

In choosing to position our analysis in the intersections between techno-science, ecocultures and spirituality and by focusing on aspects of 'nature', which represent a 'beyondness', we are, as hinted, moving beyond the traditional scope of feminist science studies. While ecocultural themes have been embraced by these studies from Merchant (1980) to Haraway (1992), analyses of spirituality seem, at least at first sight, to be alien to the field. Grounded in social constructionist, poststructuralist or in other ways materialist thinking, major trends in feminism have committed a fair number of calories to keeping spiritual ecofeminists, goddess-worshippers and the like at a safe distance. Haraway's final words in her famous cyborg manifesto, 'I would rather be a cyborg than a goddess', testify to this (Haraway 1991: 181).

Nevertheless, one striking similarity between the discourses of feminist science studies and aspects of spirituality does catch the eye. In spite of pronounced differences and the wish to maintain a distance, feminist science studies seem to have one urge in common with spiritual eco-feminism. Both desire to subvert mechanistic science's image of nature as passive, inert other and to let the agency and subject-status of non-human others co-write the discursive universes of science.

A shared target of several otherwise different feminist science critiques is the discursive killing of non-human nature that has been brought about by modern science. Merchant (1980) mourns 'the death of nature', and pinpoints the historical moment of this holocaust in the scientific revolution of early modernity; her goal is to make it clear that a rethinking is possible and long overdue. Keller deconstructs the scientific discourses of nuclear physics and molecular biology and the way they have exorcized mystery from nature's 'secrets of life and death' (Keller 1992: 39ff.); she also praises Nobel Prize winner Barbara McClintock for her dialogical approach that allowed the corn molecules she studied to 'speak' to her (Keller 1983). Birke (1994) turns against the biological sciences' reduction of animals to subjectless beast-machines. Haraway criticizes the widespread discursive positioning of the natural scientist as 'ventriloquist' for a passive and muted non-human other (Haraway 1992: 312). Although she warns us that nature is a difficult concept, whose ethno-specific genealogies have to be borne in mind, she also confesses to her belief in its agency, its status as 'material-semiotic actor' (Haraway 1991: 200). According to her, non-human nature is a 'witty agent', to be compared with Coyote, the American prairie wolf, who plays the role of trickster in Native American myths (Haraway 1991: 199; Haraway 1991a; Penley and Ross 1991).

It would, of course, be a distortion to collapse feminist science studies into spiritualist thought but, conversely, a sheer denial of certain resemblances also misses the point. The affinity, when it comes to questions of the agency and subject-status of non-human nature, seems to be especially clear in Merchant's holistic understanding of nature as imbued with life and in the scattered references to the mythic Coyote-figure in Haraway's texts. Indeed, Haraway's Coyote marks out the borders between her construction of wild nature and that of feminist goddess-worshippers. Coyote is invoked to act as an ironic, non-gendered alternative to an essentializing cult of nature as 'primal mother' (Haraway 1991: 199). But Coyote also seems to be interpellated into Haraway's texts because Cyborg needs a wild cousin, who - like the goddess - can tell stories of a spiritual agency beyond human intervention.

In this book we will explore a new hybrid: feminist cultural studies of science and spirituality. But, as the references to the discussion of nature's agency in feminist science studies discourses show, we follow a line of thought that can be traced in embryonic form here.

Philosophy's Shadows and the Female Divine

The most important theoretical impulse behind our approach to spiritual themes comes from French poststructuralism, primarily Irigaray, Cixous and Kristeva. Over the years, several French poststructuralists have touched on 'philosophy's shadows' (Berry and Wernick 1992: 2): the sacred, the spiritual and the divine, through their exploration of concepts such as *jouissance*, ecstasy and the sublime. Irigaray in particular brought a thought-provoking slant to the discussion, asking what the lack of access to a divine mirror means for the female subject (Irigaray 1993).

Although the sacred has thus been on the agenda of French post-structuralism for a number of years, it was a long time before it began to attract the attention of a broader audience of poststructuralist scholars. It is, for example, symptomatic of the Anglo-American situation that a collection on postmodernism and religion from the early 1990s speaks about an 'unexpected emergence' (Berry and Wernick 1992: 3) and a 'recently revived interest in religion [...] that has surfaced within the new postmodernist [...] intelligentsia' (ibid.: 57). As Berry and Wernick observe, spiritual thought, the shadow side of thinking, was othered by Enlightenment *ratio*, but this othering continued in post-Enlightenment philosophies. However, as we approach the Millennium, it is no longer a prerogative of narrow circles of Parisian intellectuals, marginalized New Age scholars or feminist goddess-worshippers to theorize new-religious insights. By contrast, spirituality and mysticism seem to impose themselves with increasing power on the post-Marxist agendas of secularized Western intellectuals as well as to participate forcefully in the final devaluation of the special Marxist version of secular materialism in the former Soviet Union.

The emergence of the sacred and the spiritual within secular, post-structuralist thought is a sign of this changing situation (Berry and Wernick 1992; Wyschogrod 1990). We may also note that New Age spirituality has become an object of interest to cultural studies in the 1990s. It is suggestive that a comprehensive survey of cultural studies includes a chapter on 'New Age Technoculture' (Grossberg et al. 1992: 531–56) and that critical but elaborate discussions of New Age mysticism from a cultural studies point of view can be found, for example, in Coward (1989), Ross (1991) and Hess (1993). Another collection, whose explicit aim is 'to fill the gap that exists in the scholarly literature' on the New Age (Lewis and Melton 1992: x), testifies in much the same way to the growing fascination with the New Age movement as a cultural phenomenon.

Our book is informed by a comparable commitment to a theoretical widening of the scope of cultural studies, and a desire to move beyond an exclusion and othering of the sacred, the spiritual and the divine. We want, on the one hand, to transgress the paradox of much postmodern cultural critique that displays a disbelief in Enlightenment thought while simultaneously giving in to its rules when it comes to the repression and rejection of 'philosophy's shadows': spiritual thought. On the other hand, we do not want to be snared by the traps of universalism and essentialism, which characterize a major part of New Age and spiritual feminist thought.

This is our reason for choosing to draw inspiration from French post-structuralism, and in particular from the works of Irigaray, Cixous and Kristeva, in our analysis of New Age astrology. This approach makes it possible to keep clear of acting as an auxiliary arm of Enlightenment repression and at the same time to avoid siding with the universalist, essentialist, and sometimes extremely phallogocentric truth claims of New Age astrology. Irigaray's notion of the female divine will, for example, allow us to highlight the desire for a feminine elsewhere, exposed by New Age astrology, while deconstructing the essentialist notion of a Great Cosmic Mother, which, in different forms, is conjured up by both patriarchal and feminist astrologers.

Feminism, Story-telling and Extraterrestrialism

A shared feature of the otherwise different texts of Haraway and Irigaray, from which we have drawn inspiration, is that they make the boundaries between theory and literature permeable. This is the case as far as their writing styles are concerned, but it applies to their reading strategies as well. Irigaray reads philosophy as psychoanalytic narrative (Irigaray 1985a), while Haraway interprets science as 'story-telling practice', likening, for example, biology to Romantic literature (Haraway 1989: 4–5). With all their theoretical and political differences, their common goal is nevertheless to create critically disruptive and deconstructive reading positions. By tackling philosophy and science discourses from these oblique angles, both Irigaray and Haraway generate eye-opening denaturalizations. At the same time, their reading strategies make it possible to avoid both the pitfall of simplistic either/or, good/bad dichotomies as well as the impasse of having to choose between one-dimensional standpoint criticism or political relativism.

Inspired by these disruptive reading strategies, we transliterate the discourses of space flight, astrology and dolphins into various narrative genres. The aim is to make critical interventions by the creation of oblique reading positions, which differ from the ones immediately offered by texts that, for example, are explicitly asking to be read as science fact reports or spiritual doctrines. For much the same reason, we mix readings of scientific reports, astrological doctrines, spiritual revelations, etc., with texts that willingly expose their fictionality, such as novels and films. In the conscious blurring of these genre-boundaries, we follow Haraway in particular in her double move, when, deliberately reading 'out of context' (Haraway 1989: 377; Strathern 1987: 251ff.), she transcribes science fact discourses into a branch of science fiction, while provocatively 'converting' science fiction texts into a kind of science fact (Haraway 1989: 5).

Our choice of extraterrestrialism as thematic pivot has much the same background as our focus on story-telling and reading 'out of context'. Being outside the world of terrestrial everyday life, extraterrestrialism also involves oblique perspectives that may sustain the creation of disruptive reading positions. So the two strategies we use are both rooted in the wish to carry out a feminist meditation on contemporary culture from strange angles that will be capable of stirring up inconvenient and improper questions.

As far as the extraterrestrial perspective is concerned, we are particularly inspired by feminist appropriations of science fiction. The genre demonstrates that the extraterrestrial wilderness, whether cosmic or oceanic, constitutes an evocative backdrop for stagings of hyperbolic and grotesque extrapolations from contemporary culture. In the hall of distorting and diffracting mirrors created by an alien environment that is totally dislocated from the everyday world, selected features of this mundane and familiar setting may be effectively scrutinized, denaturalized and questioned. Recycling Robert Scholes's analysis of science fiction as 'fabulation' on a different world, designed to make us confront our own in a cognitive way (Scholes 1976: 46ff.), Marlene Barr coins the term 'feminist fabulation' to characterize feminist science fiction and its re-readings and revisions of patriarchal myths:

> Feminist fabulation, a new reading practice, critiques patriarchal master narratives. It is feminist metafiction: fiction about patriarchal fictions ... Feminist fabulation is feminist fiction that offers us a world clearly and radically discontinuous from the patriarchal one we know, yet returns to confront that known patriarchal world in some cognitive way. (Barr 1993: 10–11)

We absorb into our work an analogous reading strategy to the one Barr ascribes to feminist science fiction. Hence we read not only fictional but also non-fictional (scientific or spiritual) discourses on the wilderness of extraterrestrialism as fables that reflect current constructions of the gender/race/nature nexus in a hyperbolic and grotesque form by situating them in an alien environment.

To Widen the Geographical Map of Cultural Studies

Since their beginnings in the 1960s, cultural studies have had a marked Anglo-American focus. So have feminist cultural studies. This state of affairs is the result of the history of the concept and its emergence in a British context. However, cultural studies need not, of course, remain within this restricted territory. They are able to act as 'genuinely international phenomena' (Grossberg et al. 1992: 11). We venture into this potential when we base our discussion of the three icons – the spaceship, the horoscope and the dolphin – on American as well as Russian[3] discourses and narratives.

This double gaze unveils certain asymmetries between the conditions for studying the two cultural areas. First of all, the availability and accessibility of sources and critical studies are often greater in the USA than in Russia. This is true not only of those with a feminist approach, which, in Russia, have had to overcome many more obstacles to publication than in the West, but also of others. Although the censorship that supervised the Soviet world of media and manuscripts is long gone, the policies of concealment and the ideological monopoly of the old Soviet state are still casting long shadows.

The example of space flight provides a good illustration of this. While the military side of American space flight has largely been camouflaged beneath a mask of openness towards the mass media and the public, embodied by NASA as an allegedly civil organization, Soviet space flight was, from its very first days, deliberately shrouded in the kind of secrecy and misinformation that reveals its military character. For instance, the rocket specialist Sergei P. Korolev, who masterminded the Soviet space triumphs in the late 1950s and early 1960s, had to remain a mystery man, unknown to the world during his lifetime. Similarly, the name of the Soviet launching site, Baikonur, was chosen with the purpose of misleading the public as to its whereabouts,[4] and the launches themselves were so secret that not even the cosmonauts' families were informed before lift-off. As a consequence of this huge difference in policies, there are plenty of media portrayals and public stories of individual American astronauts from the 1960s onwards, including critical ones, available for analysis, allowing us to explore American myths of the masculine space hero; but it is far more difficult to document and contextualize the Soviet versions. Due to heavy censorship and a long tradition of doctoring reality with textual makeup, the latter appear uniformly hagiographic in the sense that they reflect only the official, ritualized ideology of the militarized 'red right stuff'. It is precisely this hagiographic character that the Russian author Victor Pelevin,[5] to whom we will return in Chapter 9, so aptly exposes in his satirical novel, *Omon Ra* (1992/1996), which is dedicated to the 'Heroes of the Soviet Cosmos'.

Another striking asymmetry that has affected Eastern and Western cosmology stems from the different ways in which the Soviet Union and the USA reproduced the ideologies that are meant to keep large, mission-oriented institutions together. In accordance with its technophilic belief in productive forces as carriers of progress, the Soviet government created a uniform and abstract picture of the big mission assigned to space flight. Although permeating the institutional walls of 'big science', this set of monotonous abstractions was apparently unable to mould the mindscapes of its staffs into an organizational unity in the way that the US government and NASA have jointly achieved. Rich in high-flown rhetoric, yet deprived of the glamour of things, of the lush décors and seductive desire radiating from the spin-off commodities that act as personal and societal encouragements in the USA, the Soviet authoritarian monologue on the mission in space has failed for decades to deliver the evocative commonplaces that could generate a unifying iconography in organizations such as the Institute of Cosmic Research (IKI), which we visited in Moscow in 1991.

The collapse of the Soviet Union at that time only underlines our point. There were no internalized imageries strong enough to hold the nation's body together. In the case of institutions like IKI, this meant that the official purpose of the space enterprise ('to benefit mankind') was not transformed into the invisible mind-web that makes up a community consciousness. Aside from distant, utilitarian goals, the universe that the state depicted in its official slogans on the big mission of space flight left nothing except a vacuum for the individual imagination to fill. The cosmography the IKI staff presented to us during our interviews was as a result less uniform than the one displayed by the Americans, but more coloured by private, individual and self-made fantasies. An unexpected paradox seems to arise from this comparison: the totalitarian regime fosters signs of individualism, whereas the democratic one gives birth to uniformity. Because of its authoritarian and abstract character, the former neither would nor could generate the community spirit that bonds large, mission-oriented organizations into a homogeneous whole within which the public imagery is closely allied with that of the individual; the latter, conversely, succeeded very efficiently in creating such an organizational unity. NASA has thus been capable of internalizing and regenerating the missionary quality of its national goals, an achievement that depends on the staff believing, as dedicated actors, in the master narrative of the enterprise.

However, amid these differences, our double gaze also unveils a discourse of sameness that emphasizes some striking continuities between the two cultures, including their in many ways homonymous master narratives of space flight.

Notes

1. Haraway emphasizes that the acts of deconstruction engendered by cyborgs differ from the traditional poststructuralist definition. While poststructuralist deconstruction, as conceived by Derrida (1987), is a textual process, cultural studies of technoscience have led her to 'a gesture of materialized deconstruction that literary Derrideans might envy' (Haraway 1997: 102). For a further discussion of Haraway's notion of deconstruction and the cyborg concept, see Lykke (1997).

2. Note on terminology: 'cosmos' is the preferred term in Soviet space flight. 'Outer space' or simply 'space' are the terms normally used in the USA.

3. At times our use of the name Russia also covers the Soviet Union.

4. Geographical confusion formed part of the official Soviet strategy. Thus all more or less accurate maps of the Soviet Union disappear around 1930 only to return in 1990.

5. An excellent interview with V. Pelevin may be found in Laird (1999). It is part of the historical irony that when Pelevin's satirical depiction of the Soviet Cosmos as nothing but Potemkin façades came out, even the sky into which Russia launches its piloted missions was no longer what it used to be. Today it belongs to Kazakhstan, the rightful owner of the gigantic Baikonur Cosmodrome after the breakdown of the old Union. In 1994, a long-term lease agreement was signed, transferring control of the cosmodrome to the Russian Space Agency.

Amazing Stories I–III: The Spaceship, the Horoscope and the Dolphin

Amazing Stories is the title of the first pulp science fiction magazine published in the USA. It was founded in 1926 by an émigré from Luxembourg, Hugo Gernsback, who later lent his name to the Hugo Awards, given each year to the best works of science fiction. The idea for *Amazing Stories* grew out of his obsession with stories of futuristic hardware, for which he first coined the term 'scientifiction'. Another inspiration came from adventure pulps and magazines such as *Weird Tales*, which told stories of the supernatural. With *Amazing Stories*, Gernsback established a trend. In the wake of its publication, many more popular SF magazines sprang up, with such dashing titles as *Science Wonder Stories*, *Air Wonder Stories* and *Astounding Stories of Super-Science* (Scholes and Rabkin 1977: 36–7).

We have borrowed Gernsback's title as the heading for a number of stories that we tell in between some of the chapters in order to spotlight the amazement, the feelings of disbelief and wonder, that we, as implicated strangers, often experienced during our research on the foreign cultures and unfamiliar domains into which we ventured. The condensed form in which the spaceship, the horoscope and the dolphin icons are presented in the following cluster of stories, is meant to serve as a general appetizer; it should tune the reader in on amazement as part of the critical reading strategy that we lay out more clearly in Chapter 2.

Touch the Moon!

In a specially constructed vault–cum–laboratory beneath Johnson Space Center in Houston, Texas, behind a 14-ton door strong enough to meet Bank Protection Act requirements, the American government treasures one of its most precious relics. Here lie NASA's lunar rock samples, or at least the major part of them.

With NASA's flair for publicity that rivals that of Hollywood or the Catholic Church, the public is informed about the lunar samples in an exhibition that demonstrates their significance not only as scientific objects and precious stones, but also as holy relics. The lunar vault is open to visitors, and presents itself as a hybrid of a laboratory, a bank safe deposit and a chapel. The chapel-like character is emphasized by an 'altar' bearing a small piece of lunar rock that has been removed from the Pristine Sample and graciously located in the public space of the vault. Here, visitors are offered a kind of Holy Communion. Emblazoned with the words 'Touch the Moon', the plate in front of the 'altar' invites you to reach out your hand and touch the 3.8 billion-year-old piece of lava stone.

To ensure that we, the amazed public, recognize the extraordinary significance of this communion, the plate goes on to explain the touchstone's symbolic meaning. We are told that we have the opportunity to touch 'a priceless artefact from one of history's greatest voyages of exploration'. The touchstone, the plate instructs us, symbolizes 'both our past and our future on the space frontier'. It can allow us to reconnect with primordial times, when the surface of the Moon was covered with molten lava flows, and it is also intended to act as 'a reminder that one day in the years to come, humans will return to the Moon to establish a permanent base, where they will live, work, explore and gain new knowledge for the people of Earth' (Johnson Space Center, text accompanying exhibit of lunar touchstone).

With its many references to the Apollo astronauts who picked up the rocks and the scientific insights gained by their heroic acts of exploration, the lunar vault seems to convey the message that spaceman has turned the cosmos into a cyborg laboratory. It gives us to understand that he can control even primordial extraterrestrial matter as well as construct his own cosmic future. The visitor's touch is staged as the palpable proof of this. In much the same way as the Catholic Church ensures that believers experience in a literal sense the incorporation of the heavenly/human body of Christ, through the dogma of the transubstantiation of bread and wine, so NASA makes use of the special power of enunciation of the touchstone. The touch is designed to appeal to the public's sense of mythic realism. The stone is intended to perform not only as a symbol of the Moon, but as the Moon itself. When we touch the stone, we, the visitors, are brought into direct contact with this other world and allowed entry into the spaceman's cosmic laboratory.

A Coincidental Meeting

Our first meeting with the Russian astrologer Vera appears to be the result of a coincidence. However, according to Vera, it is a highly meaningful coincidence. She invites us into her amazing reality, and takes our breath away with her exposition of what this coincidence signifies. To her, the meanings of the macrocosmos are inscribed in our meeting, and we are the cosmic messengers from whom she expects great things.

In any case, whether the coincidence is meaningful or not, it certainly takes us by surprise to find Russian astrologers in the place where we meet Vera, although the setting has a very 'cosmic' air. It is an autumn day in 1991, and we have set out to visit Moscow's counterpart to Disneyland or the Epcott Center in Florida: the grandiose exhibition and amusement park, VDNKh (the Exhibition of Economic Achievements) that was built in order to celebrate the techno-economic successes of the Soviet Union. Our goal is the gigantic 'Cosmos Pavilion', which is acclaimed as the park's central and most popular attraction, with close to ten million visitors every year. Over the decades since its opening in 1966, this pavilion, the monumental encapsulation of the 'conquest of space', has heralded the bright future of cosmic communism.

In the big exhibition area the 'Cosmos' is located as the triumphant end point to which all roads lead: the point where the apotheosizing finale of the tour is supposed to take place. Expectantly, we approach the pavilion, which looks from the outside like a hybrid of a church and a fortress. But inside an anti-climax awaits us; everything is in a mess, and most of the exhibits are covered or in other ways swept into limbo. A sign informs us that the Soviet Cosmos is presently undergoing repairs. This former 'mirror of the future and progress' now reflects only the chaos and decay of the Soviet Union in its final days.

From the deserted Cosmos, we stroll back towards the exit of the exhibition area, but suddenly our attention is caught by one of the other impressive pavilions where, by contrast, the installation of new life seems to be in full swing. Alternative medicine, healing and occultism have here totally ousted the Soviet techno-triumphs. Now we finally meet the cosmos, although in a very different form from the one we came to see. Together with other prophets of the New Age, an astrological company has set up a stand, from which Vera and her colleagues cast horoscopes and proffer other kinds of celestial consultations.

Vera welcomes us warmly, as though she has been expecting us. Later she explains that she was supposed to have already left, but 'something' persuaded her to stay at the stand this afternoon. On this particular day, she has Venus in the ascendant, so she knew that something important would occur. When we appear on the scene, she immediately understands that we are THE EVENT. 'It had to happen,' she says. Nevertheless, she debates with herself whether she could perhaps be mistaken. Maybe we are just a little too amazed to be suddenly cast into this unfamiliar role of cosmic messengers; maybe we insist too much on not being particularly important. At any rate, doubts arise in Vera's mind. Are we the event the cosmos has sent her this grey autumn day, or was it in fact the young man who had approached her earlier about selling a device to measure bio-energy? She tells us that she did not have time to talk to the young man because she was preoccupied with the horoscope of a client, and he had left again quickly. Nevertheless, her intuition makes her think that it was a significant incident. The young man had probably designed the instrument himself, and it might turn out to be an important invention. Such devices are rare. Finally, however, Vera settles on the solution that the young man will probably return some other day, and that we must be the unique event to which the cosmos has guided her this autumn day. She kindly invites us to visit her in an apartment that serves both as a day-care centre and meeting place for Vera's astrology group. A couple of days later, we spend a pleasant Sunday afternoon there, interviewing Vera and one of the other astrologers about the amazing stories the cosmos conveys to them. We are pleased to get our very first interviews with astrologers, but it is not easy to be cast in the unaccustomed role of cosmic messengers that Vera keeps thrusting upon us, although we emphasize that we do not consider ourselves fit for it.

Even at the end of the afternoon, Vera is still confident that, as celestial messengers, we must possess some particular kind of occult or esoteric knowledge, and her expectations are especially directed towards the one of us who does not speak Russian and who has therefore been silent during the interviewing. In a paradoxical way, this language barrier has increased the astrologer's intuitive feeling of a mysterious connection, and made her deeply expectant of communication on a level higher than ordinary language. In pregnant silence, she seats herself close to the muted visitor, and indicates by gestures that she wants to have her palm read. It is hard to convince her that neither of us, whether deprived of speech or not, can teach her the astrology of the hand (as palm reading is also called), or any other occult or esoteric secrets. She cannot bring herself to believe that the cosmos would create a meaningful coincidence like our meeting without some significant ulterior purpose.

This is a Trick!

> Within the next decade or two the human species will establish communi-
> cation with another species: non-human, alien, possibly extra-territorial,
> more probably marine, but definitely highly intelligent, perhaps even intel-
> lectual. (Lilly 1962a: 15)

These words were written in 1961 by John C. Lilly, a medical doctor and
brain specialist. It is the opening line of his book *Man and Dolphin*, which
describes his research on methods of interspecies communication with
bottlenose dolphins as experimental subjects. Lilly is the principal author
of the post-Second World War dolphin script and it is through his work
that enormous interest was first generated in these animals, whose existence
had attracted little scientific or public attention up until then. He set up
his own Communication Research Institute with laboratories in Florida
and the Virgin Islands, partly funded by the American National Science
Foundation, and at that time he was already making headlines. He
confronted the amazed public with the possibility that dolphins might
learn to speak a human language, and he frequently told journalists and
others that he was convinced of the animals' high intelligence, which was
perhaps even superior to his own. In 1960, the amazing story of Lilly and
his dolphins hit the front page of the *New York Times* (21 June). The
following year, the full extent of his ideas was unfolded with the publication
of *Man and Dolphin*, an event that was heralded by the extremely influential
Life magazine in a widely read feature (28 July 1961).

Like the designers of the Apollo project, Lilly was obsessed with the
challenge of mapping and controlling totally unknown spaces, in this case
the *terra incognita* of the huge, 'human-like' dolphin brain. But, like Vera,
who searched for cosmic messengers, he was equally absorbed in his desire
to trace a 'genuine' language capacity in this wild and alien environment,
and was convinced that dolphins had been endowed with a will to communicate intelligent and meaningful messages to humans. In this way, the
story of Lilly and his endeavours to speak with the dolphins encompasses
central aspects from both of our first two amazing stories. Lilly's project
is also an appropriate illustration of the ambivalent oscillation between
cannibalizing and sacralizing that characterizes late twentieth-century
attitudes towards wild others.

An incident that occurred while Lilly was working with test animals
Numbers 9 and 10, Baby and Lizzie, exposes the doubled vision that
manifests itself so insistently in this new dolphin script, and specifically in

Lilly's work. Numbers 9 and 10 were the first animals with whom Lilly experimented in the Virgin Islands laboratory. He had flown the two dolphins in from Florida. Lizzie, who was named after Lilly's wife, Elisabeth, had been rather badly injured in transit. Furthermore, she seemed to have contracted some kind of infectious disease, and she clearly did not feel at home in the laboratory's dolphin pool. She would not eat, and had to be force-fed by stomach-tube. Of course it added to the worries of Lilly and his team that all the previous animals in the test series (Numbers 1 to 8) had already died or been seriously damaged as a consequence of their experiments. Now the outcome was once more about to be painful death and bodily decay rather than sublime intellectual conversation.

However, before Lizzie died, Lilly tells with awe, something strange happened. Since his work with test animal Number 6, he had been convinced that the dolphins mimicked the human sounds they heard. As part of the experimental setting, therefore, every sound in the laboratory, airborne or underwater, was recorded and later analysed. When Lilly played back the tapes in slow motion, to his own astonishment he reached the conclusion that the dolphins in an 'eerie' way also 'copied' human laughter and even certain English words (Lilly 1962a: 157–8). But the finding that amazed him the most was the phrase that he and his team seemed to hear when they listened to Lizzie's last recording. She may, he relates, have mimicked the sentence 'It's six o'clock!' which had been uttered by someone to remind him that he was going to be late for dinner due to the extra work of force-feeding Lizzie. However, he 'was caught first by another "meaning"' of Lizzie's words. To him it seemed as though she said: 'This is a trick!' (Lilly 1962a: 158).

In Lilly's imagination, Lizzie's final act before expiring was to transgress the role of mimicking beast-machine, and to begin to convey intelligent messages of her own. The ambivalence could hardly be clearer. On the one hand, Lilly's ventriloquism constructs Lizzie as a docile test animal whose behaviour 'proves' that the doctor's agonizing experiments are scientifically meaningful and his thesis about dolphin intelligence and linguistic abilities correct. On the other hand, Lizzie appears in Lilly's story as a sibylline figure, to whom such a trivial pursuit as the search for scientific 'proofs' is but 'a trick'. In the doctor's fantasy, she becomes the bearer of a 'higher' truth which, as a kind of last will and testament, she wants to bequeath to him and other humans in distress. Indeed, Lizzie's last 'words' were not wasted on Lilly, who eventually converted to the New Age.

2

Between Amazement and Estrangement

The discourses on the spaceship, the horoscope and the dolphin are linked by the theme of extraterrestrialism. When we use the critical strategy we introduced in Chapter 1, and read them 'out of context' (Haraway 1989: 377; Strathern 1987: 251ff.), we can articulate this similarity in another way. Addressing the non-fictional discourses of our material as though they were narratives, we can read these alongside the truly fictional ones from the perspective of literary theory and borrow analytical tools accordingly. In line with this approach, we will look at the theme, extraterrestrialism, from a genre viewpoint and revisit the commonalities and differences of the stories in this light.

From this perspective, the extraterrestrialism of the three icons' stories places them in the literary genres of romance or fantasy. Along with science fiction theorist Robert Scholes, we define these genres in a broad sense: as an umbrella for different types of stories that join hands in insisting upon 'a radical discontinuity between [their] world and the world of ordinary human experience' (Scholes 1976: 46–7). The purpose of this disjunction, Scholes comments, is to confront the well-known sphere of everyday life from new angles. In the most basic form of romance or fantasy this effect is achieved by a spatial dislocation to 'another world, a different place: Heaven, Hell, Eden, Fairyland, Utopia, The Moon, Atlantis, Lilliput' (Scholes 1976: 47).

Another science fiction theorist, Darko Suvin, proposes the term 'narrative of estrangement' (1979: 20–1) to describe the same inclusively defined genre. He wants to emphasize the non-familiar and non-everydaylike setting in which the story takes place. He links his definition to the concept of estrangement, first coined in Russian formalist theory (Shklovsky 1990) and politicized in Brecht's theory of the theatre. In this context, it refers to literary techniques that de-automatize and de-naturalize the reader's perceptions of the world: 'A representation that estranges[1] is one which allows us to recognize its subject, but at the same time makes it seem unfamiliar' (Suvin 1979: 6; Brecht 1964: 192).

Dislocation to extraordinary and otherworldly places is a feature that works well as a description of our stories of cosmic and oceanic extra-terrestrialism. In this chapter we shall, therefore, subject them to a genre analysis that is informed by Scholes's and Suvin's definitions. From the oblique angles of a literary reading, we shall draw a map of the patterns of similarities and differences that characterize the master narratives of the spaceship, the horoscope and the dolphin.

In our analysis, we find it worthwhile to keep both Scholes's and Suvin's terms in mind. Suvin's 'narrative of estrangement' is apt to evoke images of unfamiliar and alien environments, which are implied in the concept of extraterrestrialism, whether applied to outer space or to the world beneath the ocean surface. Scholes's terminology may in return call forth associations with the combination of the romantic and the fantastic which, in different ways, characterize the rhetoric of the master narratives of space flight, New Age astrologers, dolphin scientists and dolphin-lovers. Furthermore, while 'estrangement' indicates critical denaturalization in the tradition of Russian formalism and Brecht, 'romance' and 'fantasy' may signal an alliance with wonder and amazement. In this way, the two terms may supplement each other.

Besides the genre category, we shall borrow one more direction-finder from the inventory of literary theory in order to map the stories of our three icons. This is the concept of the fable. The fable of a story is the condensed structure of its course of events in terms of logic, chronology and central theme. As part of our mapping of the genre differences and similarities, we shall produce a survey of the fables on which the stories of the three icons are based in the discursive fields of space flight, New Age thought, cetaccan research and popular culture. Typically, each of these fields is structured by one or two master fables that recur in different forms in various materials, fictional and non-fictional, textual and non-textual. In this chapter we shall illustrate each of these master fables with examples, which we call prototypical because they crystallize many central features of the stories. In order to catch the prototypical dimension, we have chosen to focus on simplistic, fictional examples from popular culture, even though this approach has the disadvantage that it engenders a distinct imbalance in favour of American examples because of the USA's hegemonic position on the scene of popular culture.

A related purpose of the chapter is to point out the relationship between fable and genre, demonstrating how the fables can be described in terms

TABLE 2.1 Main features of the master narratives of the spaceship, the horoscope and the dolphin icons

Spaceship	Horoscope
a) Genre • The masculine adventure story • Science fiction • The fairy-tale of the questing hero	a) Genre • The spiritual journey guided by the 'Eternal Feminine' • The fairy-tale of the hero who is acted upon
b) Fable *Driving forces*: • To imprint the cosmos with human meaning • Command-control: to will, to know, to know-how *Central theme*: • 'To conquer space'	b) Fable *Driving forces*: • To be imprinted by macrocosmic meaning • Coincidences: to abandon yourself to cosmic guidance *Central theme*: • 'As above, so below'
c) Self–other relationship • Cannibalizing	c) Self–other relationship • Sacralizing

Cyborg dolphin	Noble savage dolphin
a) Genre • Science fiction: alien encounter SF and cyborg SF	a) Genre • Pastoral novel • Romantic noble savage story
b) Fable *Driving forces*: • To imprint the animal with human meaning • Schooling; body modification *Central theme*: • 'Uplift', 'Education in humanity'	b) Fable *Driving forces*: • To be imprinted with animal wisdom • Fight between good and evil, nature and technocivilization *Central theme*: • 'Return to nature'
c) Self–other relationship • Cannibalizing	c) Self–other relationship • Sacralizing

of sub-genres of the narratives of romance/fantasy/estrangement. To anticipate the result of the genre-analysis, we shall premise a remark about the involved sub-genres. They are: the science fiction story, the adventure story, the spiritual journey, the pastoral, the Romantic noble savage story and the fairy-tale. These all take place in extraordinary, otherworldly and exotic settings, suited to create estrangement as well as amazement. Table 2.1 presents a survey of the sub-genres, and how they relate to the three icons. A detailed analysis can be found in the pages to follow.

Another anticipatory remark concerns the fables. When we interpret their driving forces and central themes, and take into consideration the self–other relationships they put on display, two opposing pairs emerge (see Table 2.1). As we will show, the stories of the spaceship, the horoscope and the dolphin fit so neatly into such pairs that they seem bound to each other in patterns of reversal and negation. The world of the New Age master narrative appears as the inverted world of the space fable, and vice versa. The latter is about 'civilized selves' wanting to imprint the cosmos with human meaning, while the former, conversely, represents a human longing to be the object of macrocosmic meaning imprints. The in-appropriate contiguity established by the mutual negations of these two sets of tales is emphasized by the polysemy of the dolphin icon, which enacts the same kind of reversals, circulating endlessly between the position of subject and object of the human self.

The Space Age Adventure: To Leave Human Marks in Outer Space

Since its early beginnings, a central theme of the master fable of both American and Soviet space flight has been the 'conquest of space', which means that the crucial driving force of the space adventure is to leave marks in outer space – to imprint the cosmos with human meaning. In spite of its dubious colonialist connotations, the 'conquest' metaphor is still used in the 1990s. An example is the Astronauts' Memorial at NASA's Kennedy Space Center. It was erected in 1991, as a tribute to the heroes and heroines 'who have made the ultimate sacrifice believing the conquest of space is worth the risk of life' (Astronauts' Memorial inscription).

The conquest story implies a fundamental shift in human perspectives from an Earth-bound existence to a new life in outer space. 'Yesterday the Moon, Today the Space Station, Tomorrow Mars', the explanatory inscrip-tion told us, when in 1998 we visited Kennedy Space Center's Processing Facility for the new International Space Station that will replace the Russian *Mir*. Embedded in a pompous rhetoric, the space fable situates humanity at the threshold of a new era, the cosmic millennium that will make us citizens of the Galaxies and transform old-fashioned *homo sapiens* into *homo spaciens* (White 1987: 172).

Prototypical versions of this master fable abound in both American and

Soviet space discourses, and it is celebrated in hyperbolic form by its monumental presence in the two capital cities. These national monuments will serve as illustrations here.

'The Space Mural – a Cosmic View'

Washington, DC, the seat of the US government, has emblazoned space flight in the National Air and Space Museum. This is part of the Smithsonian Museums, a large complex of buildings that dominate the National Mall between the Capitol and the Washington Monument. Within this complex, the Air and Space Museum enjoys a particularly prominent location neighbouring the Capitol. On view is the glorious American history of aero- and astronautics, illustrated by many historic highlights such as the Wright Brothers' Flyer from 1903, the machine in which Charles Lindbergh crossed the Atlantic Ocean in 1927, the command module of *Apollo 11*, which in 1969 carried the first men to set foot on the Moon, a 'touchstone' from the lunar rock samples, and so on. In order to ensure that every visitor, even the most ignorant foreigner or naïve primary schoolchild, fully understands how to interpret these illustrious proofs of American power, masculine heroism and technoscientific genius, the main entrance hall displays a large and dramatic mural, which concentrates the central features of the American space master narrative. 'The Space Mural – a Cosmic View', by Robert McCall, is a visual exegesis of this narrative blown up to proportions designed to underpin its significance and splendour. The L-shaped painting has a horizontal section 22.9 metres long, and a vertical section 17.7 metres high.

The 'Present' and 'Future' sections of the mural tell the fable of the human imprinting of the cosmos, while the first section, 'The Past', dramatically depicts the primordial beginnings of the universe in the Big Bang. The latter appears as a chaotic natural background for 'The Present' human order that has two *Apollo* astronauts standing on the Moon with the Stars and Stripes in a central position. 'The Future' launches 'spaceship Earth' (Fuller 1981; White 1987: 95) drifting over the lunar surface together with the command module that carries the third astronaut involved in the mission. Above the Earth, a radiating cross represents the Sun casting 'its radiance upward, to the galaxies and a new destiny for mankind' (Explanatory plate, National Air and Space Museum).

The will to leave human marks in space leaps to the eye of the spectator as the driving force in the story. It is unmistakably embodied by the astronaut soldier-hero (Dawson 1994) and conqueror, who plants the Stars and Stripes in the lunar soil. As his cyborg-twin or magic helper, the gadget-fetishistic representation of the big lunar landing craft is designed to confront us with the sublime technoscientific knowledge and know-how of the nation that made this event possible, while the cross of solar rays in the upper part of the vertical section signals divine participation. The knowledge, willpower and heroic virility of the USA, which happened to have God on its side, produced this unique event in human history that has forever imprinted new meaning on the cosmos – this is the message that the mural, with an almost breathtaking naïvety, wants to convey. In other words: Cybergodfather & Sons re-created the Universe.

'To the Conquerors of Space … '

The Muscovite counterpart to McCall's Space Mural consists of a 100-metre-high obelisk, erected in 1964 and dedicated to the 'Conquerors of Space'. It is located on top of the Memorial Museum of Cosmonautics, which was opened as a celebration of the twentieth anniversary of Yuri Gagarin's historic flight when he became the first human in space. Both the obelisk and the museum form part of the monumental district of Moscow, where we also find the Avenue of the Cosmonauts, the futuristic Hotel Cosmos and the exhibition and amusement park VDNKh containing the Cosmos Pavilion (whose political deconstruction we described in our second Amazing Story: 'A Coincidental Meeting'; see pp. 46–7). We will use the obelisk and the museum as our next illustration of the space narrative.

The titanic pillar of the obelisk bears at its summit a silvery rocket that conveys to the spectator an impression of something surging into space with massive power and acceleration. Part of the visual effect consists in blurring the view of the rocket from ground level. The speed and energy involved in its launch appear so immense that we, the spectators, who are still languishing in the 'cradle of Earth', can only take leave of the adventurous and heroic 'conquerors of space' by looking in amazement and awe at the rocket's trail of 'smoke'.

Below the obelisk the museum invites the public, in return for its adulation, to enter into the lofty environment of the 'conquerors'. The main exhibition hall is constructed so as to give the visitor the feeling of being inside a spaceship. The display areas perform as imitations of the spaceship's bull's-eye observation windows, and mirrored podia of polished stainless steel are supposed to create an illusion of weightlessness. Furthermore, the monumental vitrage at the end of the hall is illuminated with blue, orange and yellow – 'space colours'.

The message equals that of McCall's Washington mural. The whole setting gives us to understand that, in entering the museum, our perspective has shifted: the future in space has begun. Being inside the spaceship, we have left the nursery of Earth-bound toddlers for the adult world of *homo spaciens* that has been opened up for us by the conquerors. Carrying not the Stars and Stripes, but the Hammer and Sickle, they have already imprinted the cosmos with Soviet meaning.

One exhibit in the Moscow museum even brings to mind the quasi-religious aspect of McCall's painting, although here it has a more mystical than explicitly Christian tinge. In front of the vitrage we encounter a five-metre-high bronze cosmonaut who towers against the background of a gigantic sphere unfolding the twelve Zodiac signs. This 'space era pioneer' (Solomko 1994: 8) resembles the cosmic man, who in Renaissance astrological depictions signified the interconnectedness between the human and the cosmos. Like his Renaissance predecessor, the cosmonaut spreads out his arms to touch the Zodiac with his hands and, whether intended or not, the gesture lends him something of the cast of a Jesus-figure, giving the visitors his blessing. So even if the Soviets did not have God on their side, they had at least the benediction of a Jesus-like Cosmic Man!

The Masculine Adventure Story

In terms of genre, we may read the master narrative of space flight with the science fiction story of the extraterrestrial voyage as model. Like such stories, the space fable is located in a futuristic, extraterrestrial setting, a 'world apart' (Malmgren 1991). In McCall's version, the central action takes place on the Moon, while in the Moscow Museum we are invited inside the spaceship of the 'conquerors'. The logic of the space fable is, moreover, based on what Suvin calls a *novum*, which he defines as a basic feature of the science fiction genre. It is an important technological or social innovation that is cognitively validated, but not necessarily possible by contemporary standards (Suvin 1979: 63). An already existing *novum* involves the possibility, created by rockets and spaceships, of travelling beyond the familiar gravity-bound sphere of Earth, but speculatively the space fable also envisages the emergence of other grandiose *nova* that, in a not too distant future, will expand the human sphere of interest to an intergalactic scale. The effect of the science fiction novel can be linked to the aesthetic ability of the *novum* to create an elsewhere that mirrors a high-tech future, which fascinates because it is, at one and the same time, both amazingly different from the everyday world of the reader and potentially possible. The same is true of the space fable. Even for sceptical implicated strangers like ourselves, who find both McCall's space cartoon and its Muscovite counterpart unintentionally comical in their super-nationalistic, self-glorifying and phallocentric gigantomania, it is difficult not to be awe-stricken when reminded of the extraordinary and fabulous voyages beyond the borders of the known world to which they refer.

Intertwined with the science fiction story, two other genres suggest themselves as paradigms for the space fable and its story about the great extraterrestrial voyage. These are the fairy-tale of the questing hero and its ramification in the modern adventure story. Both involve travels to strange, otherworldly and unknown places far from home, which test the ability of the protagonist to overcome great dangers and meet incredible challenges. Together, the two genres give a clue to the analysis of the conqueror-protagonist of the space fable.

As described by Vladimir Propp (1975), whose fairy-tale theory strongly influenced structuralism and semiotics (Greimas 1983), the questing hero is the protagonist of one type of fairy-tale. He is the kind of hero whose project generates the course of events of the story. In the fairy-tale magic helpers endow him with three important modalities or action-generators – will, knowledge and know-how – so that he can accomplish the project successfully. When the fairy-tale scheme is transferred to the adventure story, the questing hero is made the standard protagonist and at the same time inscribed in a modern cult of supermen, who by individual personality, and not because of magic helpers, are empowered by invincible will, knowledge and know-how. It is obvious that the protagonist of the adventure story shares these features with the hero of the space fable. Whether posing as soldier-hero who plants the Stars and Stripes in the lunar soil or as Soviet 'conqueror' who has left the 'cradle' of Mother Russia far behind, he incarnates the questing adventure hero.

In his analysis of the modern adventure story, literary scholar Martin Green (1990, 1991, 1993) critically describes it as a tale about the white, male hero, who embarks on dangerous journeys for nationalistic and imperialist purposes. He traces the genre back to *Robinson Crusoe* and discusses various types, for example the frontiersman stories (well known in both American and Russian literature). He defines adventure stories as modern fairy-tales. They are, he writes, 'folktales of white nationalism and empire' (Green 1990: 4), allied to a specific kind of modern masculinity that flows from the 'high-spirited' experience of exerting power 'beyond the law, or on the very frontier of civilization' (Green 1991: 3). The adventure story represents a 'liturgy of masculinism' (Green 1990: 6), intersecting with a 'liturgy for the cult of potency and potestas – the social management of force, the exertion of power, material and moral' (ibid.: 5).

Green's description fits well as a characterization of the space fable. It sustains the suggestion that the adventure story and the fairy-tale are both part of the underlying script that created the image of the astro- and cosmonaut supermen. Like Green's adventure heroes, the astro- or cosmonauts perform as mythic national romantic heroes, acting beyond the frontiers of civilization in the wilderness of hostile space, allegedly 'in peace for all mankind', although always carrying with them their national flags to mark their presence in the new territories.[2] Furthermore, the hero of the American and Russian space fable is strikingly masculine. The great 'first steps' of the human journey into the cosmos (the first human in space, the first humans on the Moon, and so on) are, over and over again, in history books, space museums, etc., celebrated as having been taken by 'men of the right stuff' (Wolfe 1988).

The New Age Pilgrimage: To be Pervaded with Macrocosmic Meaning

With similar high-flown rhetoric to the spaceship fable, the master narrative of the New Age articulates prophetic visions of a radically reconfigured relationship between the human and the cosmos. But while the former presents the new cosmic connection as an intentional human imprinting of outer space, the New Age fable depicts it as the opposite. Here cosmos is the subject and the human the object of imprinting. We should, this fable instructs us, stop trying wilfully to control and command the world; instead, we should recognize the symbiotic relationship between macro- and microcosmos, and accept that meanings emanating from the macrocosmic 'above' pervade the microcosmic 'below': body and psyche.

Another difference between the two is that the spaceship fable stages the coming of the new epoch as a result of the voyage into outer space, whereas the entry into the Promised Land of the New Age follows from the exploration of inner, mental spaces. The master fable of the New Age tells of a mental journey into realms of the spiritual and the occult that were exorcized by the Enlightenment and modernity. This fable is about a reinvention of allegedly ancient knowledges and practices, such as the old astrological tenet: 'as above, so below'.

Astrological thought plays a central role in this fable, although it should be stressed that New Age discourses are highly eclectic. They mix heterogeneous elements from many different sources within both Eastern and

Western traditions of occultism and mysticism. But the idea of the interconnectedness and synchronicity between macro- and microcosmos, which dominates the astrological world view, runs as a *leitmotif* through all the New Age stories. In influential versions of the fable, the astrological calendar itself initiates the Great Mental Journey that takes humanity and the Earth from the Zodiac sign of Pisces, which began at the time of Christ, to a new epoch: the Age of Aquarius, which will make our existence flow with love, peace, cosmic harmony and higher human consciousness, 'the mind's true liberation' as the popular song 'Aquarius' from the rock musical *Hair* was promising decades ago (Ragni and Rado 1970).

Celestine Messages and Meaningful Coincidences

Together with our second Amazing Story on our coincidental meeting with the Muscovite astrologer, Vera, the worldwide best-seller and super-didactic American novel *The Celestine Prophecy* (1993), by James Redfield, will serve as illustration of the New Age fable. Both Vera's interpretation of our meeting and Redfield's book exemplify with utmost clarity how the New Age fable turns the space narrative, of the human subject who imprints meaning on the cosmos, upside down. In Vera's and Redfield's universe, it is the cosmos that fills the human with new spiritual insight, and the narrative structure of their stories rests exclusively on sequences of events that are determined by the occurrence of meaningful co-incidences, arranged by the macrocosmic forces. The command-control paradigm of the space narrative is totally suspended, as is the belief in scientific rationality, know-how and the laws of mechanistic causality.

Redfield's novel has not distinguished itself by any literary qualities and neither, strictly speaking, does it deal with astrology. We chose it as proto-type example because of its global popularity, which is reflected in an amazing publication history, and because, with a simplicity that borders on the naïve, it illuminates a very basic New Age tenet: the belief in the fundamental importance of meaningful coincidences. Since this belief is a prerequisite for the use of occult 'tools' such as astrology, the I Ching, tarot, etc., which aim at interpreting coincidences, the book can be con-sidered as an elementary manual for novices in all these branches of 'New Age science' (Spangler and Thompson 1991: 83). As such, it was also recommended to us by one of our astrologer-interviewees. It is, moreover, typical of the mix of activities in which many New Agers are engaged that Redfield practises as an astrologer as well as writing. He sells personalized audio-tapes, based on interpretations of the astrological data of his readers

(Redfield 1993: 247). So astrology is evidently an integral part of his universe.

The novel was distributed privately via a PO box before it was eventually bought by a publisher for $800,000; for over three years it was included in the *New York Times* best-seller list, with eight million copies sold in 35 countries. It has given rise to innumerable discussion groups and fan circles, and has been followed up by another hit novel, *The Tenth Insight* (Redfield 1996), a handbook, *The Celestine Prophecy. An Experiential Guide* (Redfield and Adrienne 1995), and another non-fictional book, *The Celestine Vision* (Redfield 1997), which elaborates on the philosophical background of the novels.

Prophecy depicts a New Age pilgrimage. It takes the protagonist, a somewhat naïve male American sociologist and counsellor, Redfield's *alter ego*, on a spiritual journey to exotic Peru in a quest for the celestial wisdom of an ancient manuscript that can reveal how to reach a mystical unity with the cosmos and save the world through intuitive, spiritual insight. A bad guy (with the ordinary Danish name of Jensen[!]) plus a narrow-minded and conservative segment of the Catholic Church of Peru, supported by the government and the army, try to hinder the quest for the manuscript. But together with a bunch of good, white middle-class guys (plus a few women!), all with Anglo–American names, and some insightful Catholic priests (the good Fathers), Redfield's protagonist overcomes all the obstacles set up by Jensen and the Peruvian government, army, etc. The key to the success of the good guys is that, contrary to the bad ones, they follow the hints of meaningful coincidences instead of yielding to reductive scientific theories and religious dogmatism. The grandiose and spiritually elevating landscape of mountains and rain forests which, like glamorous brochures for ecotourism, excludes the disturbing presence of tourists or locals not authorized to take part in the protagonist's project, provides a symbolic representation of the 'higher' macrocosmic forces of life that orchestrate the coincidences. These forces teach the protagonist how to give up wilful control and instead follow his intuition and the hints offered by the coincidences. Together with magical helpers (the good guys and the good Fathers) and antagonists (the bad guys) who, in a fairy-tale-like way pop up unexpectedly only to test the protagonist's belief in his new insights, the 'natural', cosmic beauty of the landscape guides the protagonist towards a new elevated level of existence, which he afterwards makes a vow to spread to other people.

The moral of the story shows that the pattern of meaningful co-incidences, which constitutes the main driving force in *Prophecy*'s journey, is the vehicle for guiding us towards a higher spiritual level of life. The resulting new kind of consciousness is promoted as the key to social, ecological and spiritual salvation for mankind in the twentieth and twenty-first century.

A World of Reversals

The New Age master narrative often consciously reflects the fact that it represents a world of reversals compared to the scientific world view to which the space narrative adheres. Redfield's novel explicitly invites its middle-class American readers to opt out of the scientific mainstream culture in which they were brought up. The novel is not only about learning to live with the mystical teachings of the ancient Peruvian manuscript; it is also a manual of ways to unlearn the command-control paradigm as well as the outlook of modern science that reduces 'nature' to mindless matter in mechanical motion. The protagonist's voyage through the Peruvian wilderness is at the same time an inner journey into unknown mental landscapes that opens up new ways of seeing, sensing and acting in the external world. Thus, the novel depicts an otherworldly journey on an inner as well as an outer level, and in this way it inscribes itself in the classic genre of the spiritual hero-journey.

As this genre is interpreted by Campbell's Jung-inspired analysis of its figurations in ancient myths (Campbell 1968) and in a spiritual feminist mode by Göttner-Abendroth (1980), it has important overlaps with the fairy-tale. What is at stake, however, when the ancient genre of the spiritual hero-journey is revived as New Age master narrative, is a different fairy-tale model from the one we saw activated in the space adventure story. In the New Age fable, the modalities or action-generators of the tale of the questing adventure hero are substituted by those of the opposite type of fairy-tale described by Propp (1975), the one in which the protagonist is being acted upon and led forward by 'higher forces'. To will, to know and to know-how have – as in an act of reversal – left the stage in favour of opposite modalities such as abandoning oneself to cosmic guidance, to be open to intuitive wisdom occurring naturally in one's mind, to be in a meditative mood. The aim is no longer to imprint the cosmos with human meaning, but, conversely, to be imprinted by cosmic wisdom. The New Age fable maintains that when the protagonist reverses the modalities, i.e. gives up the will to control and engages in a spiritual journey following the hints of macrocosmic meaning conveyed to her/him in the language of the coincidences of everyday life, exciting things begin to happen; mental change will then begin to spread out from her/him in ever-widening circles. To unlearn the modalities of a modern hero and identify with the opposite ones is, thus, exactly what Redfield's protagonist is taught by his co-incidentally determined voyage to Peru.

Another important reversal that opposes the New Age fable to the space narrative bears upon the construction of the external environment of the otherworldly setting. Described in terms of genre, this opposition can be highlighted by Suvin's distinction between the estrangement of the science fiction story and that of 'metaphysical genres' (Suvin 1979: 20), to which the combination of spiritual journey and fairy-tale that we find in Redfield's novel appertains. Like science fiction, the 'metaphysical genres' escort their protagonist to an otherworldly setting, but they differ in that the alien world 'is actively oriented towards the hero' in either a positive or a negative way instead of obeying the laws of physics. They confront us with a world in which these laws are denied, and where 'physics ... in some magical or religous way [is] determined by ethics, instead of being neutral toward the hero' (ibid.: 19). With a slight twist of Suvin's arguments, we may describe the differences as follows: the space narrative glorifies the human self because it successfully instrumentalizes the laws of physics in the service of cosmic expansion; the New Age fable, conversely, locates its protagonist in the navel of a universe that, without any side-glances to physics or causality, concentrates all its parental attention on the guidance of this particular individual!

A third reversal concerns the pattern of genderization. Like the space narrative, Redfield's novel and its spiritual journey are a rather phallocentric affair: it is primarily the brotherhood of good guys and benevolent fathers who are called by the higher cosmic forces to bring along spiritual elevation and new harmony. But the phallocentrism of the prototype New Age fable differs from that of the space narrative. In contrast to the masculine hero of the latter, whom the technoscientific will drives to imprint his meaning upon the cosmos, Redfield's angelic boy scout network is guided by values such as intuition, mysticism and interconnectedness, which most New Age texts bluntly identify with an essential 'feminine' principle.

It is popular among New Agers to invoke 'The Universal Feminine' as representation of alternative value systems. Along these lines, the opposition between technoscience and intuition/mysticism/occultism is often articulated as a dominating masculine *vis-à-vis* a repressed feminine principle. Some versions of the New Age fable reconstruct this gendered opposition as a complementary figuration. An imbalance has occurred in favour of the masculine *yang*-principle, but this will be rectified when the repressed feminine *yin*-principle returns with the dawning of the New Age. Like Redfield, the American physicist Fritjof Capra achieved almost instant fame for advocating this notion in his international best-sellers (Capra 1982, 1991).

In a way, these New Age constructions reverse the gendered mythologics and value systems of the space discourses. 'Universal Man' and his brother-hood of adventurous 'right stuff' heroes are replaced by the soft and spiritual values of 'Universal Femininity'. But as a prototypical example, Redfield's novel confirms once more the often made observation that the close embrace of a 'feminine' position and of essential 'feminine' values does not automatically imply an annulment of phallocentrism and patri-archal modes of thought. However, it should also be noted that many feminist goddess-worshippers and astrologers contribute in alternative ways to the 'feminization' of the qualities that the New Age is said to bring. The position of these feminists will be revisited briefly in Chapter 6.

Dolphin Fables of New Age and Space Age: Between Pastoral and Science Fiction

While the spaceship icon of American and Soviet/Russian space flight discourse and the horoscope icon of New Age cosmology can each be related to one dominant fable, the dolphin icon resists the singular in so far as it engenders at least two distinct fables. Since contemporary dolphin stories involve a lively activity of boundary-crossing between modern high-tech science discourses and ancient myths and legends, the dolphin can perform smoothly in roles that otherwise exclude one another: as both cyborg and noble savage. In the prototypical cyborg dolphin story the animal is being imprinted with human meaning, whereas the master fable of the noble savage dolphin tells a story of an alien figure conveying profound cosmic wisdom to humans in distress.

The Dolphin as Noble Savage

According to the latter fable, the distress stems from civilization that has severed the connections with the animal world. Typically, the storyline opens with images of what has been lost: a series of scenes that in our culture automatically signal a natural sublime state of original bliss. De-picted in highly aestheticized ways, the free and joyful oceanic life of wild cetaceans radiates an aura of awe and sacrality that is often enhanced by the absence of humans. Thus the human spectator may be kept away, hidden in a space-off position (as in McCulloch's 'Earth Dolphins' photo), or relegated to the off-stage role of the implied author/reader in the case of a textual representation. The apparent absence of humans is clearly intended to render the scenery reminiscent of the Garden of Eden at the beginning of the Golden Age, before human intrusion foreshadowed the Fall. When humans are allowed into this initial, idyllic imagery of the story, they will have to express the feeling of being 'honoured' by the presence of the animal and to show the appropriate attitude of awe (Ocean 1997: 19). At other times, the spectator or narrator enters into the primordial scene in order to voice a human desire to transgress the alienation caused by civilization – as in the following example:

> I envy them [i.e. the whales], envy their life and the ease of their connections. I wish to be of them, yet my thoughts, my ideas, become obstacles to the possibility of that experience. (McIntyre 1974: 221)

The human narrator of these stories is motivated by a longing to merge with the dolphins or whales, to live in their 'innocent' world and to be imprinted by their 'natural' wisdom. But also on the agenda are the barriers that (techno-)civilization has erected against a return to this Paradise. As the first section of the fable discloses the original bliss of an oceanic Garden of Eden, so the next one brings the Fall: a violent act disturbs or destroys the paradisic state. The violence is perpetrated by agents of civilization who in the USA are usually depicted as insensitive, brutal machos or white, male capitalists, while in Russia they may appear as representatives of the inhuman Soviet system.

To be Imprinted with Cetacean Wisdom

In Ken Grimwood's popular science fiction novel, *Into the Deep* (1996), ancient Greece witnessed a blissful unity between humans and marine mammals. Apollo's priestesses at Delphi were imprinted with cetacean wisdom and taught the animals' moral concepts, their social organization and governing precepts by means of telepathy, or 'Mind-Linking'. However, these 'Teachings' were viciously interrupted by 'barbaric, non-Linking' humans who took a specific pleasure in butchering women and children as well as whales and dolphins. Only after 2,000 years of violence and cruelty, when an environmental disaster eventually threatens to destroy all life in the sea, does the global, sentient network of the large whales, which constitutes the semi-divine 'Source-Mind' of the world, decide to commission the intelligent and helpful dolphins with the task of re-establishing contact with some of the 'land-walkers'. Since three young children who are selected by the marine mammals all possess the talent for telepathic communication, their minds are easily imprinted with the cetacean message: 'Harmony'. Decades later, these three people play a crucial role in saving the globe. Particularly important is the marine biologist, Sheila (her gender and profession both emphasize her bonds with the body of the sea); driven by the dolphin message, which gradually surfaces from the depths of her unconscious, and also by John Lilly's books on communication with dolphins, she finally manages to translate the complex cetacean language into human pictures. In more ways than one, Sheila re-enacts the part of the priestesses who long ago performed the sacred rituals of the oracle of Delphi. Not only does she understand and disseminate the warnings from the oceanic womb of the Earth, but she was present at the Kennedy Space Center when *Apollo 11*, namesake of the ancient dolphin God, was launched to the Moon in the 1960s, certainly a sacred moment in the space programme. Furthermore, it was during this lift-off that she received the message of Harmony, and originally became imprinted with cetacean wisdom.

In the final pages of the novel, the global wound is healed: undergoing an education in dolphinity, humanity leaves the death-world of violence and weaponry in order to embrace the altruistic life-world of dolphins and whales. With the restoration of Eden the stage is set for the return of God. The global consciousness, the 'Source-Mind', created by the whales seems to enter into contact with other planetary group minds: 'there may even be a galaxy-wide or larger aggregate consciousness, a limitless, truly godlike greater sentience pervading the universe – and eternally seeking out newly self-aware worlds, like ours, to join it in jubilant immortality' (Grimwood 1996: 377).

Thus the noble cetacean savages who draw virtues directly from nature provide *Into the Deep* with a happy ending (stage three). In other versions of the fable the endpoint comes already with the tragic stage two, where technocivilization and so-called 'progress' show their evil faces. This is the case, for example, in the Siberian author Yuri Rytkheu's *When the Whales Leave* (1977), to which we shall return in Chapter 8, and in the Canadian naturalist Farley Mowat's semi-documentary novel *A Whale for the Killing* (1978), which describes the meaningless killing of a trapped pregnant fin whale on an island off the Newfoundland coast. The whale murderers are a group of locals, who have become alienated from the traditional lifestyle of the islanders by the industrialization process of the 1960s. The death of the whale seals the locals' final expulsion from the symbolic Paradise, the island as the enclosure of original innocence. When the divine dies, Paradise is lost.

Pastoral Precursors

A clue to understanding the fable of the cetacean as noble savage comes from the pastoral novel, which reached a peak in pre-Romantic Europe. The 'return to nature' philosophy, combined with the consciously lachrymatory and spiritually elevated style of, for example, Bernadin de Saint-Pierre's best-seller *Paul and Virginia* (1788/1989), the most famous pastoral novel of early modernity, seems recently to have been revitalized in stories of animals threatened with extinction. Dolphins and whales fit the genre well, since they appear designed to represent the innocence of the 'uncivilized other' combined with an inherent capacity for goodness and 'natural' wisdom. The Eden of the eighteenth-century pastoral novel, with its pure and innately good characters living in a blissful state contrasted against evil and corrupt civilization, would today appear old-fashioned and comical if applied as a paradigm for stories with human characters. However, when the humans are substituted by touching and glamorously aestheticized images of wild animals, the ancient model evidently regains its strength, confirming the rule that, as reinvented nature becomes more widely perceived as the norm, so wild nature is more thoroughly transformed into an emblem of the innocent, the unpolluted and the sacred.

Intertwined with the pastoral novel, the noble savage tradition of European Romanticism also serves as an obvious model for stories about cetaceans. As described by Fairchild (1961), the Romantic movement initiated a critical renewal of the pastoral and re-authenticated the noble savage tradition, which stemmed from several sources: from the travelogues of explorers (from Columbus to Captain Cook), from the philosophy of a 'return to nature', and from medieval and classical conventions such as the legend of the Golden Age. In a departure from these sources, women, children, peasants, Native Americans and other non-whites were constructed as bearers of an inherently sublime wisdom, to which a 'natural' state of existence supposedly gave rise. There are obvious parallels here with present-day re-inventions of dolphins and whales: with a spotlight on their 'big brains' and 'no hands', the marine mammals easily merge with the classic noble savage figure who seems to 'lack' the prerequisite of technoscientific civilization, yet possesses a wisdom that transcends rational intelligence.

Although somewhat different, the pastoral and the Romantic noble savage story form an interlaced pattern of genre models for one strand of late twentieth-century dolphin and whale stories. The common denominator is the celebration of the 'pre-civilized' other as moral and sacred ideal for civilized selves in search of a 'natural and non-alienated' elsewhere.

The Dolphin as Cyborg

In opposition to the dolphin as noble savage fable, the prototypical cyborg dolphin story features an 'uplift' (Brin 1996) from an animal to a humanoid state of being, an 'education in humanity' (Lilly 1962a). An important theme in both fables is the quasi-humanness of dolphins and whales. But while, in the former fable, this quality makes the animal a fitting guide to lead humans back from alienating civilization to their supposed 'natural' origins, the boundary-position in the latter fable rather transforms dolphins into challenging and attractive objects of techno-scientific experiments in humanization and imprinting of human meaning. In this way, the two branches of dolphins fables perform as reversals of each other.

The genre model of the cyborg dolphin fable is the science fiction story of the alien encounter, but with a specific modification. Contrary to the popular trend within this SF sub-genre of depicting aliens as hostile, dolphin stories show the human self encountering a friendly and devoted other. Moreover, cyborg dolphin stories describe encounters with alien others who, although bodily different, are nevertheless 'highly developed' according to human parameters, i.e. in terms of intelligence and language skills. As in the spaceship fable, the narrative structure builds upon a *novum*: in this case the cognitively validated possibility of communication with an 'intelligent' alien species of sentient beings.

The standards of communication in the fable are basically human. Therefore, it is an integral part of the story that the alien is measured in human terms and imprinted with human meaning. The course of events displays the many small steps that the successful 'uplift' of the animal to a humanoid status requires in terms of learning human ways of living, speaking and thinking. This will often imply that it is transformed into a cyborg, i.e. modified technologically, to be able to participate in the communication. The varying degrees of cyborgification represent another dimension of the *novum*; it characterizes the futuristic setting that such advanced body modifications are possible.

'Uplift' and 'Education in Humanity'

As prototypical illustration we have chosen the cult novel *Startide Rising* (1996), by the American SF writer, astrophysicist and NASA consultant David Brin. Like other SF stories about dolphins, such as Anne McCaffrey's *The Dolphins of Pern* (1996) or William Gibson's *Johnny Mnemonic* (1995), Brin's novel takes as its point of departure the evocative dolphin script created by Lilly's famous attempts to teach his dolphins English in the early 1960s, which we introduced in our third Amazing Story and revisit in Chapter 8. Within this trend, one reason for choosing *Startide Rising* as prototype is Brin's link with NASA, but another is the novel's status as the dolphin-lovers' cult book; a comprehensive dolphin reference database lists it as 'the all-time cetacean sci-fi favorite' (cf. Feuerstein 1998).

Startide Rising is one of Brin's novels about 'uplift' from one evolutionary stage to another. 'Uplift' means that a 'higher' species, a so-called 'patron species', using genetic manipulation and other technological modifications, makes a 'lower' species of sentient beings, a 'client species', fit for space travel and for participation in the ancient galactic civilization. The rules for the 'uplift' of one race by another and the relationship between patron and client species constitute the founding principles in the universe of the novel. In this way it presents itself as a novel about interspecies communication, which at the same time functions as a metaphor for intercultural communication between various kinds of 'selves' and 'others'.

Startide Rising narrates the story of a spaceship staffed by seven humans (of whom some are products of conscious genetic change), 130 dolphins and one chimpanzee. The animals have been 'uplifted' by humans. They function as scientists, engineers, and space pilots on a more or less equal footing with the humans. Sometimes they do, however, relapse into atavistic, i.e. 'pre-uplift', behaviour, and this causes conflicts in the novel. Another part of the drama unfolds through the encounter with the alien, spacefaring races who have ruled the galaxy for billions of years. Most of these age-old and technologically superior races, some of which physically resemble 'lower' terrestrial species (birds, reptiles, etc.), consider humans to be a primitive bunch of annoying 'natives' who are very strange for two particular reasons. First, humans have not been 'uplifted' by a superior race, but have done it for themselves. Second, they treat their client species, the cyborg dolphins and the chimpanzee, as their equals instead of enslaving them as all the other galactic races have done.

In showing cyborg dolphins in charge of the complicated technoscientific tasks necessary for space flight, and in allowing humans to encounter technologically superior galactic races with the appearance of animals, the novel flirts with a post(hu)man position. It advocates a retreat from human specialness (cf. Steels and Brooks 1995), a break with the humanism of modernity and the hierarchy that it constructed between universal man and 'his' others (e.g. animals). Along the lines of the cyborg anthropology (Gray et al. 1995: 341ff; Haraway 1997: 52) and the technophilic techno-critique that followed in the wake of Haraway's cyborg manifesto (Haraway 1991), *Startide Rising* in one sense promotes the cyborg as a rebellious figure that deconstructs the anthropocentric and phallogocentric values of humanism. But at the same time, Western humanist values pervade the novel: humans are presented as different from all other species; like the protagonist of the American Dream, they are self-made and democratically minded. While the dolphin as noble savage fable places the dolphin above the human as a standard to which 'we' should adapt, the cyborg dolphin fable conversely tends to place humanity above all other species.

To Read out of Context

We have now introduced the prototype fables of the spaceship, the horoscope and the dolphin, and the genres involved, as a framework for the more detailed presentations of the icons and reading of their stories in the following chapters. Before we end this chapter we shall, however, briefly sum up the question of reading strategies.

In a book with the significant sub-title: 'Om forbløffelse' [On amazement] (Hastrup 1992), the Danish anthropologist Kirsten Hastrup points out that critical distance and amazement should be balanced against one another in the anthropological project. This balance is also important for the reading strategies we advocate. Relying both on Scholes's term, narrative of romance, and on Suvin's narrative of estrangement, we try to evoke a double perspective that gives room both for the wonder and amazement that an extraterrestrial perspective is likely to evoke, and for critical distance. But as far as the latter is concerned, we shall add a few remarks to Suvin's definitions.

We shall first emphasize that 'estrangement' and 'critical distance' should not be collapsed into each other. Extraterrestrialism and otherworldliness create distance and estrangement, but this does not in itself make up a critical approach. Suvin distinguishes between the estrangement caused by 'the metaphysical genres' (fairy-tale, myth, fantasy, etc.) (Suvin 1979: 20), and that of genres such as science fiction and the pastoral that, according to him, relate to a cognitively validated world (Suvin 1979: 8–9). While the former genres close around a metaphysical truth and leave space only for spiritual meditation, wishful thinking and escape from the everyday world, Suvin maintains that the latter possess potentials to act as critical eye-openers. In particular, he gives priority to the cognitive estrangement of the science fiction story, which may lead us to revise taken-for-granted viewpoints when we use its estranged world as a mirror for the familiar one. This is due to the 'totalizing ("scientific") rigor' (Suvin 1979: 6) that he ascribes to the non-trivial trends within the science fiction genre.

We find Suvin's distinctions between different kinds of estrangement illuminating, but we do not share his belief in 'scientific rigor' (even though he puts the term in quotation marks). According to the social constructivist and postmodern science critiques, to which we adhere, a point of departure in a scientifically validated estrangement would just lead to the installation of a new kind of metaphysics – a new kind of master narrative. We agree with Suvin when he notes that spatial dislocation in itself is not enough to create a critically estranging platform, but neither is a scientifically validated estrangement in his sense. The critical estrangement we suggest as reading strategy is, therefore, different. It is linked not to beliefs in a metaphysics of science, but to the de-naturalizing and de-automatizing effect of readings 'out of context' and of a focus on story-telling practices rather than scientific 'truths'.

Another aspect that we would like to stress, as far as our reading strategy is concerned, regards the configuration we have created by juxtaposing the stories of the three icons. As the binaries in Table 2.1 indicate, the proto-type fables of the spaceship, the horoscope and the dolphin are closed stories that each claims to enunciate a truthful account of the relationship between human selves and wild others. So even though they may appear as both amazing and estranging – when we read them out of context, and when we meditate upon their extraterrestrial content and naïve enunciations of high-flown truth claims – they can still maintain a certain closure and resist the intrusions of other 'truths', as long as we look at them one by one. But if, instead, we read them as a configuration, then patterns of reversals and negations, a carnival of circulating meanings, are put on display. We see this as yet another way to create critical estrangement and de-naturalization. Each of the poles in the binary pairs makes its opposite seem non-evident.

Our configurative reading produces its own de-automatizations. The analysis of the binaries and patterns of reversal shows that the fables of the three icons, when juxtaposed, may articulate a contemporary oscillation between two opposing kinds of self–other representations and suggest how late twentieth-century minds are caught in an ambivalent pattern of cannibalizing and sacralizing *vis-à-vis* the global commons. On the one hand, the stories of the spaceship and the cyborg dolphin demonstrate an unrestrained will to imprint the 'wild' commons and their inhabitants with human meaning. We define the self–other relationship that is implied here as 'cannibalizing' insofar as the difference of the 'wild' other is meant to be consumed and transformed into an exploitable resource for or image of the human self. On the other hand, the horoscope and dolphin as noble savage fables tell tales about a completely reversed obsession – about modern human selves who present themselves as desperately longing to become imprinted with non-human meanings, with cosmic or animal wisdom. We shall distinguish this kind of representation as 'sacralizing' in the sense that it constructs the other as a norm to which the human self should adapt.

The distinction we make between 'cannibalizing' and 'sacralizing' self–other representations should not, however, obscure the fact that 'sacralizing' often appears to be a different mode of 'cannibalizing'; we discussed this in our interpretation of McCulloch's picture in the Prelude. Nor does a 'cannibalizing' self-representation exclude the involvement of strong acts of sacralization; our analysis of the space narrative will illustrate this.

Notes

1. Contrary to the Willett-edition of Brecht's texts (Brecht 1964), Suvin uses the translation 'estranges' instead of 'alienates'. We follow Suvin's translation, which is more correct, since it takes into account the difference between German *verfremden* and *entfremden*.

2. The plaque that was left on the Moon together with the American flag after the first lunar landing bears the inscription: 'Where men from the planet Earth first set foot upon the moon, July 1969, AD. They came in peace for all mankind.' It is signed by the crew members and by President Nixon (Wilford 1969: 303–4). Part of the space race was a competition to demarcate the lunar landscape with national emblems. Already in 1959, the Soviet emblem was scattered onto the Moon.

3

The Big Mission

'Once I started into it, I got the rocket fluid in my blood.' (female NASA employee, Kennedy Space Center, Florida)

'For me, it is my life.' (male IKI employee, Institute of Cosmic Research, Moscow)

The American and Russian space narratives are told so homogenously that one might half expect a smiling, transnational chief script-writer to appear at the end of the dramatic course of events. In this chapter we shall re-tell the master narrative as we heard it articulated by the 26 women and men we interviewed at the Institute of Cosmic Research (IKI) in Moscow, at NASA's Kennedy Space Center in Florida and at the adjacent Space Camp for youngsters, in the early 1990s.[1] Although certain national and gender differences do distinguish the narrators, their stories are very alike. Two strongly marked features function as homogenizing factors of the individual stories: the cross-national idea that space exploration represents a magnificent human 'mission', and the implicit recycling of the masculine adventure story to frame this noble goal.

In the imaginary of our interviewees in both East and West, the missionary character of the enterprise is clearly marked. The space hero and his large-scale backup team of scientists, technicians, workers and administrators on Earth are presented as united in their dedication to a common objective: the successful accomplishment of a big mission of utmost importance to the nation and to the future of all mankind. These imaginary representations reflect the fact that the organization of space exploration in both countries is typical of the trend towards mission-orientedness that has been part of the development of 'big science' in the twentieth century. An important feature of this kind of research is an explicit goal 'expressed in terms of a contribution to society reaching beyond the laboratory' (Galison and Hevly 1992: 265). The term 'mission' reveals a genealogical root in wartime projects such as the American Manhattan Project and the Soviet rocket research, carried out by engineers and top scientists who were imprisoned in special camps during the Second World War. But 'big science' projects, organized as societally or commercially defined 'missions', had already before the war entered the research of civil society – although it often seems difficult to draw a hard-and-fast line between civilian and military purposes (DeVorkin 1992). NASA, as an allegedly civil organization that nevertheless cooperates with the military, provides a good example of this (cf. Von Bencke 1997: 37). As a consequence of the very direct interaction with mission funders – in many cases the state – mission-oriented research will often couch in a master narrative that legitimates and motivates it explicitly in relation to broad national, sociocultural or commercial goals. The dedication of space flight to a 'big mission' – allegedly undertaken for 'all mankind' – is one of the background features accounting for the homogeneity which, as discussed in Chapter 1, is even more visible in our American than in our Russian interviews, due in part to the turbulent political situation in Russia in the early 1990s.

The second homogenizing feature characteristic of the space narrative is the inscription of the project in a national-romantic adventure story with a remarkably fixed and unchanging structure.

As discussed in Chapter 2, the space fable fits the narrative scheme of the adventure story, and it is based on the same driving forces – to will, to know and to know-how – that narratology attributes to the fairy-tale of the actively questing hero. Accordingly, the entire space project, including its most spectacular protagonists, the mythic national heroes, seems permeated by an invincible will to large-scale accumulation of sublime technoscientific knowledge, matched by the unfolding of a gigantic potency and know-how. A new meaning will hereby be imprinted on the cosmos, demarcating it as a place to go to.

Although individual NASA or IKI employees may rebel, now against one part of this narrative and now against another, it is as if, in the 1990s, the general script is still surrounded by such a halo of sacrality that any substantial adjustment would appear as a serious heresy to the believers in the Big Space Mission of mankind. In order to underline the conspicuous similarities we mix the Russian and American, the female and the male voices in the following presentation.

To Devote One's Life to the Big Mission

To work with space flight is perceived as being something special. The master narrative of space exploration plays an important role for those involved, both in the West and in the East. Our interviewees might perhaps not fully agree with all the space activities or space goals of their country but, to all of them, the project of civilian space flight in general, the great boundary-crossing journey out into the universe, represents a decisive and important step in human evolution.

The perception of this step as something quite unique and sublime is reflected in the fact that, to a majority of our interviewees, their involvement in space flight assumes the character of a personal quest. They see it as a mission to transform *homo sapiens* to *homo spaciens*, and have more or less devoted their lives to this cause.

This kind of outlook seems to be especially pronounced in the somewhat older generation, who have taken part in the development of space flight from its infancy and right through the years of pioneering adolescence in 'the great decade', 1960–70, when the space race between the USA and the Soviet Union reached its first peak. 'Once I started into it, I got the rocket fluid in my blood,' says JoAnn. She is an engineer and began to work at NASA back in the 1950s, when she was 17. At the time of the interview, she has a leading position at the Kennedy Space Center; moreover, she is one of extremely few women to have been involved in the Apollo Project of the 1960s. JoAnn sees a deep symbolism in having touched some of the artefacts that have remained on the Moon. Every time she looks at it, she relates, she thinks about these things, and the human footprints that she spent ten years of her life to assist in imprinting into the lunar dust. To her, the abandoned objects and the imperishable footprints represent her most important mission in life: to help ensure the possibility of a cosmic exodus when the sun explodes in billions of years' time. To secure life – not necessarily human life, but what we today understand as life in the broadest sense – to give it a chance of survival somewhere else in the universe, constitutes in her view 'the ultimate good' of space flight. The first Moon landing, and her own contribution to this accomplishment, set up a milestone on the long road towards this goal. By the end of the interview we, as the former infidels, are converted by encountering a true missionary, and agree that there is something special in the fact that we can now go back to Denmark and tell of our shaking hands with somebody who has touched artefacts that are still standing on the lunar surface. After this interview, the Moon seems only a handshake away!

Speaking of space flight in missionary terms, many of the interviewees indicate that they have pursued this particular career since childhood. Often the choice was made due to the influence of spectacular, historic events. *Sputnik* had an enormous impact on the recruitment of technicians and scientists to space jobs in both the Soviet Union and the USA. The same is true of Gagarin's flight and the first Moon landing. The Russians draw much attention to the wave of enthusiastic faith in the future that was unleashed all over the country after the triumphs in space. The older ones recall the experiences they had at that time; the younger mention how their parents' enthusiasm is vividly imprinted into their memories. The beeps of *Sputnik* and the parade in Red Square after Gagarin's flight in 1961 functioned as a collective rite of passage in the same way as the American TV transmission of the Moon landing did in 1969.

Nikolai, who has worked as an astrophysicist at IKI for almost 20 years, belongs to the generation who, as teenagers, witnessed both *Sputnik* and Gagarin's flight. These two events, he says, left 'tremendous marks' in his mind. He is the son of two victims of the purges in the 1930s (he was born in Siberia), and as such he did not appreciate the propaganda that proclaimed the space triumphs as victories for the communist system. But, he goes on, these great and unique events in space did speak for themselves. To his generation, they came to represent something sublime and unparalleled. They became an important symbol of a field in which his country could excel. He points out that, against the background of a poor standard of living and the multiple hardships of life in the post-Stalinist society of the 1950s, the technoscientific advances represented by *Sputnik* and Gagarin's spacecraft gained a special significance. They added a new dimension, which he describes as spiritual, to this tough life. Perhaps they came to embody promises of a different existence for the whole of humanity, materially and spiritually enriched, and he emphasizes that they became decisive in his choice of career.

Sputnik also made a huge impact on Irene, who works as a doctor at Kennedy Space Center, specializing in the biomedical problems of humans in space. She tells us how, by the age of nine, she had already decided that she would devote her life to this field. Deeply impressed by the launchings of the *Sputnik*s in the late 1950s, she eagerly devoured all the TV broadcasts she could find on technology and science. 'That's what I will do,' she said to herself while watching a medical doctor from the Air Force describe his job during a transmission on the preparations for the American space programme. Irene held firmly to her decision, although she had to break through many barriers to achieve her goal. In more ways than one she belongs to a minority within NASA: she is African–American as well as female. In addition, not wanting to do military work, she had difficulties in finding a civilian biomedical space programme. That she nevertheless succeeded in making a career, she ascribes to her determination and her dedicated perseverance. She never relinquished the decision she made at the age of nine, and thus her dream came true.

Although the feeling of being part of a big mission is particularly pronounced in the generation that experienced the start of space flight in the 1950s and 1960s, the younger staff members also frequently emphasize their feelings of working for a glorious mission of exceptional significance to humanity.

At 20, Sergei is still a student. When we meet him, he is engaged in trainee service at IKI. He very much wants to continue working with space flight after his graduation from the Moscow Institute of Aviation. To a certain degree, his reasons are similar to those of the much older Nikolai. Nor is Sergei's enthusiasm due to any sympathy for the communist regime. During the coup against Gorbachov, which took place a couple of months before this interview, he demonstrated in favour of democracy in front of the White House, where the parliament sits. His desire for a job in the space programme is rooted in the belief that this is a field where his country has accomplished magnificent things and enriched humanity. It is also important to him that he is a child of the Space Age. To have grown up at a time when society was capable of huge technoscientific achievements has provided his generation with great self-confidence, he states. In his view, our capability of travelling into outer space proves our ability to solve the problems on Earth, and he wants to contribute to this.

Much the same attitude is expressed by Shannon, a 32-year-old computer science engineer at NASA. She too is convinced about the Big Mission embedded in space flight. She informs us that her friends sometimes blame her for trying to make them proselytes of the space programme in an 'overzealous' way. But she truly believes in its crucial significance for the evolution of the human race. Since her childhood, when she ardently followed all the details of the Moon landing on TV, she has been seized by an unshakable belief in the USA's historic mission in space. She has been brought up in a strongly patriotic spirit, and it means a great deal to her that her job is relevant to both her nation and to humanity. Her work for NASA, she feels, enables her to combine these two aspects in an ideal way.

The Adventurous Journey

One icon that almost all of our interviewees, in both East and West, identify as an essential image in the master narrative of space flight is the figure of Columbus. They view space flight as a re-staging of the Renaissance's adventurous voyages of discovery beyond the ultimate frontier that the ocean to the west represented to those European rulers, merchants and explorers.

The symbolic parallel between Columbus and present-day voyages through the hostile and unexplored cosmic ocean is particularly clear to the Americans, since it resonates with a canonized, historic theme with which our American interviewees feel a natural bonding. But the comparison is by no means unfamiliar in Russia either. In the official Soviet history of space flight, Gagarin was called 'the cosmic Columbus', and although the idea of a new world inscribed in a cosmic communism does not receive much applause from the IKI staff today, most of them acknowledge the parallel with Columbus. In the shifting political landscape, this icon remains an appealing symbol for what many Russian intellectuals perceive to be a fundamental feature of the Russian mentality: unlimited dynamism, perpetual movement and messianic nomadism (Boym 1996: 157ff.). This image of the self as a dynamic explorer, a conqueror with an extraordinary mission, was also celebrated in the name of the communist organization for children that was founded in the early 1920s: Pioneers.[2] At the present time nearly every adult Russian has in childhood been a member of this pioneer organization to which Gagarin, 'the cosmic Columbus', allegedly sent his last thoughts before the lift-off that was to re-affirm his status as a 'pioneer', an 'explorer' and 'trail-blazer' (Gagarin 1971: 63f.). One Soviet book on this space hero is simply entitled *The Pioneer of Pioneers* (Kopylova and Yurkina 1962).

Olga, a 23-year-old radio engineer and programmer at IKI, exclaims spontaneously: 'Yes, of course' when we ask her about the analogy between space flight and Columbus's voyage. The question prompts her to mention one of IKI's *perestroika*-born projects, in which ordinary people are encouraged to send in their preferences on things to be explored in space. Olga seems very excited about the perspectives this project opens up for democratic access to the new cosmic world's inexhaustible fund of the thrilling secrets that are so important for human evolution. She is happy that IKI and space flight are now blazing a trail whereby 'anybody can become a Columbus and make his or her own discoveries'. Olga is confident that humanity will not only put questions to the universe, but that in time we will also go out to settle the distant planets.

One of our American interviewees has a distinctly negative attitude towards the idea of everybody encroaching on Columbus's or the astronauts' preserves, and as such he appears on one level to be Olga's diametric opposite. Dr B, as our NASA guide calls him, is a medical doctor. His career at NASA goes back to the days of the Apollo Project, when he was a part of the team behind *Apollo 17* and the last Moon landing in 1972. For almost two decades he has been in charge of the biomedical department at the Kennedy Space Center. Dr B's categorical rejection of the notion of a democratically open outer space stems from his pessimistic view of human nature. According to him, Earth's problems with pollution, overpopulation and much more have been allowed to grow to insoluble proportions because of human folly and prejudice. The only effective way out, he suggests, is a cosmic exodus of a select few who can start all over again somewhere else in the universe. It is his hope, and the goal of his work, that a chosen group consisting of highly intelligent and scientifically minded individuals will one day populate the cosmos – and found a new world on a sustainable basis.

Olga and Dr B are extremely different. Nationality, age, gender and, not least, their views on life and human beings radically separate them. Nevertheless, they have one substantial thing in common. They both see undreamed-of possibilities opening up via the magnificent voyages of discovery signalled by the Columbus analogy. Their common belief, that we will attain an extraordinary and sublime world if we technoscientifically pursue our will to exploration and engage in the adventurous journey across the cosmic ocean, is one they share with many other interviewees.

The High Frontier

A network of related notions play distinguished roles alongside the Columbus image in elaborating the master narrative into which our interviewees inscribe their work. This network includes 'the frontier', 'the wild' and 'the enigmatic'. Such concepts, clearly, are present in the Columbus myth, but these three notions carry much wider significance as well.

To the Americans, the idea of the universe as 'the high frontier' or 'the new frontier' has a strongly national-romantically coloured meaning. The frontier concept has deep roots in American history. Referring to the expansion towards the west in the nineteenth century, 'the frontier' represents the myth of the borders to the 'Wild West', which challenged pioneers with promises of fertile land, gold and a new life. At the same time, 'the frontier' also signifies the way into a tough, dangerous and unknown world. This outlook has influenced the sense of national identity so strongly that the myth of the frontier as being indispensable was even canonized in American historiography in the first half of the twentieth century. As the frontier disappeared into the waves of the Pacific Ocean, the American historian Frederick J. Turner set up a national monument to it, with his 'frontier' thesis.[3] His argument, which became immensely popular, specified the frontier to the west as the matrix of American democracy and national character. The disappearance of the frontier, Turner warned, could seriously damage the development and identity of the nation.

Seen from this perspective, the USA has been lacking a frontier that could regenerate the national spirit for many decades now. As if in a healing response to this, the master narrative of space flight came forward with alluring offers of a new mythical frontier. Under the title *The High Frontier: Human Colonies in Space* (O'Neill 1978), a well-known professor of physics, Gerard O'Neill, impressed by the national successes in space of the 1960s, contributed yet another enthusiastic chapter to the history of the US frontier myth. Even better, O'Neill's new frontier wholly overcomes the problems raised by Turner. In contrast to the old frontier, which was eventually devoured by the ocean, the new one borders onto a 'wilderness' of cosmic dimensions that is, in theory at least, open to endless expansion.

To ourselves, born and raised in a small nation that has to resort to the somewhat shabby myths of the Vikings for a national-romantic icon to represent the legendary voyage into the wild unknown, the frontier myth sounds very alien. By contrast, to our American interviewees, this myth is an unquestionable part of their national identity. 'What has permeated the US since it was founded is going to the unknown,' JoAnn points out. She considers the quest for the unknown, for new knowledge and adventure, to be part of her national heritage. In others, this heritage has become so much second nature that they even consider it to be an essential characteristic of 'universal man's' biology. Dr B's version of the frontier myth goes as follows: 'Man has always moved outwards ... If there was an ocean, we sailed across it. If there was a continent, we walked across it. All this space out there ... we will somehow sail across that to get to the other physical body ... we shall go there. It's the nature of the beast.'

In several discourses, a Turner-like argument pops up not only in a form aiming to highlight the frontier as a positive challenge, but also in a negative version: what will happen to humanity if we ignore this challenge? One of several to voice this aspect, Irene strongly underlines the likelihood of intellectual degeneration should we fail to constantly confront new horizons. As if echoing Turner, Shannon states that, since there is no more room for expansion on Earth, we must venture into outer space to regain the pioneering spirit of former times. The cosmos is now 'the natural course of advance'.

A major theme in the frontier myth concerns the expansion of the territory that we, in a physical, social and scientific sense, can define as being domesticated – that is, the territory that we are able to utilize for our own purposes. An expansion into the universe will, according to some of the interviewees, solve our demographic problems; others refer to visions of mining the Moon and the asteroids as a means of overcoming the shortage of natural resources on Earth. As part of this line of utilitarian expansionist arguments, the revolution in communication technologies, which depend on orbital satellites, is also emphasized.

All of these *leitmotifs* appear in the legitimization of space flight for utilitarian goals. But the desire for domestication represents only one side of the frontier myth, and should by no means eliminate the existence of the frontier itself. In the cosmic-scale version of the frontier myth, the universe should simultaneously be domesticated and remain a challenging gateway into the unknown.

Ross, who, with a PhD in ecology, is in charge of an ecobiological research programme being carried out for NASA by a private company, brings out this ambiguity very strongly. One of his key arguments concerns the human need for contact with a vast, non-domesticated nature, a pristine wilderness. Originally, he had not believed in the necessity for manned space flight; he felt it would suffice to launch robots. But his work at NASA has convinced him otherwise. He is now confident that human experiences in space are indispensable, for they add a subjective interpretation that no robot could come up with. When explaining to us why we as humans need to go into outer space, he refers to the ecological offshoot of the American frontier debate, to one of the classical preservationists, Aldo Leopold, who co-founded the American Wilderness Society in 1935. Seen from a utilitarian point of view, the wilderness is unproductive. Yet, Ross ponders, recycling Leopold's ideas, as humans we need a wilderness into which we can venture. It evokes the curiosity and urge for exploration that constitute basic traits of our being human. If we are not challenged into permanently developing this curiosity, we will degrade to the level of mere robots. To Ross, manned space flight thus brings the human into contact with a truly vast and magnificent wilderness, the incarnation of a sublimity that, by and large, we can no longer find on Earth. The contact with outer space has given us 'high hopes', he says, sounding in a way like Nikolai the Russian astrophysicist, to whom *Sputnik* and Gagarin brought a 'spiritual dimension' into everyday life.

The Enigma

In many ways, the stories told by our Russian interviewees seem very similar to the American ones. The complete spectrum of utilitarian goals also appears in their discourses. But there is a difference, in that the Russians pay a great deal of attention to the lack of spin-offs from their space enterprises. As they speak admiringly of popular American products, from moonboots to Velcro, they envision a future in which democracy and the market economy will sustain the entry of space-linked inventions into the daily lives of ordinary Russians.

Another difference is directly connected to the political situation in Russia in the autumn of 1991. Where the Americans are able to merge their utilitarian views with popular national-historic themes, the Russians' attitudes to their space mission are marked by the collapse of official values that accompanied the disintegration of the Soviet state and communism; the cosmonaut as heralder of a cosmic communism is consigned to monuments and museums. In contrast to their US colleagues, our IKI interviewees drift in limbo as far as a national-political mission is concerned. This does not, however, mean that they have lost all their aspirations. Like the Americans, they firmly believe in the Big Mission of the Cosmic Columbus for the benefit of all mankind. In their view too, this space explorer will provide us with infinite quantities of new resources and knowledge. But when the Russians depart from a strictly utilitarian description of the mission's significance, a picture develops that is more heterogeneous and searching than the American version. The imaginary cosmography of the latter draws heavily on a collective, national icono- graphy of the cosmification of the human race to which NASA, with a knack for constructing imageries almost worthy of Hollywood, has con- tributed generously. In comparison, the images with which the Russians flesh out the master fable of the Big Mission appear more individual and self-made.

Amid this Russian heterogeneity, a common iconography, a new over- individual image of the universe, nevertheless emerges as a homogenizing factor. The imagery that, to them, best specifies the contact brought about by the voyage of discovery across the cosmic sea is that of the enigmatic, the mysterious, the unknown. The Americans, too, often refer to explora- tion of the unknown as the goal of space research. Still, there is a national difference. In the imaginary cosmography of our NASA interviewees, the unknown seems less imbued with the enigmatic, the essentially mysterious, than it is in the minds of the Russians.

This difference stands out clearly when, for instance, we compare Ross and the young Sergei. To Ross, the existence of the wild and unknown is, as we have said, a fundamental condition of life. However, he concedes without any reservations that he is bothered by the idea of there being something ultimately incomprehensible about the universe. He says that he conceives of God as a metaphor for the universe's ultimately incomprehensible order but, with an apologetic laugh, adds to this that he has difficulties in worshipping an enigma. Therefore he has to 'cheat' by scientifically solving the divine mystery: 'I have trouble bringing myself to worship it ... I try to cheat to understand it.' By contrast, the young Sergei claims to see the universe as a great and, perhaps, basically incomprehensible, infinity that cannot be grasped by means of earthly standards: 'To reduce one's concepts of it to something connected with the Earth, that is stupid,' he underlines.

Contrary to the majority of the NASA interviewees, who seem to shun mysticism, the IKI staff members readily volunteer their fascination with the infinite mysteriousness of the unknown. They also oblige us with various personal versions of the kind of speculations that, as we shall see in Chapters 4 and 7, have had a firm grip on the minds of both American and Russian top scientists, who, as part of space research, became hooked by the prospect of finding extraterrestrial intelligence in the universe. Several of the IKI interviewees earnestly ponder the many UFO stories that at this time are proliferating without restraint in the Russian newspapers. Dr Vasiliev, head of the technical department whose guests we are, elaborates on the theory that evolution on Earth may be a consequence of extraterrestrial activities. To a certain degree, he is inclined to believe that it may stem from visitations from space. Others speculate on a super-intelligence or super-civilization in the universe that is observing us and, regulating our behaviour and movements on Earth, is using us as an experiment. Often, this unknown is explicitly surrounded by an aura of spiritually tinged mysticism. For example, Zhanna, an engineer and construction team leader at IKI, suggests that what we call 'God' may be such a super-civilization. Victoria, a mathematician who has been engaged in space projects since the 1950s, tells how, while calculating the orbit of the first *Sputnik*, she had the thought that there might be something of the presence of God in it.

Like their colleagues at NASA, the IKI staff evidently strive for scientific explanations of the enigmas with which space flight confronts them. But generally, they are more open than their American counterparts to speculative and spiritual conceptualizations of what might be hidden in the cosmic ocean. It seems as though the atheistic-materialist philosophy, the official state 'religion' of the Soviet Union, has been no more than a veneer over a repressed, spiritual layer that is about to return with a vengeance. The dichotomy between science and non-science, upon which the modern world view is based, emerges as fissures and fractures in the discourses of our Russian interviewees. Typically, they speak in an ambiguous both/and mode, where the universe overspills a scientific world view that cannot entirely contain it. On the one hand, they willingly discuss strange cosmic phenomena inaccessible to scientific thought; on the other, in the light of their professed rationalistic, atheistic materialism, they deny the very existence of the mysterious. Victoria's discussion of the divine manifesting in the orbit of *Sputnik* is a good example of this fractured discourse. Having seriously and thoughtfully put forward her ideas of the presence of God in the trajectory, she hastens to retract her words and claims that they are only a joke, since she is an atheist.

Meanwhile, in the USA, it appears to be almost offensive to the scientific self-consciousness of the NASA staff to imagine that there may be something unknown, something out of reach of a physical or, at the very least, intellectual domestication. Another explanation of the pronouncedly rational outlook of the majority of our NASA interviewees is perhaps, paradoxically enough, to be found in the relative strength of the American New Age movement, which may have made the narrators of the space narrative anxious to distance themselves from views that could be mistaken as non-scientific mysticism.

As we will show in later chapters, a mystical and spiritual undercurrent also pervades the American context, but, at the same time, it seems to be much more taboo than among the Russians. The case of the late Carl Sagan, distinguished scientist and NASA consultant, and one of the prominent figures in the search for extraterrestrial intelligence, may illuminate this American ambiguity. Sagan was, on the one hand, known for his fierce rejection of anything that smells of New Age and mysticism (cf. Penley 1997). On the other hand, he was obsessed, to put it mildly, by the idea of communicating with the ETs, a position that, as a New Age writer ironically observes, could lead to rather paradoxical situations:

I have watched him [Sagan] foam at the mouth while attacking a flying saucer contactee buff at a conference at Lindisfarne [a famous New Age Association in New York], but his whole imagination is dominated by images of extraterrestrial 'Contact'. (Spangler and Thompson 1991: 83–4)

To Will, to Know, and to Know-how

Whatever the differences between our Russian and American inter-viewees, the basic form of their stories is, nevertheless, fundamentally the same. At play are the three modalities: to will, to know, and to know-how, which also direct the questing hero of the fairy-tale.

The extraordinary will to transgress the borders of the unknown is, in one sense, already built into the technology, just as the pull towards the divine was embedded in the European cathedrals of the Middle Ages. The booster rockets, the spaceship, the complex technological apparatus as a whole, are constructed with the aim of realizing this will to demolish the barriers against human advance. At work is the will to transgress such essential elements of our earthly existence as gravity and our bodily dependence on the Earth's biosphere.

Many of our interviewees in both the USA and Russia compare the driving force of their space projects to the motivation of a mountaineer: the will to show that the apparently impossible can in fact be accomplished. Yet the feats performed by the astro- or cosmonaut are, in contrast to the mountaineer's, described as being the result of collective, technoscientific teamwork of unprecedented magnitude and complexity. The flag on a mountain peak testifies to the will of an individual; the Stars and Stripes on the Moon, however, renders to many at NASA – and at IKI, too – positive proof of the human collective will to overcome all physical and existential limitations. When, during the interviews, we air our scepticism about the Moon flags, alluding to their connotations of conquest, national-ism and colonization, our point of view is in most cases rejected. Almost everybody, whether American or Russian, spontaneously approves not only of the flags, but of all the physical imprints of human activity left behind on the Moon, seeing them as positive symbols of human will and know-how. The only one to disapprove is a young Russian man.

Zhanna, for instance, says that these artefacts are terrific, because they have imprinted the Moon with a new human meaning: 'They prove that man was there.' In no way does it upset her feelings of national pride that the footprints on the Moon were made by American boots: 'The important thing is that man has been there.' Ross tells us about the heated debates he has had with his friends; he totally disagrees with their view of the artefacts left on the Moon by the Apollo astronauts as mere 'garbage'. In his eyes, they represent the will to do the best we can to establish contact with the wild and the unknown to which he ascribes so much significance.

To JoAnn, the will to overcome seemingly impossible barriers and to

infuse space with human meaning assumes particularly magnificent proportions. She connects it with the control of human destiny. While
witnessing the first successful launch of an American satellite in 1958, a
few months after the *Sputnik* shock, she was changed, she says. Observing
the rocket racing into the night sky and absorbing the knowledge that this
small US-made satellite was going to orbit the Earth, she felt different. She
describes the feeling as 'a sense of greater control over your destiny' and
compares it immediately with the fear and powerlessness that the Cold War
called forth in so many people at that time. To gain control over destiny
was, in that context, about her nation achieving a position as the technoscientifically and militarily leading superpower. However, when JoAnn
speaks in the 1990s about control of destiny, after Mikhail Gorbachov's
perestroika and after the fall of the Berlin Wall, the words have a much
more far-reaching significance. The will to control destiny that space
technology now embodies for JoAnn concerns the peaceful cooperation of
the entire globe and the will to tackle all the many problems that, in her
opinion, space exploration can solve for humanity. The final item on her
long-term agenda is our total emancipation from the Earth's biosphere and
a cosmic exodus prior to the death of the sun. Undeniably, this is a project
of will and control of gigantic dimensions!

In the space fable as in the fairy-tale, the will and the know-how belong
together. The realization of the tremendous will embedded in space flight
presupposes a matching know-how. Sure enough, the ideas put forward by
our interviewees on the extraordinary will, do match with corresponding
notions of an omnipotent know-how.

Underlining their insight as professionals into the deep complexities of
this technology several do, indeed, on the one hand, point to the high risks
that such complicated machinery necessarily involves. The NASA staff,
for instance, consider it an expression of naïvety when ordinary people,
implying that technology can be infallible, interpret the *Challenger* disaster
in 1986 as a serious undermining of their techno-optimism. Both the
Americans and the Russians distance themselves from simplistic beliefs in
unfailing technologies, but they are, on the other hand, in the grip of an
extremely strong faith in the enormous technoscientific forces that we, in
their opinion, may eventually develop if we continue along the path that
space technology has opened up.

The idea of a technology so advanced that we may one day bring to life
a dead celestial body and make it habitable sounds in no way unfamiliar to
JoAnn. She considers the bioengineering of other planets or terraforming
(the artificial generation of a biosphere on a lifeless planet) to be a natural

and quite realistic progression. This is a vision she shares with the majority of our interviewees. Few doubt that humankind will settle permanently 'Out There', either by means of terraforming other planets, or by the construction of space stations. Many voice an amazingly firm belief in our capacity to develop the techno- and bioscientific know-how required to adapt our bodies to alien extraterrestrial environments.

As an astrophysicist, Nikolai extends his thoughts, fantasies and emotions very far out into the universe. Even though he does express a certain reservation regarding the scope of our space projects, the limits he sets to how far we may go into the cosmos seem so distant that his perspectives become as far-reaching as those of JoAnn. His concepts of the future are likewise deeply anchored in his faith in human technoscientific know-how. His reservation, he explains, stems from our being existentially located 'in a jail of space and time'. By this, he means the enormous distances involved in interstellar travel that make it physically impossible for us to travel very far from the Earth, even if such a journey were to last for the lifetimes of several generations. Since we cannot travel faster than the speed of light, it would take us around 100,000 years just to cross our own galaxy. In his view, therefore, although space flight has endowed humanity with a great freedom – to go off to other planets – the opening up of this free space has also, he insists, emphasized how very limited our range of action is. However, as if not quite prepared to accept the limitations he has himself sketched, he eventually leaves the door ajar to speculations on possible new technoscientific discoveries that may in the future enable us to break out of 'the jail': 'Maybe you won't need to carry all the physical particles of your body, but using some informational transfer you can go out there,' he speculates.

When JoAnn envisions gigantic terraforming projects on other planets and Nikolai contemplates voyages beyond the laws of physics as they are known today, we pass into the realms of the speculative. But the speculative discourses voice a belief in a future where a super-potent technoscience of immense reach will materialize. The grandiosity of these speculations bears witness to the great impetus that space flight has given to both the American and the Russian dream of a sublime technoscientific know-how.

Just as the gigantic and sublime dimensions of the will and the know-how match one another, knowledge, as the third of the modalities or action-generators at play in the space adventure story, also refers to something extraordinary in the minds of our interviewees.

As with the other two modalities, sublime knowledge is likewise enfolded into the technology. If the technological know-how in the stories of our interviewees assumes a touch of the sublime, then this has an effect on the knowledge invested, and vice versa. But powerful knowledge doesn't only feature among the built-in prerequisites of space flight, it is also, to many of our interlocutors, one of the noblest goals of their enterprise. Alongside the desire for expansion, for new frontiers and contact with the 'wilds' or the 'enigmatic', the quest for sublime knowledge is a recurring theme. Frequently, staff at both space centres underline this aspect of basic research as being much more important than the utilitarian arguments that aim to legitimize the huge national investments in space flight. To take part in this quest for knowledge is, for almost everybody with whom we speak, a highly motivating factor.

The Masculine Hero

Both American and Soviet space flight carry a heavy iconographic tradition connecting the prototypical space hero with an extraordinary masculinity (see Chapter 2). It is a tradition with roots stretching back deep into the infancy of space exploration.

With only one single exception, the entire collection of early space heroes, greeting present-day visitors with their cosmic smiles from the innumerable photographs in American and Russian space museums, are men – although apparently not ordinary men. From Gagarin's flight to the Apollo Project and the Moon landings, the great space events of both countries are presented to the public as the stories of supermasculine, almost superhuman heroes. According to the narrative logic, the gigantic will, knowledge and know-how must be embodied by superheroes who can represent the quintessence of legendary masculinity, the 'men of the right stuff' as Tom Wolfe (1988) called them in his book on the first astronauts and the military test-pilot environment from which they were recruited.

'The right stuff', required to gain an admission ticket to 'the true fraternity', was something unmentionable, a taboo that, in that setting, created a clear division between those who had it and those who did not. Wolfe explains the concept as follows:

> [I]t seemed to be nothing less than *manhood* itself. Naturally, this was never mentioned, either. Yet there it was. *Manliness, manhood, manly courage* ... there was something ancient, primordial, irresistible about the challenge of this stuff, no matter what a sophisticated and rational age one might think he lived in.
>
> Perhaps because it could not be talked about, the subject began to take

on superstitious and even mystical outlines. A man either had it or he didn't!
(Wolfe 1988: 22; italics in the original)

Although this description refers to American space history, the myth of
'the true brothers of the right stuff' was no less pervasive in the Soviet
Union (cf. Pelevin 1992/1996; Graham 1990: 180–1; Lebedev et al. 1973).
Without a touch of irony, the cosmonauts could be staged as heirs to the
'Real Man', the legendary fighter pilot and war cripple Maresiev, who lost
both legs in combat, and whose heroic deeds later during the Second
World War had convinced millions of readers of a popular novel about his
life that a real Soviet man did not need legs either for dancing, or for
flying. On prostheses such a man could do anything (Polevoi 1970). At
other times, the space heroes were simply referred to as 'the cosmic
brothers' although this brotherhood included the world's first space woman,
Valentina Tereshkova. However, her mission was clearly not meant to lead
women to the stars, but to emphasize the manliness and cool courage of
her colleagues. The still generally accepted depiction of this first female
cosmonaut as a vomiting,[4] weeping disaster serves to highlight her steely
counterparts as possessing the genuine 'right stuff'.

This extreme worshipping of masculinity that pervades the history of
space flight influences our interviewees in different ways. Some express a
strong wish to replace the old masculine iconography with a new, gender-
mixed one. This applies especially to the female NASA employees.

JoAnn, for instance, is active in promoting women on many levels within
space flight. She refers to the joy she felt when a very complicated operation on a space station was performed by two women. At first, she says,
she had only seen two competent astronauts at work. But suddenly, she
was struck by the fact that this was the first space operation ever conducted
without male assistance. Such examples, she claims, demonstrate the on-
going change in the status of women, although men still vastly outnumber
women, both in space and in the work teams on the ground. JoAnn has
listed the statistical improvements in a report (Morgan and Ragusa 1987)
that she, as mentioned in the Introduction, proudly presented at the
Women's Studies World Conference in Dublin. JoAnn is thoroughly optimistic about future prospects, and argues that new technology constantly
creates new jobs that are not tinged by old prejudices and gender stereotypes. Moreover, a specifically equality-promoting factor is built into outer
space as a workplace. For weightlessness, she points out, eliminates any
physical advantage of strength men may have. Space is thus the natural
site for complete equality.

However, some of JoAnn's female co-workers voice less optimism. They are generally in agreement that women are gaining a foothold within NASA, but barriers and prejudices are, they say, still easy to spot. One woman, who has otherwise been outspokenly pro-NASA, relates how, in her opinion, the female astronauts are not being taken entirely seriously. She does not like to admit it, but these women are being laughed at behind their backs, and jokes are made in tones that are never used when the subject is a male astronaut. A few female astronauts who have accomplished something extraordinary do gain respect within this environment, but they then find themselves pushed into the role of 'token woman'. Another woman mentions that 'the old boys' network' is still going strong. All in all the general impression we get fully matches Penley's observations: that NASA in the 1990s is still 'repeating itself, unable to think about women in space' (Penley 1997: 55).

A complete contrast to the female NASA employees and their wish for a change in the iconography lies in the discourses of the male IKI staff. With two exceptions, they all believe that space flight is literally a man's job.

Dr Vasiliev is very frank about his commitment to the old patriarchal school. He openly professes his belief in home and motherhood as women's true vocation. When asked to characterize himself, he refers to his profound dislike of women who smoke and of 'nursing fathers' – that is, fathers who stay at home to look after a sick child. We listen carefully for any note of irony in his tone, but there is none. Gender hybrids seem to be his favourite targets. As to the question of female cosmonauts, he warms to his subject as he describes an occasion in the early 1970s when he put a female audience in its place while giving a lecture in France. He was asked if the Soviet Union intended to launch another woman cosmonaut. With visible pride, he recalls how he replied with a categorical 'no'. He argued then, and argues again now, that the job of a cosmonaut is hard and dangerous and, playing his trump card, he informs us, as he did the dumbfounded French women, that 'in principle, a man does any job better than a woman'.

Dr Vasiliev was born in 1934, and was therefore young when space flight came onto the public agenda in the 1950s. But such views, which in no way fall short of the American myth of 'the fraternity of the right stuff', are certainly not a prerogative of his generation alone. Whatever their age, the majority of the male IKI employees believe that masculinity and space flight are two sides of the same coin. 'There are too many women in space flight. After all, the cosmos is a man's job,' one 25-year-old radio engineer maintains. Others among the young men make up their minds a little more hesitantly, but in the end they also conclude that 'men are better suited' for the hardships of space flight. This attitude, which is countered only by a minority of two, becomes so monotonous that the female IKI employee who has been assigned as our guide, and who is present during the interviews, begins to show signs of embarrassment; during an interval, she tells us that this is getting to be too much.

Between these two poles, occupied by the American women and the Russian men respectively, we find the American men and the Russian women. In contrast to their Russian colleagues, the American men are clearly so affected by the precepts of political correctness that they take great care not to voice any discriminatory remarks. Nevertheless, their stories on gender problems are much less pronounced than the ones told by the NASA women. The Russian women evidently favour equality but, with one exception (a woman who had wanted to be a cosmonaut herself), they are altogether satisfied with the existing gender division of labour in space.

Our questions on space flight and gender thus generate response patterns in which cultural and gender differences interfere. But these very different answers confirm, each in its own way, that the iconography bonding the extraordinary will, knowledge and know-how with 'men of the right stuff' is still brooding over space flight.

That space flight represents a cultural enclave where the heroic master narrative of the masculine superhero has been able to survive unchallenged far longer than in many other places is confirmed by the interviews we conducted at the Space Camp for youngsters that is located near the Kennedy Space Center.

Almost one-third of the children aged ten to thirteen at the camp are girls. According to the staff, there is little difference between the two sexes in their response to Space Camp activities; both are equally eager to learn and discuss what it means to be an astronaut. However, the girls are often surprised when they are confronted with the masculine iconography on display, so distinctly genderized that it can neither be hidden nor explained away. Since the space heroes are men, the girls who are interested in space flight have difficulties with role models. One of the teachers, Debbie, says that this collision between the traditional iconography and the girls' search for role models has the effect of making some of them very gender-conscious. She illustrates this with an anecdote: 'I used to give a lecture about this space suit from the Apollo mission. We talk about the little portable bag, the urine collector. And, well, this is a man's bag, because women did not go to the Moon, and sometimes they [the girls] are startled by that.'

Notes

1. Our interviewees belonged to the academic staff of the space centres. The majority had technoscientific backgrounds as computer scientists, engineers, biomedical doctors, biologists, astrophysicists, etc. Altogether we interviewed twelve Russians (five women and seven men) affiliated with the Institute of Cosmic Research (IKI) in Moscow, and fourteen Americans (nine women and five men); eleven were affiliated with NASA (the Kennedy Space Center) and three (two women and one man) with Space Camp Florida. The purpose of the American space camps is to get youngsters hooked on the idea of space exploration. The camps are sponsored by, among others, the Mercury Seven Foundation. (The Mercury Seven were the first American astronauts.)

2. With the fall of the communist regime, this organization was dissolved, but there are presently – in 1998 – plans being made to set up a new one retaining the old name, Pioneers.

3. Turner first put forward his thesis in 1893 at a meeting of the American Historical Association, and later published it in his book *The Frontier in American History* (1920/1996).

4. Patricia Cowings, director of the Ames–NASA Psychophysiology Laboratory, ridicules the scientific work that stereotypically claims women to be more susceptible to motion-sickness than men (see Gray et al. 1995: 96).

4

Terraforming: Farmers in the Sky

During the 1940s, a significant *novum*, terraforming, began to appear in the works of Western science fiction writers. It is a major theme, for example, in Robert Heinlein's novel *Farmer in the Sky* (1950), in which Ganymede, one of Jupiter's moons, is transformed into a new Earth, a new Terra, and populated by colonists from Earth. Since that time, the idea of fertilizing barren planets and filling the heavens with duplicates of Earth has occupied the minds not only of many SF writers, but of scientists and engineers as well. They dream of redesigning existing planets, asteroids and moons, and of creating new ones. These are the thrilling visions made possible by space flight and, the scientists stress, the technology required for such tremendous feats of planetary engineering is not so very far beyond what is possible today. In the confident words of one space salesman and NASA consultant: 'many of the now-sterile worlds of the Solar System can be rebuilt into new Earths' (Oberg 1981: 260).

In this chapter, we shall highlight the will to cosmic technopower, shifting our perspective from the personal lens of our interviewees to a general review of some of the grandiose master plans for galactic-scale cyborgification that have emerged within the framework of Russian and American space flight. We take Foucault's notion of bio-power to be our theoretical framework, but extended from human to planetary bodies and artificial life in outer space. Focusing on body regimes, Foucault (1978) described the will to administer, regulate, optimize and multiply life as a basic principle of modern society. We shall discuss how space flight allows fanciful ideas of new kinds of bio-power to proliferate: from life management on a cosmic scale to radical recodings of bodies as cyborg-machines.

As part of the story, we shall also unravel the ambivalences that, since the early years of space flight, have surrounded the introduction of the master plans for planetary and galactic scale bio-power. On the surface, the scenario looked clear and straightforward: the so-called 'sterile worlds' of the cosmos, the 'barren deserts of space', were to be fertilized and harvested in a way similar to that in which the terrestrial wildernesses have been conquered and civilized. In the USA, this approach tied in nicely with the frontier mythology of the 'Wild West', while in the Soviet Union it found resonances with the traditional Russian colonial desire that fitted so well into the Marxist myth of the productive forces as carriers of progress.

However, the concept of farming the sky, of extending the colonial enterprise to the heavenly realms, appears to be neither so obvious nor so simple as the old-fashioned conquest of terrestrial territories. For the colonial analogy, which aims at normalizing and naturalizing the coming deeds of the cosmic Columbus, has clashed with religious taboos. Acts of heavenly creation are already copyrighted by the Fathergod that most religions, including Christianity, worship. As a result, some American, and even some Soviet, discourses have implied that if we are to intrude into the realm of the divine, if we are to take profane possession of something so otherworldly, then the sacred has to be reordered accordingly. This dilemma results in interference between two different kinds of scripts. The modern, secular one describes technological man striding boldly across the cosmos, creating his own new cyber-Earths and skies. In contrast, the Holy Script(ure) reserves heaven as the traditional dwelling place of a fatherly god, the divine master of creation in comparison with whom even technological man shrinks into insignificance.

The intertextual compromise between these two very different stories has led to the construction of a new divinity: the cosmic cybergod, whose high-tech spirit and terraforming agenda seem fit to serve as a role model for the sky-rocketing visions of the spacefaring nations.

Bio-power: From Human to Planetary Bodies

In Foucauldian analysis, bio-power defines a specifically modern kind of power relations that 'materially penetrate the body in depth, without depending even on the mediation of the subject's own representations' (Foucault 1980: 186).

The ultimate rationale of bio-power, according to Foucault (1978), is the political regulation, management and control of life and life processes. At stake is a 'Power over Life', as opposed to the 'Right of Death' wielded by the sovereign of pre-modern societies (Foucault 1978: 133ff.). The pre-modern sovereign had the right and the absolute power to dispose of the lives of his subordinates, a power that was often exercised in condemning them to death. Modern power relations, by contrast, are built upon sophisticated technologies that give control over life, regulating individual bodies as well as the reproduction of entire populations. Even weapons of mass destruction, such as the atomic bomb, Foucault emphasizes, are constructed with the explicit purpose of ensuring the survival of populations; the enemy has to be extinguished as a people in order that one's own population may live. 'If genocide is indeed the dream of modern powers, this is not because of a recent return of the ancient right to kill; it is because power is situated and exercised at the level of life, the species, the race, and the large-scale phenomena of population' (Foucault 1978: 137).

Foucault's bio-power has two basic forms. First, it centres 'on the (human) body as a machine' (ibid.: 139); it brings a machine-like discipline to human bodies so they are able to fit smoothly into the capitalist apparatus of production. Second, it focuses on 'the species body, the [human] body imbued with the mechanics of life and serving as the basis of the biological processes: propagation, births and mortality, the level of health, life expectancy and longevity, with all the conditions that can cause these to vary' (ibid.: 139).

Foucault's use of bio-power is aimed at discourses on the management and regulation of human bodies and sexuality. But if we shift the focus from Foucault's concern with the history of sexuality during the eighteenth and nineteenth centuries, and extend it to the bio-political agendas of the post-Second World War period, we see that bio-power develops a much broader significance. Population policies, so-called 'population control', have not lost any of their bio-political importance. But this is only one aspect of late twentieth-century bio-politics. 'Over-population', 'food crisis', 'environmental destruction', 'pollution', 'energy crisis', etc. are today represented as a complex network of life-threatening problems that require interrelated bio-political interventions on a planetary scale. In other words, the new bio-political world order – as anticipated for example by the UN's Brundtland Commission (WCED 1987) – is envisioned as an order where not only human bodies, but also the global body of the Earth, are disciplined and regulated for the benefit of 'all mankind'.

We suggest that the gist of this new world order can be aptly articulated by an expanded version of Foucault's concept of bio-power, and also that space flight has given an important impetus to its construction. As Bordo has pointed out (Berry and Wernick 1992: 165–81), it is no coincidence that the opening paragraphs of the Brundtland Report position its subject of enunciation – the global 'we' of the UN – in 'our' new panopticon of outer space. Nor is it chance that they celebrate space flight which, having given 'us' access to this privileged view, for the first time in history allows 'us' to set in place the planet-wide regime of life management that is designed to prevent imprudent human activity from further threatening the health of the fragile Earth body:

> In the middle of the 20th century, we saw our planet from space for the first time ... From space, we see a small and fragile ball dominated not by human activity and edifice but by a pattern of clouds, oceans, greenery, and soils. Humanity's inability to fit its doings into that pattern is changing planetary systems, fundamentally. Many such changes are accompanied by life-threatening hazards. This new reality, from which there is no escape, must be recognized – and managed. (WCED 1987: 1)

Later on in the report, in the section on 'the global commons' (ibid., Chapter 10: 274ff.), the message becomes clear: space flight and space technology can play a vital role in monitoring and protecting the 'health' of the planet and in ensuring its 'continued habitability' (ibid.: 274). The Space Age heralds the advent of global-scale bio-power.

The idea of monitoring life on Earth from the space panopticon is as old as space flight itself. The first satellites with television cameras were launched in the 1960s to assist in weather forecasting. Today, satellite-mediated technology has developed into a service so familiar that 'we', all Earth's television viewers, hardly notice when TV meteorologists sky-rocket us to the elevated position of the weather satellites as part of their peda-gogical presentation of tomorrow's forecast. Many other sophisticated Earth Watch projects have been developed since then by various space agencies, utilizing orbital technology. In the 1990s these have culminated in the 'Mission to Planet Earth', launched as an international space project and as one of NASA's four strategic enterprises. It is dedicated to 'gaining a full understanding of Earth's systems and the effects of natural and human-induced changes on the global environment' (NASA: Mission to Planet Earth home page 1998). This big 'mission', designed to understand the 'total Earth system', is a significant demonstration of the way in which the extension of the scope of modern bio-power to the planetary body is being articulated, both as science and as a serious bio-political agenda for the spacefaring nations of the late twentieth century.

The term terraforming, as it is used in the discourses of both science fiction and science fact, suggests primarily a duplication by technoscientific means of our own biosphere in the faraway wilds of the universe – that is, the construction of cyber-earths or even of artificial planets. However, the word also implies a blurring of boundaries between bio-power in outer space and on Earth. In the discourses of the promoters of terraforming, Terra, the prototype for the whole project, is not only discursively constructed as a model to be imitated elsewhere; she is also considered as an object of transformational intervention herself. In the techno-optimistic discourses engendered by space flight, there seem to be only minor obstacles to overcome before the step can be taken from planetary monitoring and management to complete reinvention. Ideas for re-creating Earth as, for example, a Garden of Eden have clustered around the terraforming concept. The reconstruction of Earth as an enormous wilderness park or recreational area has been part of the speculations of several scientists engaged in space projects in both East and West. Among them is the well-known physicist and NASA consultant, Freeman Dyson. In his book, which bears the remarkable title *Disturbing the Universe*, he suggests that 'Earth may be treasured and preserved as a residential parkland, or as a wilderness area, while large-scale mining and manufacturing operations are banished to the moon and the asteroids' (Dyson 1979: 232–3).

In the East, an influential Soviet Moldovian philosopher and member of the Soviet Academy of Sciences, A. D. Ursul, advocated a similar division of the cosmos into a celestial industrial sphere and a terrestrial recreational zone (Ursul 1990: 154–5).

The notion of terraforming, of extending the regime of life management and bio-power to planetary bodies, may therefore be just as relevant when speaking of Earth as when speaking of other worlds. While Earth is proposed as the blueprint for terraforming in outer space, the discursive construction is at the same time blurring the distinction between Earth and other planetary bodies. On an imaginary level, bio-power is extended to life management of galactic dimensions. This is exactly what Dyson is proposing in the quotation above, which stems from a chapter equally astonishingly entitled: 'The Greening of the Galaxy' (Dyson 1979: 225ff.).

Civilizing the Deserts of Earth and Space

In order to demonstrate in detail how this discursive blurring of boundaries between bio-power on Earth and in outer space works, we shall look at two Russian examples: a film, *White Desert Sun* (1970), which has been a favourite of cosmonauts for decades, and a book promoting space flight, *Where All Roads into Space Begin* (Borisenko and Romanov 1982). Both clearly re-use the country's imperial Orientalist discourse in their efforts to communicate the vision of how to 'bring landscapes to life' (cf. Greenleaf 1994: 108ff.). In a rephrasing of one of Edward Said's observations on Orientalism (Said 1979: 96), it could be said that the Russian fund of clichés about the conquest of 'eastern' territories in the early nineteenth century multiplied itself into the Soviet promotion of a future expansion into outer space.

White Desert Sun is an 'eastern', the Russian equivalent of a Hollywood western, focusing on the 'wild east', those vast tracts of land comprising the former Soviet Central Asia. The film was lovingly adopted by the cosmonauts, and a viewing of it included into the rituals that the space hero in waiting had to perform prior to his flight.

Chronicling the installation of a procreative social order into the lifeless void of a desert, the film loyally – although with a touch of irony – reproduces the traditional Soviet propaganda that depicts the 1917 Revolution as a kind of societal lift-off. The bonds of feudal-Muslim enslavement of the desert region are broken by a passing Red soldier-hero, and thus the rules of life replace the realm of death. Hence the desert is seen to be heading metaphorically in the same direction as the blond protagonist, Sukhov – towards the flourishing meadows of voluptuous Mother Russia. The imaginary re-shaping of the old order and of the hot, barren landscape openly rests on sexist as well as racist representations; in a parallel with classical Hollywood westerns, there is no trace of political correctness in dealing with gender and race. The film's transformations are foreshadowed at the beginning by two contrasting images of femininity. On the one hand we are introduced to the soldier's dreams of his blossoming sweetheart: a young, typically Russian peasant woman in watery pastures far away; and on the other to the parched desert through which the hero is passing on his journey home. The sandy landscape over which he walks is sculpted to resemble a woman's body. The connections between terraforming and the redistribution of sexuality become even more clear when a harem, condemned to death by its evil husband, Abdulla, is freed, and the battle over the women's future begins. Almost single-handedly, the Red soldier wipes out the savage natives, icons of the old infertile desert society. Dissolving the childless, barren harem and encouraging the women to enter into monogamous marriages, the blond hero prepares them for the life-affirming world of his own civilization. If death and stagnation were the emblems of the old desert-woman, her newly liberated bodyscape is oriented towards fertility and progress.

The struggle between good and evil is embodied in the highly racialized figures of the blond and noble Russian, Sukhov, *vis-à-vis* the dark and cruel Abdulla.[1] Furthermore, if we use a Foucauldian framework of interpretation, Sukhov as rescuer and controller of life and Abdulla as cruel sower of death are prototypical representations of the dichotomy between modern bio-power and the pre-modern power of death, as seen from the self-glorifying position of the modern hero. As the symbol of a huge wrist-watch on the white man's arm indicates, the outcome is determined in advance. Modernity and History, understood as technology-compatible and transcendental Time, are allies with which the hero shares his impersonal, machine-like drive. For although the soldier-hero relates to the desert in his sharing of its thirst, he never succumbs to nature. His name, Sukhov, suggests dryness (*sukhoi* means 'dry'), as does his desire for his dream-girl, buxom Mother Russia. Not once in the film does a drop of perspiration moisten his forehead, nor does a grain of sand ever stain his impeccably clean uniform. Unlike the desert or the vengeful Abdulla, the hero made of the 'right stuff' knows how to master nature and transcend the body. All his desires are cool and controlled.

In 1998, seven years after the collapse of the Soviet empire, *White Desert Sun* was still an essential ingredient of the pre-flight rituals (Fedorov 1998: 5). Not only did the cosmonauts take a fancy to this film, but its dialogue even entered into the professional language of the space community. During flights the cosmonauts often quoted phrases from it in their communications with mission control, using particular sentences as a code to avoid possible misunderstandings. One cosmonaut asserts that, after using such quotes, 'everything would be clear to everybody' (Savinych 1983: 46).

One answer to the question of why this film became an imaginary the cosmonauts could internalize lies in the desert's geo-cultural representations. As a mythical icon of sterility and death, non-terraformed desert wilderness long ago came to symbolize the barren world of pre-Revolutionary Russia in Soviet ideology. But even if this desert had ceased to exist, other deserts continued to signify stagnation and to challenge the pioneering sons of the new society. The deserts of the Soviet Far East or the icy wastes of the Arctic North were perceived as frontiers to be conquered and civilized as proof of permanent revolutionary progress and expansion. Among the role models cosmonauts were expected to name in their public appearances, the flyer-heroes of the 1930s, who had 'conquered the polar deserts' of the Arctic, ranked very highly. Especially popular was Chkalov, the first pilot ever to make a transpolar flight (Gagarin 1971: 69; Savinych 1983: 67). With the dawning of the Space Age, the cosmos itself began to be perceived as 'the deserts of space', a name that, with its connotations of emptiness, underlined the secularized view of space endorsed by the Soviet regime.[2] Hence the desert is the real field of operations for a cosmonaut. Like the soldier-hero of the movie, space man is ultimately commissioned to transform the 'hostile' and 'barren' deserts into a living world, akin to the sacred homelands of Russia.

The mythical terraforming of earthly deserts as a symbolic anticipation of a cultivation of the sky recurs in other space flight discourses: for example, in the story of Baikonur, the military cosmodrome in Kazakhstan from which all the cosmonauts were launched. Our second example of boundary-blurring between the terraforming of Earth and outer space is the book promoting this cosmodrome as the symbol of the Soviet space enterprise: *Where All Roads into Space Begin* (Borisenko and Romanov 1982). The long-range perspective outlined in this text is that, by means of space flight, man can start 'harnessing the wealth of nearby planets for the benefit of the entire human race' (ibid.: 86). However, the main point of the narrative is to show that the terraforming of a huge tract of desert into a cosmodrome of itself anticipates these future riches. When, in 1955, 'an army of builders' led by a 'field commander' and construction engineer began the construction of Baikonur, one of the largest projects ever to be undertaken in the Soviet Union, the newcomers were met by a desert region that symbolized all the lifeless backwardness of the non-terraformed world of yesteryear. The starting point for the conquest of the wilderness was a tiny station where trains, symbols of the arrow of time, rarely stopped. The majority of the settlement's few houses were but small and 'mud-plastered', marked both by gravity and the dusty infertility of the desert soil (ibid.: 33).

As the terraforming evolves through all the hardships brought about by the extremely 'hostile' environment, the vast desert gives way to what the authors perceive as an oasis, a garden city, a town of roses and rockets, already halfway out of this world. No longer are the housing and the production sectors of the cosmodrome grounded in an ordinary earthly existence; rather they are re-named within the narrative as a 'living module' and a 'production module'. They have become the inhabited parts of a spaceship, associated with the creation of a new world, a new Earth, floating in the nothingness of the universe. 'Suddenly out of nowhere a green isle – Baikonur,' the authors enthusiastically exclaim as their aeroplane, having passed over the ocean-like 'greyish expanses of the desert', finally reaches its destination (ibid.: 11). By transforming the void of wilderness into spaceship garden earth, the (male) Soviet mind, he implies, has once more proved its ability to replay the god-trick of creating life from dust.

Human and Divine Will to Cosmic Bio-power

Space flight discourses blur the boundaries between projects of life management and bio-power on Earth, and in outer space. But these are not the only boundaries that are being renegotiated. So too are the ones between human and divine bio-power.

Let us reconsider the heavenly panopticon, the 'God's eye' position, to which space flight and space technology gave access. During the formative years of the Space Age, it was constructed on a deeply ambivalent basis that echoes the keynote of cannibalizing and sacralizing. Situated within this panopticon, man seemed both small and great, simultaneously the humble pupil and the dominant master. The new mental map of the universe, to which we return in Chapter 7, could be used to sustain both views. According to the modern, secular story-line, the protagonist of which boldly takes off to terraform the galaxy, the ventures into space were essentially a prolongation of the colonial activities of humans on Earth. Via the frontier myth in the USA, and the myth of the historical progress of productive forces in the Soviet Union, the new technological adventure was made to appear unavoidable and exciting, not to mention conspicuously simple. The dead and barren 'deserts of space' might, after all, be subjugated almost as easily as the deserts of Earth. In this discourse, technological man is envisioned as the future master of the universe, already capable of restructuring and re-creating the solar system:

> In the second half of the twentieth century, the inhabitants of the planet Earth are beginning to change the over-all organization of the solar system. For billions of years, our planet had only one moon. Now, many artificial satellites orbit the Earth. In the not-too-distant future, artificial satellites may be orbiting our natural moon and other planets of our solar system. (Shklovsky and Sagan 1968: 467)

The view presented by these two scientists, a Russian astrophysicist and an American astronomer, reflects the widespread perception of the first *Sputnik*s in 1957 as nothing less than 'man-made moons'. As opposed to the natural one, such artificial moons could symbolize the farthest reaches of terrestrial technocivilization, now extending into the cosmic wilds.

Yet another aspect of cosmic bio-power as a technological feat of impressive proportions was engraved on the sky when the USA launched a so-called 'talking satellite' in the closing days of 1958. This launch may be considered a spectacular attempt to outshine the triumph of Laika, the communist mongrel bitch who became the first Earthling to orbit the globe. For the first human voice to travel around the earth had a quite differently elevated and empowered tone from that of Laika's imaginary barking: it belonged to President Eisenhower who, from outer space, broadcast his Christmas message of 'peace on earth and good-will toward men everywhere'. However, the voice of the Great White Chief resonated with the words of the Almighty, the Great White Father, in more ways than one. The satellite that relayed the benevolent message incarnated of itself the will to expose an entire enemy population to death in order to ensure national survival: it was an Atlas missile (an ICBM), designed to carry nuclear warheads over intercontinental distances. Unfolding the dual per-spective of power over life and death on a global scale, this Celestial President not surprisingly supported the belief in techno-man's ability to manufacture quasi-divine wonders: 'Through the marvels of scientific advance, my voice is coming to you from a satellite traveling in outer space' (*New York Times*, 20 December 1958).

Nevertheless, the visions of such intrusions into the traditional domain of God were at the same time so daring, so obviously transgressive that they called for a second story-line to adequately renegotiate man's place in the universe in relation to the sacred. In this discourse, techno-man acknow-ledged his being, after all, only a techno-infant, a mere novice in the new world of science and technology, and so the sacred became invested with the characteristics of a benign high-techno-father (see, for instance, Cam-eron 1963; Tovmasyan 1965). The themes of man as but a small and humble pupil who is being ruled by higher, technologically sublime, forces, thus intertwine with a readjustment of the divine. Seen through the rationally scrutinizing eyes of the writer who first popularized the original cyborg concept of Clynes and Cline, Arthur C. Clarke, this second narrative could be explained in a relatively simple way. According to him, it was only a half-truth that man had invented the tool. Rather, 'tools invented man' (Clarke 1964: 202). We could add that in this case the spaceship invented not only space man, but also the gigantic projects of planetary engineering or terraforming that have been envisioned by scientists and semi-scientists since the late 1950s. Written more as a profession of faith than a provoca-tion, Clarke's statement points bluntly towards a universe that is no longer governed by the old-fashioned, 'crossed-out' god of the classic scientific world view (Latour 1993). In the new order of the Space Age, the retired watch-maker, who was needed only for an occasional repair to the celestial clock, is ousted by a very different divinity, energetic and enterprising – the Cybergod. In contrast to the distant clock-maker who supervised the universe of Kepler, Descartes and Newton from the outside, this high-tech divinity is an active and communicative terraformer, as omnipresent in time as in space.

The Cybergod entered space science discourses in both the USA and Soviet Russia around 1960. Representing a new entrepreneurial spirit in the skies, this superior being brought along a cosmos that contested the one known so far on a fundamental level. Perceptions of the differences between the cosmic natural and the cosmic artificial became unstable, the one beginning to merge confusingly with the other. Our own small satellites, the 'man-made moons', might, for instance, have numerous, gigantic fore-runners in orbit that we have naïvely and mistakenly believed to be natural. Shortly after the first *Sputnik*s, the prominent Russian astrophysicist I. S. Shklovsky thus ventured the idea that the two moons of Mars, Phobos and Deimos, with their unnaturally low density, might be artificial – huge, ten-million-ton, Martian-made satellites, rigid and rocky on the outside, and yet hollow within (Shklovsky and Sagan 1968: 373). Although the launching of such enormous structures might well surpass 'the fondest dreams of contemporary rocket engineers', such feats would offer no serious problems to 'a technical civilization substantially in advance of our own', as the American astronomer Carl Sagan noted some years later when he endorsed the hypothesis of his Russian colleague and co-writer.[3] Conceding that the non-natural moons were more likely to be mute testaments to an ancient civilization than signs of a 'thriving contemporary society', the two scientists opened up the possibility that the Martians, turning into a nation of spacefarers, might have left their home planet for good.

These trail-blazing Martians may be seen as emblems of the Cybergod. Like them, He is believed to have come into existence long before mankind, as evinced by His superior level of development in science and technology. By further association with traditional images of a fatherly God, the cyber-divinity was sometimes posited as the original Terraformer and, con-sequently, as the very masculine Creator of life on Earth. Clearly these modes of thought reflected both the deeply patriarchal settings of the space sciences and also the urge to legitimize space man's own ventures into the heavens. During the early years of the Space Age, the astronautic mind still felt the need for some kind of moral justification for his bold dreams of seeding and terraforming the 'barren bodies' of space. The notion that life might indeed have been seeded on our own planet by higher beings from the stars not only made Earth into a model for other, as yet lifeless celestial bodies; it also gave an impetus to visions of future space settlements by loosening the bonds to Mother Earth and psycho-logically facilitating our departure (see Romanyshyn 1989: 23). If, as the theory implied, Earth were only a dead and passive receptacle for the enterprising life-genes from above, if she were merely a bowl of 'prebiotic soup', then ideas for our return to the intelligent and splendid realm of the Father would seem natural as well as tempting.

Panspermia or the New Genesis

These ideas relating the origins of life to a Cyber-Godfather led to an updated, and in a way truly seminal, theory of how life began on Earth: the concept of 'panspermia' re-entered the stage of science. The 'sperm' in question had a certain impact on the subject of terraforming and also bluntly demonstrates how phallogocentrism, gigantomania and destabilized boundaries between Man and Cybergod merge in the space flight discourses on life management and bio–power. It therefore seems appropriate to sketch the genealogical table of these 'little guys' as one scientist approvingly called panspermia in the 1998 documentary *It Came from Outer Space* (Discovery Channel).

The concept of panspermia as generator of life was most fully elaborated at the beginning of this century, when a distinguished Swedish chemist and Nobel Prize winner, Svante Arrhenius, took up the idea in a book (Arrhenius 1907) that was later issued in English as *Worlds in the Making* (1908). Here he suggested that the Earth (or other planets) had been impregnated by life-bearing spores that migrated through space, speeding from one celestial body to another. These spores, thrown out from a planet by 'volcanic force' or the like, were imagined to be driven by radiation pressure from the sun and other stars. The necessary precondition for conception was simply that the planet receiving the semen should be ready to 'shelter organic life'. As a result of this interstellar migration, Arrhenius reassuringly asserted, life in the universe had no end. Although living beings on any given planet would die out when conditions became inimical, their essence would live on in the creatures propagated by the panspermia from their parental planet elsewhere in the universe. From this outlook, cosmic life came to seem very much like the stable, ceaselessly colonizing, patrimonial family so cherished during Victorian times. 'Sperm' from one parental celestial body gave rise to 'children' on another; these children reproduced similarly, and so on *ad infinitum*. Carried by the panspermia floating through the cosmic womb, heading for a planetary 'shelter', life would go on eternally.

Arrhenius's perception was, naturally, influenced by his own time and by the world in which he lived. The Old World of those days was sending living beings by the thousands over the oceans to the New Worlds of America and Australia. The colonial powers were also busy in their endeavours to spread life and civilization to the colonies as well as keeping their empires together. The 'humanization' of space and the 'export of life' into space, advocated by pro-space activists several decades later

(O'Neill 1978; Elias 1990), was by no means a novel idea. However, Arrhenius's thinking differs from theirs in that he takes nature, the human body, as the root metaphor for the bonding of the universe. His mode of terraforming is still situated within the framework of 'natural procreation'. In his discourse, tools had not yet invented either man, or his sperm.

Let us now proceed to some updated versions of his theory. Here the natural has been ousted by the artificial. Just as the borders between the moon and the satellite had begun to blur, so the traditional division between naturally and artificially generated life was collapsing. Now, artificial insemination on a galactic scale became conceivable.

By 1960 the spaceship, icon of the Cybergod, had revived interest in the panspermia hypothesis, the credibility of which had eroded over the years.[4] At the First International Space Science Symposium, the geneticist J. Lederberg added the dimension of Space Age technology to Arrhenius's organic concept when he pointed out that 'rocket-impelled spacecraft' had 'furnished a mechanism for producing artificial panspermia' (Goldsmith 1980: 43). In other words, space man was now able to engage in an export and import of life throughout the cosmos. Intentionally or otherwise, he could implant the spores of terrestrial life on distant celestial bodies, and his spaceships could equally well carry alien micro-organisms back to Earth. Visions of creating life on other planets by means of 'infection' or 'seeding' were put on the scientific agenda (with Venus, of all places, serving as the very first imaginary target; see for instance Fogg 1995: 25). And, of course, what space man was able to do now, the enterprising Cybergod might already have done a long time ago.

Various lustful fantasies of a barren Earth herself being infected or seeded by alien astro- or cosmonauts popped up in the Space Age sciences. For example, in the American 'garbage' hypothesis, terrestrial life was the result of a picnic held by visitors from an advanced civilization on the 'virgin' Earth. A primordial crumb, left in the party's refuse, might thus be the ancestor of us all (Shklovsky and Sagan 1968: 211–12). On the Soviet side, not surprisingly, it was suggested that we may stem from the activities of 'highly organized cosmonauts' who were conducting well-planned experiments – not dissimilar, it seems, from the Soviet five-year plans – on foreign celestial bodies (Konstantinov 1972: 17; Shklovsky 1976: 321). Jointly, scientists from the two superpowers wondered whether these divine aliens intended to prepare the Earth for colonization or merely wanted to distribute their genetic code, so that the 'evolutionary patrimony would not be irretrievably lost' in the event of a disaster on their home planet (Shklovsky and Sagan 1968: 212). In each of these visions, the living Earth, including ourselves, descended from a Being whose superiority was founded on the technologies on which artificial panspermia depended – rockets, spaceships and computers (at that time tellingly nicknamed 'Giant Brains'), as well as knowledge and control of the genetic code.

Dismissing the prevailing view that earthly matter had generated life on its own, the theory of artificial panspermia revitalized and rephrased the dichotomy between mind and matter. If the 'semen' of life were transmitted in microbiological codes programmed by a superior techno-logical intelligence, then Earth provided only the pre-biotic, the pre-life environment, for these genes to evolve in. And insofar as the genetic code is usually seen as a dictionary or language,[5] the mind in question was also authoring our planet by writing a text that, like the Word in Christianity, imprinted meaning and logos onto an otherwise mute and senseless world.

The artificial panspermia theory held a certain attraction for several scientists because it offered one possible explanation for the enigmatic universality of the Genetic Code. Indeed, it attracted no less an authority on genetics than Francis Crick who, with James Watson, had 'decoded' the structure of DNA. It was Crick who came up with the quintessential version of the New Genesis. In 1973, assisted by the prominent chemist L. Orgel, he invented the term Directed Panspermia (translating 'panspermia' as 'seeds everywhere') to describe the ancient Cybergod's encoding of life on our planet. Almost a decade later, he even published a book, *Life Itself* (Crick 1981), outlining his astonishing vision. He speculates that, long ago, Earth was covered by a 'pre-biotic ocean', a 'primitive soup' or 'chicken bouillon' containing no life, but filled with small organic molecules that could serve as 'food' and 'raw materials' to sustain the pioneering life genes when they came raining down from above. Hence, this ocean of thin organic soup was passively 'waiting for life to get going' (Crick 1981: 105). Mean-while, we are invited to envisage a higher civilization inhabiting an alien galaxy very far away. Having reached technological maturity billions of years before Earth was terraformed, this civilization would be interested in colonizing the universe through the means of interplanetary fertilization. Filling his rocket with generative cells, this Cybergod targeted the Earth's passively waiting, as yet sterile, womb and launched his frozen semen. After the arrival of the tiny colonists, emissaries of Technological Mind, life began to multiply and grow in the nourishing 'soup' of the virgin planet which was thus made (or, we suggest, raped) to become Mother Earth.

What Crick and Co. are advocating is the idea that our genetic heritage comes not only from the stars, but from the heavenly, high-tech Father we have named the Cybergod. Although Crick speaks out against our own 'infecting' or 'polluting' of other celestial bodies, the warning sounds somewhat hollow in the light of his own infectious obsession with Directed Panspermia as the procreator of life on Earth. Moreover, his writings confirm that a certain kind of self-replicating panspermia does exist, at least in the imaginary and textual interchanges between fathering minds; Crick's views are not very different from either Aristotle's theory of conception where the sperm alone created life in the womb, or from the Christian narrative of creation.

Out of the Cradle

The next entry into our inventory of new kinds of bio-power evoked by space flight concerns discourses about the escape from gravity and a new artificial cyborg-life in weightlessness. These stories present us with one more cluster of ancient phallogocentric images of the sacred and the profane articulated in the language of modern high-tech culture.

The imagery sustaining arguments for a departure from Earth feeds on the ancient cultural dichotomy between a Heavenly Home, associated with a wise and omnipotent Father God, and a barren, fallen World governed by the concerns of low and mindless (female) nature. In some Space Age discourses this opposition was transposed into a confrontation between 'gravity' as a property of enslaving matter and 'non-gravity' as an icon of energy (the techno-scientific term for spirituality) and disembodiment. Thus the degrading and impure World was extended to encompass all the gravity-ridden worlds of our solar system in opposition to the uplifting and blissful zero-gravity of open space. When planning our future in space, advocates of this trend argued, we should construct artificial 'earths' in space instead of trying to re-engineer the forbidding and heavy celestial bodies.

The idea of building colonies in the sky as a way to escape the 'chains of gravity' goes back to the Russian schoolteacher Konstantin Tsiolkovsky, who invented the space rocket at the beginning of this century. However, Tsiolkovsky invented much more than the mere technological prerequisites of space flight. He also laid out the imagery that came to fascinate so many scientists and that pervaded the bulk of space discourses after the Second World War. This is true not only of the Soviet Union where the teachings of the Russian 'father of cosmonautics' became mandatory but also, and at first glance more surprisingly, of the USA as well. In a single, telling sentence, Tsiolkovsky articulated the metaphorical script for the Departure and in so doing he succeeded as no other space pioneer has done in stirring the imaginations of his techno-scientific heirs:

To live on them [i.e. on the heavy planets] means to shackle oneself in the chains of gravity which [on other worlds] are sometimes stronger than the terrestrial ones; it means to put up a multitude of obstacles around oneself, to be packed together on a tiny space, to live a miserable life in mother's womb. *The planet is the cradle of intelligence but you cannot live in the cradle forever.* (our italics; Tsiolkovsky 1954: 127)

It was the final sentence that really developed a life of its own; written in 1911, this cradle-image still figures in current space discourses as a high-flown rhetorical, yet evocative, challenge to break away from matter, mother and Earth and to 'become a man'. It is, for example, inscribed on the wall of the public area of the Kennedy Space Center's new, International Space Station Processing Facility. In English, this slogan usually reads: 'The Earth is the cradle of man but you cannot live in the cradle forever', or abbreviated simply to 'Out of the Cradle' (Hartmann et al. 1984).

Gravity as the emblem of imprisoning mother/matter also frames other images that continue the devalued 'womb' and 'cradle' imagery. Viewed as a very 'deep hole' (alternatively a 'deep pit' or 'well'), the gravitational field around a planet makes us 'disadvantaged' as we have to waste too much energy in order to clamber out of the devouring abyss it forms. 'Does it make sense to climb with great effort out of one such hole, drift across a region rich in energy and materials, and then laboriously climb back down again into another hole?' O'Neill, author of *The High Frontier*, rhetorically asks (O'Neill 1978: 37). As though echoing these reflections, another advocate of living in a zero-gravity zone, Timothy Leary, wishfully claimed that: 'There is no reason for us to ever climb back down into such a planetary hole again ... The original sin of "Genesis" is gravity: the fall' (Romanyshyn 1989: 27).

Contrary to traditional Romantic imagery, Home and World have exchanged genders: the sacred Home belongs to the Cyber-Godfather, while the World of gravity is left to fallen and feminine Nature. A complete liberation from the natural environment was therefore among the primary objectives (cf. Ulubekov 1984: 50). In the artificial, non-polluted 'earths', built from the raw materials of celestial bodies, the inhabitants would fully control their worlds. Here, gravity could be properly reinvented so as to suit differing needs, and the environment of the man-made heavenly bodies would consist only of carefully selected, non-offensive vegetation and animals. For instance, mosquitoes, symbolizing the itchings of the flesh, were banned from O'Neill's artificial 'garden-earths' where idyllic and pastoral landscapes with lush gardens and luxurious houses were set up in opposition to the depleted and 'polluted' World of the Earth. In contrast, the Soviet sanctuary privileged the productive forces that were taken, here as on Earth, as the governing principle for the layout of the settlement. Thus the machine dominated the futuristic visions of a cosmic communism headed by a new, superior breed of workers: tidy 'city-earths' with clean production compartments, separated by a green belt from the small, petty-bourgeois apartments that seemed amazingly reminiscent of Western European habitat ideals of the 1950s (Ulubekov 1984: 212–13).

Although these artefact 'earths' were designed for future emigration, they had, at least on a modest scale, been overtaken by events by the time these visions of a sacred refuge were written. Along with other ventures into the sky, orbiting space stations had shown that neither Gravity nor the rest of fallen Nature any longer constituted a serious hindrance to leaving behind the turbulences and troubles of an earthly life. As an example of the astonishing new world we were entering, the Soviet champion of the Departure, Ulubekov, tells of how the cosmonaut in *Soyuz-3* observed wild thunderstorms and torrential rains beneath him while he himself was sitting warm and comfortable in his quiet cabin, high above the raging of nature (Ulubekov 1984: 155). Describing space as 'the high throne of orbit' and the spaceship as 'an enclosed cylinder of magic', ex-astronaut Al Shepard similarly opposed the imagery of elevated clear-sightedness, *wonder*-ful peace and tranquillity to the turbulent and distorting 'atmosphere' of Earth (Shepard and Slayton 1995: 429). The choice of the Sea of Tranquillity as the first Lunar landing site could only underline this dichotomy. While wars and racial upheavals were tearing the Earth apart, a Tranquillity Base was set up on the Moon, for the occasion standing in for Home.

These images of raging and confusing nature showing herself to the distant and curious gaze of the space traveller may be used to identify one of the two very ambivalent, yet interrelated, thematic clusters with which the Space Age has re-created the Earth. The first, suggested by the turbulent atmosphere, is Earth as an hysterical body: an unruly, unpredictable and, from a distance, deeply fascinating body that, on the constant brink of a breakdown into chaos, seems close to the tomb, to the Fall, to death. She represents the World, the bodily troubled background, matter gripping hold of mind, against whom the blissful disembodiment of space (or space man) may be profiled. She is the empty 'womb' without a future of her own, the barren body whose displaced and empty 'holes', such as the ozone hole, must be carefully watched and scrutinized from the panopticon of the sky. She is the patient in need of supervision and medical re-engineering so that she may become a 'reservation in space', a controlled and manageable Earth with reconstructed, primordial wilderness and restored historical sites. A body of the past.

The second Earth also has its origins in outer space. It is Earth as 'the beautiful blue planet', perceived in contrast to the 'lifeless deserts of space' – 'the bright colorful home' as opposed to 'stark black infinity' (Kelley 1988: Preface). Ever since the blue planet's creation in the vicinity of the Moon in 1968, it has been lifted out of this World, sanctified as 'our only home' and worshipped as the holy Mother whose existence, however, also depends on the Son and the Father.

In this vision, one key factor in the crucial outsider position of the sons is that it implies that the 'fragile' Earth has become 'an aged mother, totally dependent on us, her children' (Koval and Desinov 1987: 8). The pictures taken from the space panopticon did give an impetus to the environmental movement and to the technology-mediated resacralizing of Earth and Nature, as we discussed in our analysis of McCulloch's picture in the Prelude. However, another factor in the significance of these pictures may stem from the fact that they are also well-suited to legitimize the escape fantasies of the Space Age. The concept of a helpless Mother Earth, an elderly beauty in distress, entrusted to the 'filial love' of space man[6] encourages the idea that only by going out can we, mankind, develop the proper attitude required to 'save her'. Moreover, when building space stations based on recycling technology, we shall, space fans claim, learn how to 'manage' or 'steward' our own natural habitat, on a planetary scale. If one term may be singled out as suggestive of Earth as the projected controlled body of tomorrow as well as the home/body we have left, it is the name of that NASA project we mentioned earlier: the Mission to Planet Earth. The Cybergod could hardly have done it better.

The Bodyscapes of Men of Steel and of their Mock Mirrors

After this exploration of the ways in which space flight discourses invent ever new ways of extending the power over life and combining it with resacralization processes, let us now return to what Foucault describes as the most basic element of modern bio–power: the reconstruction of the human body as machine. Elaborate new versions of this aspect of life management are also part of the bio–political agenda of space flight.

In multiple and unprecedented ways, the test pilots who were selected as astronauts during the infancy of the Space Age were made to demonstrate their capabilities of breaking the bonds holding them to matter, body and Earth. The autobiographical anthology *We Seven* (Carpenter et al. 1963), written when these American astronauts were still naïvely over-whelmed by their own historical significance, is crowded with examples of how coolly and self-obsessedly they endured all bodily torture in order to match their otherworldly mission and augment the technologically sublime machine they trained for years to fly. To remain cool and casually skim through a popular magazine while being baked for hours at 135°F in a heat chamber, to fall asleep in a chair in the sealed-off isolation chamber, to consent to having one's feet submerged in a bucket of ice cubes for seven minutes, or to black out in the G-centrifuge and still nonchalantly maintain the easiness of the test – all that, and much more, rendered symbolic proofs of an outright martyr-like readiness to sacrifice emotional flesh and depart from the bodyscaping powers of Earth. So non-humanly self-controlled, so emotionally self-suppressed were these steel men that they were often likened to predictable robots or 'mechanical men' (Collins 1974: 54). In the eyes of one NASA official who lived and worked alongside astronauts for many years: 'they become so disciplined they can almost dial up the emotional commodity that's needed. If they are going to a cocktail party they'll dial up to where it says, "We are going to be light and gay"' (Young et al. 1969: 183).

The image of the mechanical men gained strength from a mock-hero by the name of José Jiménez. José was an imaginary comic character created by the US writer and comedian Bill Dana around 1960, more or less simultaneously with the figuration of the first real-life space men. José appeared as a Hispanic astronaut who spoke English with 'a hilarious accent and a wispy "please-don't-send-me" attitude'. When asked in interviews during TV shows what he was going to do on his epic flight, he inevitably answered that he was going to cry a lot (Carpenter et al. 1963: 14, 182). Obviously, alien and effeminate José could not really be counted among the seven first astronauts, the men who were presented to the public as the new 'heroic breed of men' whose responsibility it was to embody America's numinous future as a superpower. Nevertheless, he came to play a major role in developing the image and the self-image of the Astronaut (at that time significantly written with an initial capital letter). The first team of astronauts, the Mercury Seven, adopted him to function as 'a handy device for relaxing the troops' (ibid.: 14). The first words spoken from the ground to the first American human in space, Al Shepard, were: 'OK, José, you're on your way'. Accordingly, Shepard's post-flight debriefing statement res-ponded: 'My name José Jiménez, Chief Astronaut, Junited States' (Benford and Wilkes 1985: 139). In other words, José seems to have created a moment of joy and laughter in tense situations. By providing a debased and blurred counter-image to the semi-divine prototypically white, Protestant, military test-pilot-turned-space-men, this timid Hispanic mock-hero affirmed the real soldier-heroes' status as 'ordinary supermen', as one Air Force general put it (Carpenter et al. 1963: 12).

The shadow figure of José accompanied the staged masculinity of 'the right stuff' in various ways. Scott Carpenter of the Original Seven Mercury Team, who went up hoping to be let in on a 'great secret',[7] became so swept away by the sublimity of the experience of orbiting Earth that his over-composed, astronautic self gave way to an emotional, erratic identity with an eventual loss of control of his corporeal as well as his surrogate bodies – the space suit and the capsule. Listening to the alleged steel man's anguished cries during re-entry, one disgusted NASA official bluntly asked whether the astronaut thought he was changing his sex (Young et al. 1969: 178).[8]

José may also be viewed as a symbolic boundary figure between space man and his earthly wife. In the popular cult of the Astronaut, beginning in the early days with *Life* magazine and continuing up to the present with the book *A Man on the Moon* (Chaikin 1994) and the film *Apollo 13* (1995), a dichotomy is invariably at play between the calm and aloof astronaut-hero who strives for the sky, and the anxious housewife who represents family, womb and earthly matters. With mythic persistence, this opposition also dominates the Soviet presentations where Gagarin's rural mother (less often his wife, a medical doctor) typically re-enacts the role of the body and of Mother Earth.

However, the Soviet Union had a much more immediate mock-cosmonaut than the USA. Putting the questions of both ethnicity and gender on the ideological agenda long before the Americans, the Communist Party launched an ethnic other, a Chuvash, as well as a woman, Valentina Tereshkova, as cosmonauts number three and six respectively. While the Chuvash, Nikolaev, codenamed Falcon, was generally accepted into the heavenly élite, the poetic Seagull, Tereshkova, was not.[9] Although the space agency realized that the preparation of a woman for this flight 'required special scientific research, called forth by the peculiarities of her organism' (Lebedev et al. 1973: 103), things went terribly wrong in outer space. Even Soviet science could evidently not cope with such organic 'peculiarities'. From soon after her lift-off, she was perceived by the infuriated Control Centre as possessing too little steel and too much earth, as being far too worldly. A recent book rather sarcastically relates all her physical complaints: her discomfort with the helmet, for instance, which she found too heavy even though, the patronizing author notes, this was simply impossible in

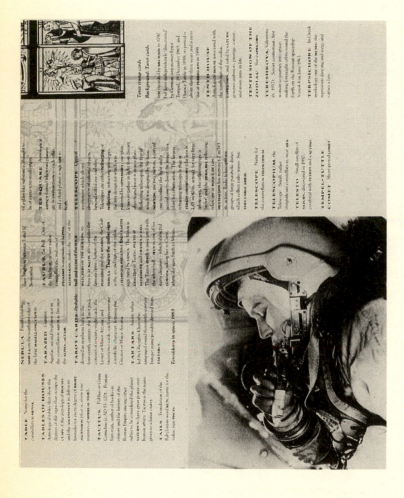

PLATE 4.1 The right place for the 'wrong stuff'? Valentina Tereshkova, the first woman in space in 1963, depicted in a New Age astrology book. (Reproduced from Jan Kurrels: *Astrology for the Age of Aquarius*, Anaya Publishers, London 1990, 2nd edn Tiger Books International, London 1992. Courtesy Jan Kurrels and Popperfoto/Nordfoto.)

her state of weightlessness (Golovanov 1994: 700). Allegedly, a crying, vomiting, disoriented and exhausted Seagull (an obvious *alter ego* for the timid José) wanted only to return home.

Her flight was depicted by the media as yet another victory for the system, but the stories of her catastrophic failure nevertheless became more or less common knowledge remarkably quickly. Having it both ways, with an impressive demonstration of liberated Soviet Woman up front and a notorious flop behind the scenes, a satisfied Korolev, the mastermind behind the space programme, could now assure the rest of the brotherhood that women did not belong in space and that he would never again venture into such an experiment. In an American magazine from 1975, nearly a decade after Korolev's death, staunch cosmonaut A. Leonov still maintained that 'by analyzing her flight, we understood that their [i.e. women's] lot is to stay on Earth' (Golovanov 1994: 701). The creation of the 'wrong stuff' was thus accomplished in a manner characteristic of the Soviet PR stunts around women's emancipation. The ideological façade of equality was upheld while discrimination flourished freely. Tereshkova's double life never ended.

Even today she is depicted by many Russians as the cosmonauts' quint-essential counter-image, helping to give credibility to the notion that men alone can escape the bonding of gravity and the materiality of body and earth.[10] By contrast, Tereshkova figures prominently in a Western New Age and astrology dictionary, *Astrology for the Age of Aquarius* (Kurrels 1992: 180). A large photograph depicts her lying in her space capsule with dreamily closed eyes. Presenting her under 'T', together with such entries as 'Tarot Cards' and the astrological 'Tables of House', the author of this book seems finally to have defined the 'right cosmic place' for 'wrong stuff'-heroines!

Back in the 1960s, however, homebound Seagull was re-caged by Soviet propaganda in a context seemingly more suitable than that offered by the space capsule. Soon after Tereshkova's flight, the Communist Party, eager to improve the somewhat tarnished image of the nation as 'one happy family', staged a celebrity wedding between her and none other than the Chuvash cosmonaut, the 'man of iron tenacity' (Lebedev 1973: 59). This cosmic marriage, set up as an official event of grandiose proportions, could also serve as a splendid icon for the Party's vision of Heaven on Earth.

From Superman to Post(hu)man Cyborg

A major purpose of the steely body of the 'right stuff' was, as we have discussed, to demonstrate its capability of transcending debased bodily matter. Nevertheless, in its own way the lift-off implied a dramatic return of the body in its fusion with the machine; a return that was paradoxically sustained by the many persistent mock-heroes.

As the space body exposed its flesh and intestines to the devices of innumerable medical tests, examinations, adjustments, probes and the like, as it was inserted into the electronic and mechanical systems of the space capsule, it began to seem like a machine in its own right. The way in which the astronautic body was fragmented and transformed into numbers and statistics exemplifies this configuration of body and machine. It also came to tickle the popular imagination as this totally decomposed body accompanied the presentation of its owner-occupier, the space hero himself, to the public.[11] Thus the rate of the space man's heart before, during and after the flight, his pulse, weight, lung capacity, blood pressure, respiration, oral temperature, blood count, the colour and gravity of his urine, and so on and on ... all of this was carefully registered and, especially in the USA, made a question of national interest. Strikingly, this act of de-composing the body became a counterpart to the reduction of a machine into small, separate parts or, as Romanyshyn has cleverly pointed out, to the dissection of a dead body, a corpse (Romanyshyn 1989: 17).

However, this analogy overlooks an important point. What the medical electronics involved in rendering the astronaut body fit for cosmic adventures is mechanically translating, by means of so many numbers and figures, is not the language of other machines or of decomposed corpses: what it electronically signifies is rather the disjointed grammar of organic speech. What it translates and interprets into the depersonalized lingo of science is nothing if not the vague murmuring of organisms in change: the whispering of blood particles, the susurration of cells, of muscles and organs at work. It is the speech of a body that, transformed into a post-(hu)man cyborg, can only be rendered intelligibly and functionally alive through technology. Inspected and explored for diseases and organic mal-functions, the astronaut becomes so dissolved in bodily fragments and in multiple voices that the boundaries of that strategic and heroic assemblage called self appear to be thoroughly transgressed (Haraway 1991: 212).

Consequently, the image of the autonomous and transcendent astronaut, a cybergod in waiting, easily merges with counter-images of earthly shadow figures that conjure up the spectres of degradation, fragility and depend-ence; images such as the mock doubles of Hispanic José, Seagull Teresh-kova, and also the chimps, monkeys and mongrel bitches of earlier flights – that is, the non-straight, the effeminate male, the hysterical woman and the domesticated animal.

These symbolic carriers of 'weak' nature(s) performed actively in the phantasmagorical show that, in the first decade of space flight, brought into focus the representations, not only of a divinely strong and self-reliant steel man, but also of a vulnerable and mortal cyborg body, completely unable to function on its own. In this performance, the space man was not the manly conqueror and explorer, taking other territories and bodies into his possession; rather, his own body had become possessed by everybody. Thus, in his book on the *Apollo 11* mission to the Moon, Norman Mailer locates a binary opposition between the masculinity of the space heroes with their elevated images as stainless steel men and the pictures of their manipulated bodies which were not only possessed and (sexually) abused by technology, science and the penetrating scientific gaze, but were even laid open for public entry. The objectifying, dissecting and knowing vision of Mailer himself provides evidence of this transgression:

> They were virile men, but they were prodded, probed, tapped into, poked, flexed, tested, subjected to a pharmacology of stimulants, depressants, diuretics, laxatives, retentives, tranquilizers, motion sickness pills, antibiotics, vitamins and food which was designed to control the character of their faeces. They were virile, but they were done to, they were done to like no healthy man alive. (Mailer 1971: 48)

Conclusion: Bio-power and the Sacred

The Foucauldian notion of bio-power gives both a rationale and a driving force to the master narratives of the adventurous space heroes, which we analysed from a genre point of view in Chapter 2 and in Chapter 3 through interviews with academic staff of the American and Russian space agencies. We have seen how space flight constitutes an important chapter in what literary scholar Martin Green calls 'the history of the white male mind' (Green 1993), and how this history intersects with Foucault's 'bio-history' (Foucault 1978: 143), an approach that may also cover the many brand new kinds of life management and body regimes to which the prospect of a cosmic exodus gives rise.

Our analysis shows, first of all, that, when ideas of calculated, cosmic-scale power over life are introduced, they produce a break with the secularization process that is considered to be a part of the modern scientific enterprise.

The Foucauldian description of bio-power and the cultural impetus to gain total control over life point towards the conclusion, stressed in particular by Evelyn Fox Keller (1992), that twentieth-century biology has aimed for a final excommunication of the 'secrets of life': for a wiping out of mystery and a definitive detachment from story-telling, speculation and religion. Keller quotes, among others, Crick and Watson, who describe the scientific quest that led them to the discovery of DNA as a 'calculated assault on the secret of life' (Keller 1992: 42). In our context, Keller's account is especially interesting because it spotlights the secularization process, which is a logical consequence of the desire for total human control over life. If humans are in charge of the processes of life, there is little space left for traditional divine mysteries.

But what Keller does not comment on is that the scientific 'assault' on Nature's traditional secrets and the ensuing erasure of the activities of an old-fashioned God, who possesses only words and other magic tools for the creation of life, leave a vacancy to be filled by a Cybergod who, in contrast, is equipped with the most advanced and super-powerful high-tech devices. Crick's invention of the directed panspermia hypothesis, after having successfully carried out his own 'assault' on the secrets of life, is a significant example of the phallogocentric re-sacralization process that is also a part of modern high-tech science.

Apart from highlighting, on the one hand, this high-tech-based 'return of the divine Father', another conclusion suggests that the cosmic high-tech laboratory, on the other hand, is a tricky place, where supermen may be heading not only for the elevated realm of the Cyber-Godfather, but also for a fall into the post(hu)man.

Notes

1. The scenario was co-authored by the Russianized Azerbaijani writer Rustam Ibragimbekov.

2. Nevertheless, among ordinary Russians the view of the cosmos, and consequently of the cosmonauts, as divine or semi-divine persisted (see Savinych 1983: 136).

3. The Soviet–American book *Intelligent Life in the Universe* (1968), by Shklovsky and Sagan, has remained the 'bible' of SETI (Marx 1988: 305). The book is a translated and expanded version of Shklovsky's Russian book on the subject (1962). In his memoirs, Shklovsky notes that while he, the main author, never received one penny in royalties, Sagan made both a fortune and a name for himself from the book (Shklovsky 1991: 251ff.).

4. The theory lost credibility after the discovery of the damage done to organisms exposed to radiation.

5. 'The Genetic Code is the small dictionary which relates the four-letter language of the nucleic acids to the twenty-letter language of the proteins' (Crick 1981: 171).

6. A declaration of this 'filial love' is also perceptible in the title of the Soviet book on the cosmonauts that NASA had translated into English: *Sons of the Blue Planet* (*Syny goluboi planety*) (Lebedev et al. 1973).

7. Carpenter implies a parallel between his upcoming flight and the afterlife as, lying atop the Atlas, he recalls how in his childhood a dying uncle talked of getting ready to 'know the great secret' (Carpenter et al. 1963: 328).

8. Carpenter was never re-assigned to a space mission. Instead, he joined the Navy's Sealab experiment, where he worked with a dolphin whose name, Tuffy (derived from 'tough'), suggests yet another mock-mirror.

9. Nevertheless, both the Chuvash and the woman were launched as part of a group flight where the cosmonaut in the twin capsule was more 'right', i.e. ethnic Russian and male. The idea of a woman cosmonaut came shortly after Gagarin's flight in 1961. Of the twenty female candidates who were selected from regional parachutist clubs, three went into training. One of them, Ponomareva, had a degree from the Moscow Institute of Aviation. In contrast, Tereshkova was a graduate in textiles, with no experience in aviation. Prime Minister Khrushchev made the final choice; however, he may well have been influenced by the agency – and heavyweights such as Korolev and Gagarin supported Tereshkova – into picking the candidate least likely to question the 'right stuff' icon. Only in 1982 did the 'cosmic brothers' get a 'second celestial sister', the fighter pilot Svetlana Savitskaya. Upon her arrival on board *Salyut-7*, the crew presented her with a bunch of flowers and an apron (Popovich et al. 1989: 120–1).

10. The job of space man still carries with it many earthly rewards, such as money and prestige.

11. See, for instance, the decomposition of John Glenn in Carpenter et al. 1963: 322–3. In the 1990s, the orbital heartbeats of Gagarin were still on display at the space museum in Moscow.

Amazing Story IV: The Dark Side of the Moon

This amazing true-life story bridges the gap between the astronautical and astrological mind. The cast of characters is the crew of *Apollo 11*: Neil Armstrong, Michael Collins and Edwin E. Aldrin Jr, generally known as 'Buzz'. Aldrin takes the leading role in the story that stems mainly from his own recollections, *Return to Earth* (1973). In its effort to debunk the images and values of Mechanical Man, this exceptional book is strongly influenced by the youth revolt of that time.

Much to his resentment, Buzz Aldrin was not designated to be the first man on the Moon in July 1969. Yet Aldrin did score his own historic first. As he backs out of the hatch and, covered with goose bumps inside his spacesuit, steps onto the Sea of Tranquillity, which exhibits a landscape of 'magnificent desolation', he immediately notices the peculiar properties of the lunar dust which, when kicked, reacts differently from sand on a terrestrial beach. But Aldrin was not only observing the effects of his moonboots on the lunar dust. 'The second thing I did', he writes, 'was record my own first on the Moon, a first that became known to only a select few.' His kidneys, he says, sent him a message of distress: 'Neil might have been the first man to step on the moon, but I was the first to pee in his pants on the moon. I was, of course, linked up with the urine-collection device, but it was a unique feeling. The whole world was watching, but I was the only one who knew what they were really witnessing' (Aldrin 1973: 235).

What Aldrin seems to be relating is that his lunar identity was not what it appeared to be. Beneath the shielding glamour of the spacesuit, radiating impressions of a knightly heroism, behind the façade of the astronautic steel man himself, his out of control bodily processes secretly mock-mirrored Neil Armstrong's historic first step, and fooled the worldwide TV audience. The only thing of which Aldrin was in conscious control was the knowledge of the debasing secret itself; he alone could decide whether or not to let it out. Or perhaps even this degree of control was

PLATE IV.I 'Do you see what I see?' (Text and photo from astronaut Michael Collins' autobiographical account of the first Moon landing (Collins 1974). Courtesy NASA.)

illusional, for the Moon appears to be so strangely interwoven into his life that it unleashed forces that eventually led him to recognize and disclose aspects of his personality that had been secret and repressed. Thus other cues in his story intensify the sense of inappropriateness that pervades this incident, creating a context that transforms it from a carnivalesque act into an Oedipal drama of truly cosmic proportions.

A clue to this palimpsestic pattern stems from his earlier perception of the lunar mountains and craters as sexual parts of the female body. When

passing over the back side of the moon, while radio contact with the Earth
was cut off, the three astronauts gazed down at the moonscape rushing by
beneath their craft, exchanging remarks that Collins in his book on the
voyage records as follows:

> Buzz pipes up. 'Yes, there's a big mother over here, too!' 'Come on now, Buzz,
> don't refer to them as big mothers; give them some scientific name.' Buzz
> ignores me and goes on. 'It sure looks like a lot of them have slumped down.'
> 'A slumping big mother? Well, you see those every once in a while.' Buzz
> decides to descend to my level. 'Most of them are slumping. The bigger they
> are, the more they slump – that's a truism, isn't it? That is, the older they
> get.' (Collins 1974: 392)

As though determined to make the meaning of these euphemisms crystal
clear, Collins continues the passage by relating a fantasy in which he is
inspecting a spaceship crew of a thousand women with 'two thousand
breasts bobbing beautifully and quivering delightfully in response to their
every weightless movement' (Collins 1974: 392ff.; see also his photograph).
So the astronauts' moon was unquestionably feminine; indeed we can go
further and suggest that the mother, the queen, whom the ancient Oedipus
married, also has a role to play.

On the way back to Earth, Aldrin becomes plagued by the mysterious
cosmic flashes that he first noticed on the outward journey, but which at
that time he quickly forgot. Now they become a veritable obsession, evoking
a state of fear and anxiety that is to be his constant companion for years
to come. According to some scientists, he says, the flashes, generated
perhaps by tiny particles of cosmic dust penetrating the astronauts' helmets
and skulls, may eventually cause brain damage and blindness. Seen through
the prism of our story, this strongly suggests that the space man is terrified
of the fatal embodiment of a vengeful moon.

Even at the astronauts' press conference before lift-off, Norman Mailer
spotted Aldrin's particular anxiety of being emasculated by 'evil moon
rays'. Mailer relates that the space man had come up with a rambling story
in which he began talking about his former rank of tenderfoot within the
Boy Scouts before jumping bizarrely to his hopes that he would not have
'a tender foot after walking around the moon' (Mailer 1971: 41). (The
name Oedipus means clubfoot.) In their discouragement of emotions and
their disregard for the sexual taboos engraved on our culture and minds,
officials at NASA never saw what it took Mailer only minutes to suspect:
the Oedipal anxiety that co-constructed Aldrin's moon.

Back on Earth, and deeply depressed, Aldrin eventually breaks down.

At a banquet for the cream of the 'right stuff', his country's most distinguished test pilots, he is publicly asked what he calls his 'anathema' question: 'how it really felt to be on the moon' (Aldrin 1973: 280). Developing hysterical symptoms, he is hospitalized. During the treatment, he comes to realize that his trauma includes a demanding, pushy father, Edwin E. Aldrin Sr, and a depressive mother who took her own life prior to her son's journey to Tranquillity Base. Incredible as it may sound, his mother's maiden name was Marion Moon.

Besides the fantastic Oedipal re-enactment, this story hints at two further layers from the realm of the imagination. First, the interconnectedness in the astronaut's mind between his parents and himself on the one hand, and God, the Virgin Mary (Marion) and the Son on the other (he was the only and adored son in a household full of females: two older sisters, the mother, a grandmother who was also a Moon). Secondly, if entry and possession are suggestive of sexual mastery – and the assault on the Moon may well be seen as rape – who in his situation would not worry that the Goddess of Fate might be eager to resettle the score?

5

As Above, So Below

A human being follows the way by which he is guided. (male Russian astrologer)

I was, in fact, a part of the Universe and doing what I was supposed to be doing no matter how difficult. (female American astrologer)

Space flight discourses construct the cosmic commons as a technoscientific playground and an appropriate scene for the heroic adventures of steel men and cybergods who are obsessed by the will to leave their mark on the universe through the expansion of human or superhuman bio-power. But when we now leave the scientific cosmos of space flight and turn to that of 'New Age science' (Spangler and Thompson 1991) such as astrology, we are met by actors who speak and act very differently from the steel men and cybergods. Seen through the lens of the New Agers, the picture of the wilderness 'above' changes radically, and other kinds of proper human attitudes are prescribed.

The actors who invite us into the New Age Cosmos are a rather heterogeneous group, belonging to dispersed circles that represent many different kinds of spiritual and occult beliefs. They do not form the kind of consensual community that, to a large extent, unites the narrators of the Russian and American space fable. Nevertheless, they share a nucleus of beliefs as far as cosmos, nature and body are concerned that makes up a master narrative as compelling and coherent as the space adventure story.

In this chapter we shall present the New Age narrative of the relationship between human self and cosmos, as it was told to us by fifteen female and male astrologers, whom we interviewed in Moscow and San Francisco in the early 1990s.[1] While retelling their stories, we shall look at the differences and similarities between the women and the men, the Americans and the Russians. The primary focus, however, will be the general framework of shared beliefs, which highlights a master narrative of an inner spiritual journey beyond the world view of modern science.

The driving forces behind this journey are modalities or action-generators quite opposite to those that characterize the space adventure story. The modalities of the fairy-tale of the questing hero – to will, to know and to know-how – are replaced in the narratives of the astrologers by those found in the other prototype fairy-tale, the tale of the protagonist who is led or acted upon by external forces (Propp 1975). Independent of gender and nationality, the stories of our astrologer interviewees were borne along by an enthusiastic dedication to act as such guided protagonists. They had consciously opted out of the scientific world view in which they had been brought up, and had rejected the mainstream cultural values of their countries which, in different ways, celebrate the will of universal man to shape his own destiny. All were eager to tell us about their will to abandon themselves to cosmic guidance, to be open to intuitive wisdom and to cultivate a meditative mood. Their stories were clearly driven by a desire to be imprinted with cosmic meaning, an emotion just as strong as the space men's will to leave their mark in outer space.

To Devote your Life to Cosmic Guidance

Mikhail, a 42-year-old Russian, illustrates his belief that he was pre-destined to become an astrologer by pointing out the connection between his life story and the position of the planets at the moment of his birth. In the late 1980s, he left his job as a computer specialist in order to become director of an astrological academy, where he lectures and gives consultations to the public. Aside from being a prolific author of articles and books, he is also active in the interregional federation of astrologers that was set up during the *perestroika* period.

Originally, however, he graduated with a degree in computing and mathematical topology. Nothing in his rationalistic and atheistic childhood environment seemed to point towards his later spiritual life. Only two things set him apart from most children: his interest in astronomy, and his Jewish heritage, which he only discovered by accident when he was ten years old. But today he perceives neither his fascination with the firmament, nor his feeling of being marginalized because of his ethnicity, as anything more than links in the long chain of coincidences that eventually led him to astrology. Seen from the normal explanations of cause and effect, he says, his astro-spiritual awakening appears to be a result of all the preceding events of his life. However, seen in a different light, it is 'as if I have walked a path that was already laid out at the moment of my birth'. In retrospect, all the coincidences in his life form a pattern of cohesive significances, a narrative whose structure only became meaningful when the language of astrology offered him a key. Inevitably, he claims, 'astrology became my natural occupation'. Mikhail feels that a higher power, the cosmic language, structured the course of his life at birth, and marked him out for this particular profession.

A similar sense of having been called by higher forces is voiced by American Stephanie, who is about the same age as Mikhail. She has broken out of a marriage and given up her job as a social worker to embark on a search for a deeper connection, a higher meaning in life. She, too, was fascinated by astronomy before turning to astrology. 'That was about ten years ago, and since then it has been my passion. I feel in a sense called to do this work.' Nevertheless, she tried for a long time to avoid her vocation because of the social stigmatization that she knew would follow, even in the San Francisco area, unofficial capital of the New Agers. Finally, Stephanie 'surrendered', she says, and at the time of the interview she has been practising astrology professionally for eighteen months.

Others articulate their vocation in a similar way; they use phrases like: 'it was probably destiny', 'I had no choice', or 'so this is my gift, this is what I am supposed to do in this lifetime and I love to do it'. To judge from their intonation and appearance, this commitment seems to be accompanied by the kind of inner peace and joy that is usually ascribed to born-again Christians.

Often their encounter with the alien world of astrology took our interlocutors themselves by surprise. It is as though they had suddenly stumbled upon a strange, exotic landscape whose dislocation from the mundane world of Western civilization made it an appropriate environment for their initiation into a higher, spiritual existence. During a journey to India, a youthfully disoriented Gregory had his horoscope cast by a native astrologer; although the casting provided him with a certain inner clarity, the prediction that one day he too would be an astrologer came as a shock to him. Suddenly he realized that, perhaps, he was meant to 'get lost in order to find his way home'. After his return to the USA, he called on a distinguished astrologer and became the Sorcerer's Apprentice.

For the Muscovites, however, who were not permitted to copy the New Age *Bildungsroman* by travelling abroad, the exotic was, in contrast, to be found much closer to home – in the underground movement. Mikhail's short journey to a metaphysically minded, subcultural study group in Moscow meant, as he recalls with a smile, that he was led down to the basement in more ways than one – to the nethermost floor as well as into the subconscious. 'It was a revelation to me,' he says. 'My atheistic education turned out to be a shell and one strong blow was enough to smash it.' In a very short time, and much to his surprise, he discovered the metropolitan underground movement, populated not by Soviet-loyal atheistic materialists, but by Soviet society's peculiar oriental mirror-shadows, the Russian Buddhists, yogists and religious philosophers.

In contrast to Mikhail's easy transition to a new life, the economist Vera's way into the world of astrological spirituality was long and tortuous (we introduced Vera in our second Amazing Story; see pp. 46–7). In the late 1960s, when she was in her twenties, she became a member of a subcultural group for whom astrology was the major interest. But the information she gained on the subject seemed at the time foggy and vague; only very gradually, having supplemented her knowledge with courses in psychology, extrasensory perception and biorhythms, did she begin, many years later, to practise as an astrologer herself.

Vera speaks only her mother tongue, and has had difficulties in obtaining any information at all on occult or esoteric subjects. Astrological books were no more available in Soviet bookshops than other religious or spiritual literature. People with interest in such things had to xerox old, pre-Revolutionary texts or to copy them laboriously by hand. Those who knew foreign languages were in a better position and often managed to get hold of books by authors such as Dane Rudhyar, one of modern astrology's founding fathers, and the younger, but no less influential, Liz Greene. However, even though most professionals, such as Mikhail, draw a strict line between 'popular' and 'scientific' astrology, it is not an institutionalized belief system with authoritative interpretations. On the contrary, each practitioner is free to endow it with new principles and hermeneutical readings in accordance with her or his own perceptions. Thus Vera has herself elaborated some new astrological concepts, and the feeling of being a spiritual systems developer has enhanced her self-confidence enormously: she now sees herself in the role of a 'fairy-tale prince who is predestined to bring her ailing people back to life'.

Vera is not alone in viewing astrology as a dynamic booster in the restructuring of her country. In his dialogue with a Russian astrologer, the very prominent author and president of the Russian PEN-centre, Andrey Bitov, claims that astrology's return with a vengeance from the long list of prohibited ideas has perhaps contributed more than anything else to the de-ideologizing of Soviet society. To Bitov, there is no doubt that the re-emergence of astrology has assisted in liberating the mind from the paranoid effects of totalitarianism: 'to believe that you are ruled by the celestial bodies is after all better than to assume that the KGB or the freemasons stand behind everything' (Bitov 1994: 7).

To be Imprinted with Cosmic Meaning

In one way or another, our interviewees all refer to a feeling of being embedded in a specific pattern of significances that is given from above; hence they perceive themselves as being constantly guided by higher forces. To feel the rhythms of the cosmos in their lives is to them a literal truth. They understand themselves to be microcosmic bodies closely inter-connected with and totally dependent on the celestial bodies of the macrocosmos. This symbiotic dependency structures their everyday lives down to the smallest detail.

In our second Amazing Story, we saw Vera pondering how to interpret our visit to her astrological stand. For a long time she wavered: were we or were we not the cosmic messengers that the heavenly constellations had promised her that day? However, Vera's indecisiveness in decoding the celestial sign turned out to be an exception rather than the rule. Several other interviewees provided us, in contrast, with examples of the natural ease with which they pick up and read the flow of cosmic communications. Mikhail, for example, claims that anyone who has been preoccupied with the cosmos for a long time, and has developed a certain sensitivity for its 'language', will spontaneously feel the changes in the macrocosmic constellations. It is then no longer necessary, he insists, to check the ephemerides (tables listing the positions of planets and nodal points) in order to know what is going on. Instead you will feel it in your body and your soul. If, for instance, he wakes up tired and depressed, he knows that this is due to the influence of Neptune or the Moon, and if the breadknife should slip and cut his finger, then that is the work of Mars. When the celestial signs are changing, so is he, and his life with him. For these reasons, he considers the practising of astrology to be the only realistic way of 'controlling' your life: it gives you insight into the laws that rule your destiny.

American Stephanie strikes a similar chord when she describes her own, extremely intimate, contact with cosmos. She already had a conception that 'as above, so below' before she was introduced to astrology, but at that time she had no language to encode her experience. Today she is fully capable of describing the synchronicity between the 'above' and her micro-cosmic self: an ascendant Cancer means, for example, that she herself will think of subjects that astrologers believe emanate from this constellation: family, needs, emotions. She feels the cosmic energies most strongly when she consciously 'tunes in':

> Every two and a half days when the Moon changes signs I definitely notice those shifts. Often within minutes I can feel that shift if I tune in, if I am quiet. If I'm running around, busy driving, then I don't know of this so much. But if I am home quiet, I feel these shifts. For example, I was sitting on the couch and the Moon was just finishing going through the sign of Pisces which is a very quiet and introspective kind of energy and as soon as it went into Aries, I got up, got into my computer, you know, got real busy and more external. Then I looked later, oh, isn't that interesting. The Moon just changed sign and I just changed energy too.

This feeling of being guided by cosmic forces is shared by our interviewees in both countries. Nevertheless, there is a national difference. While the Russians speak of the celestial bodies as being real-life, concrete, sensuous and extremely powerful agents, the Americans tend to use abstract terms that to some extent transpose the macrocosmic agency to mainly psychological and aestheticized forces. This difference between the two nationalities can best be illustrated with examples from their views on space flight and the Apollo journeys to the Moon.

One of the female American astrologers sees the moon landings as a strengthening of our bonds with the feminine archetype that the Moon represents in New Age astrology. With these journeys, she says, we signalled our readiness to enter into a broader cosmic connection that will perhaps be based on the feminine principle. Clearly inspired by the NASA iconography, she also endorses space flight as 'a giant leap for mankind', which has enabled us to see the Earth from the outside and to perceive it as a living organism without national borders, etc. One of her male colleagues, Rick, author of several books on astrological philosophy, offers another, more speculative version. To him, space flight may be an indication of human escapism, but it could also mean something quite different and positive. It may be part of a greater, galactic birthing process initiated by the cosmos itself. 'It is also like the baby starting to come out of the mother and see itself, see Mother Earth, from the outside.'

Although the higher cosmic forces are present here, the narrative perspective of these stories is primarily linked to the human mind and its cognitive functions. Even in the image of Mother Earth in labour, the viewpoint is assigned not to the planet but to the interpreting eyes of the human baby.

In contrast, these astrologers' Russian counterparts expose a cosmo-graphy in which the celestial bodies act as the only forces of significance; they are the ones that carry the narrative perspective and, acting as the protagonists, they also set the plot in motion. They do so not by rep-resenting psychological principles or forces, but by literally embodying powerful parental figures, which are cast as divine beings. In this way, the Moon of the young medical doctor, Petr, may be said not to represent but to embody the cunning intelligence of a female with absolute power: Petr understands the Apollo journeys as a scheme devised by the Moon with the sole purpose of making humans realize the insanity of the space projects. The Moon (Luna) had her own reason for 'letting the astronauts come to her', he says.[2] Petr maintains that she took them under her 'influence' because she wanted to transform their consciousness, referring to the widespread belief in Russia that the astronauts came back as com-pletely changed people. In Petr's discourse, the human is replaced as agent by the powerful Moon, who is endowed with both will and knowledge. By contrast, human will, knowledge and know-how are completely illusory as action-generators. It was the Moon who guided the space men to visit her body and then, as they were forced to acknowledge their mistake, to leave it for good.

A similar story of macrocosmic forces as embodied performers comes from 30-year-old Sveta. She has a technical education from the Moscow Institute of Aviation, and has since taken courses in extrasensory perception and astrology; she is also very interested in UFOs, which she sees as messengers from a plurality of highly advanced civilizations. She believes that one of these extraterrestrial civilizations is so advanced that it can incarnate the will of the cosmos and, consequently, rule the universe. While this is a view she shares both with the Russian 'father of cosmonautics', Tsiolkovsky, and with many of his scientific heirs at the Institute of Cosmic Research, Sveta's conclusion differs radically from theirs. According to her, this divine civilization will simply put an end to earthlings' efforts to colonize space. 'It will not allow us to pollute the planets in the way we have polluted the Earth,' she says, full of serene confidence. 'It will be stopped in time.' Hence the space projects are without any significance whatsoever: 'Everything is going to turn out the way it must, and not the way we want.'

The perspective on space flight taken by our two Americans includes a certain human agency and rationality in the general picture of higher forces at play. Moreover, the guidance that they anticipate from the cosmos has quite a benevolent and helpful character: in the USA, the cosmic guide seems ready to show some goodwill and render humans at least a

certain amount of assistance in their projects. In the Russians' case, however, humans are not only reduced to mere marionettes in the hands of the
supreme power; they are also directly rebuffed and put back in their place.
The will and knowledge of the Russian higher forces effectively exclude
the upward mobility for which the Americans expect a helping hand from
above. Roughly speaking, the American cosmos offers a carrot, that of the
Russians wields a stick.

On a personal level, the Russians are also led by cosmic forces in a
much more concrete and imperative way than the Americans. When Sveta,
for instance, began to understand the language of the cosmos, she would
receive thoughts such as: 'go!', 'do this!' or 'look there!'. She says: 'You
feel that someone is guiding you, that someone is educating you.' Sveta
gets all the instruction she needs from above, as do many other Russian
astrologers. An elderly former space flight technician, Askold, assures us
that 'no knowledge' originates within himself, not even the capability of
driving his car safely. Macrocosmic forces take over the wheel when danger
lies ahead.

However, one of the Russian astrologers strongly disagrees with the
rest of her colleagues on the despotic and interfering character of the
cosmos. Farida, who has a degree in psychology, angrily rejects interpretations such as those of Sveta and Askold. She points out that these
views are remnants of the authoritarian political system that strongly
encouraged a fatalistic attitude. 'Oh, how I hate it!' she exclaims. The
horoscope is to her nothing if not a fantastic offer to each individual to
take responsibility for her/himself and to make use of the possibilities for
self-development that are contained in cosmic energies.

The differences between the Russian and American astrological mind
are easy to find, but so are the similarities. At certain times, the Americans
too become mere instruments of a divine agency. This happens when they
perform the sacred ritual connected with the reading of a horoscope. For
example, Gregory refers to this as a ritual role where he changes from an
everyday, mundane individual to the elevated position of speaking on behalf
of higher cosmic forces. During this transformation, his appearance also
seems to change as though he becomes part of an ancient mystery play. He
feels that, metaphorically speaking, he develops a mask over his face and
a mantle of transpersonal energy over his shoulders:

> As you wear the mask, you take on the mantle of a transpersonal energy or
> power, but you are just a vehicle for that. It transcends you and you just try
> to make yourself an adequate instrument for that to happen. So when I do

read the chart, I do really feel like something shifts inside me and, hopefully, it is not just me speaking.

The notion that something or someone speaks through the astrologer during a seance is phrased more directly by Victoria, another San Francisco resident. It is not she but something else that does the readings, she insists. In her incense-scented apartment she prepares herself very carefully for her meeting with the client whose chart she is going to read. While meditating, she attempts to 'pull in' her client to ask the cosmos for permission to do what she can for the person she is waiting for.

Then the client comes and something just happens. I get very psychic and things come through me and I am able to put everything together and to integrate the whole chart. It's a magical thing and I don't think I am doing it, you know. It's someone else or something else and I am a very willing spokeswoman.

These two stories push to extremes the set of modalities that rule the astrological stage. To be imprinted with macrocosmic meaning is central to both Gregory and Victoria. They abandon themselves totally to cosmic guidance; they are wide open to the intuitive wisdom that comes spontaneously into their minds during the ritual. They are so completely receptive to celestial wisdom that even their own personalities are intended to serve only as its tools.

Astrology and Gender

Regardless of nationality, our astrologers all agree that their profession holds a very special attraction for women. As president of an astrological organization in Moscow, Farida conducted a survey that showed clearly that women, and especially middle-aged women, form the majority of astrologers' clientele and of those attending their lectures. Since their children do not need them any more, Farida says, these women finally have time for their own spiritual growth.

While Farida is vague about the exact figures in her statistics on the distribution of gender, some of her American colleagues immediately declare astrology to be an almost purely feminine concern. Among those attending his consultations, about 90 per cent are women, Gregory informs us, and his percentage is roughly matched by the estimates given by others. There is also a broad consensus as to why this is so: it is due to feminine intuition. 'I would hate to sound too feminist,' says Farida, 'but women

have a better connection with their intuition, and astrology implies intuition, not only calculations.' Much the same explanation is used in the
USA, although with the significant difference that, here, no one airs any
concerns about sounding too feminist. Quite the opposite. As we shall see,
femininity, the icon of the marginalized, deviant and intuitive, functions in
the discourses of all the American astrologers as an unambiguously positive
self-image.

Cathy, who teaches at a New Age college, is fully confident of the
natural interconnectedness between women and astrology. To her, intuition
and receptiveness, which she considers to be essentially feminine, are crucial
when it comes to reading the chart, and today, where the mathematical
calculation of planetary orbits and so on is completely computerized, they
may even be viewed as the only really important skills. Since the necessity
of carrying out complicated computations for the horoscope casting has
vanished, because the mapping of the cosmos is left to computers, women
can now, more easily than ever, apply their natural talents to reading the
signs. According to Cathy, the readings are mainly about uniting and
creating connections, for instance by drawing lines from one planet to
another, and feeling the mutual influences exerted by the celestial bodies.
'It's very connecting and complex and receptive, intuitive … It's natural
for women and not so natural for men,' she says.

To discover connections, and hence to co-weave the net of cosmic
textures, are talents that spring from the female body. (Only one person,
an American man, felt that feminine intuition originated from upbringing
rather than from nature.) The natural origin of female intuition is evident
from the roles women played in ancient European myths, the American
psychologist and New Age philosopher, Ralph, maintains. The Volva in
Nordic mythology, Pythia and the Sibyl in the Greek tales, all acted as
prophetesses and priestesses able to read signs that were concealed from
others. These mythic figures clearly indicate that, since the dawn of time,
women's natural talents have been linked to the intuitive, symbolic gifts of
prophecy that also included astrology. Women, he says, are born with a
talent for the clairvoyant and telepathic. 'Men have it too, but women
simply have it naturally. Women seem to be drawn to that.'

However, in the eyes of our American interviewees, it is not just that
women are naturally connected with astrology as clients or professionals;
astrology itself should be identified with femininity. Thus, Ralph is very
sceptical of the ancient version of astrology he sees so many present-day
astrologers reproduce uncritically. It is, he insists, an Indo-Aryan construction strongly tinged by the deeply patriarchal thought of that culture.

Accordingly, what the astrological world view needs is a feminist de- and reconstruction parallel with that which has been brought to bear on some of the natural sciences. Ralph also mentions Marija Gimbutas's feminist reinterpretation of European archaeological prehistory as an example of a science critique that could be successfully applied to astrology (Gimbutas 1982).

This revolt against the patriarchal iconography of traditional astrology recurs in the astrological system with which New Age philosopher Rick presents us. (Strikingly enough, several of our interviewees took part in the youth revolt of the late 1960s, among them Ralph and Rick; today they are both well-known authors of spiritual and ecological books.) Clearly inspired by the American goddess movement, Rick has created a feminine universe that, in the shape of the Great Goddess, appears to be in constant labour, giving birth to everything. He even envisages patriarchal culture as a manifestation of a larger feminine, cosmic 'principle', but when humanity one day gathers the courage to walk through what he sees as the birth canal of the Great Goddess, it will emerge to a 'reconnection with the feminine grounded being', he prophesies. Rick is thus extremely preoccupied with motherhood, birth and rebirth on a universal scale and, not surprisingly, he feels that psychologically he is rooted in a strongly feminine principle – which, he emphasizes, does not in the least affect his heterosexual orientation. He relates that he has had many fantastic experiences of identifying with the Great Mother Goddess when She is engaged in the process of giving birth (and this, we might add, seems to be her main occupation in Rick's universe). Generally, he believes that it is especially his feminine side that connects with the astrological cosmos: 'I have a very strong connection with the feminine inside me which I think very much informs my understanding of the cosmos and my openness to astrology.'

The identification of astrology as overtly feminine is not only based on its contiguity with traditional female characteristics such as intuition, receptiveness, mediating abilities and interconnectedness with nature. Astrology is also endowed with 'soft' female contours because it is perceived as a repressed counter-universe to the 'hard' natural sciences that are embedded in masculinity. As a resurgence of mythic thought, astrology calls to mind an alternative, womb-like cosmos that, according to Rick, threatens the masculine principle of the natural sciences:

> Of all disciplines, it [astrology] is the most scorned by conventional scientists because it is in certain ways the most feminine of sciences. There is a gender thing going on. The one-sidedly male psyche or masculine principle that

has been running the show for modern science is most scornful of the emergence of astrology because it threatens its male bastion.

The majority of our American astrologers whole-heartedly endorse the battle with the 'male bastion' and look towards the future with high hopes that it will hold the return of femininity/astrology. In spite of their continual marginalization, they feel that the cultural shifts caused by a growing feminist consciousness and by the ecological movement have led to an increasing interest in their profession. The position of Woman/ Nature is hence privileged as the place from where they try to subvert and counter the dominant scientific discourse.

In Russia, however, the picture of gender and astrology looks different. The astrologers may all admit to a specific feminine interest in the occult and esoteric that can be explained by women's superior intuition, but that is about all. Farida's cautious, yet pronounced, rejection of feminism indicates a demarcation line that is not to be transgressed – with or without the still relatively scarce computers. Femininity has no privileged position here.

Although Rybakov's impressive book (1981) on the paganism of the ancient Slavs exposed a female deity of a magnitude that could easily accommodate several goddess movements, none has emerged. Moreover, the esoteric, idealized women that hover in Russian occult belief systems seem to the spiritual mind to have little in common with the profanely enfleshed ones of everyday life. As Holly DeNio Stephens notes in her article on the proliferating occultism in Russia today, the deification of the Eternal Feminine (or Sophia) in many of these occult teachings has definitely 'not translated into reverence for women and their purportedly occult powers' (Rosenthal 1997: 374).

This is true of our astrologers as well. Mikhail is thus the only one among our interviewees to support Farida's view on the importance of feminine intuition in the readings, but he too keeps his endorsement of this idea within safe limits. Intuition is important, he concedes, since the mystical side of the soul cannot be explained by rational means alone. Cooperation between a male and a female astrologer is therefore optimal, because the 'divine wisdom', the logical-rational faculty of Universal Man, and the 'divine love', the intuition of the Eternal Feminine, can then join forces. Another Russian, the young paediatrician Petr, whose wife works as a healer and witch, totally rejects the idea that women should practise astrology professionally. Just as a man cannot be a witch, Petr reasons, a woman cannot be an astrologer. The latter deals with 'liberating the human from its cage', and such a liberating expansion can only be done by a man. Women should do the opposite – that is, preserve and keep together the human within its frame. (Nevertheless, his pronounced dislike of female astrologers does not prevent him from being vice-president of the organization that is headed by Farida.) Finally, a third male answers our question on possible gender-based differences in the approach to astrology with a rodomontade whose essential message is that women are intellectually mediocre while men span the entire spectrum from the stupid to the brilliant. Hey presto – men are the best!

While the Russian men eagerly embrace patriarchy and openly advocate misogynist notions of a kind reminiscent of the great European gender debate of a century ago, their female colleagues energetically resist the traps of labels and definitions set up by the gender discourse. They demonstrate their resistance by maintaining, for instance, that gender is insignificant, or by claiming that everybody contains femininity and masculinity – or *yin* and *yang*, as one of them puts it – in the same way that both sexual categories are present everywhere in the universe. Hence their strategy is to define themselves not as constrained women but as free humans.

All in all, the Russian gender discourse seems old-fashioned. The subversive possibilities of the concept of Woman as a loose discursive position that may assist in the deconstruction of repressive systems have not yet moved eastward.

Beneath the surface, however, the female sex does occupy the language of the male Russian astrologers with its own subversive agents. Via the grammar of gender that is so vital in Russian (nouns are feminine, masculine or neuter), another very powerful femininity is installed alongside the one that is conversely characterized by a definite lack of power. The latter emerged in the male astrologers' explicit phrases about women, while the former rises inexorably with the Moon, the feminine Luna. To most astrologers, American and Russian, the receptive and light-reflecting Moon symbolizes the maternal and emotional sphere that is connected with the past, with childhood, and hence with the distinctive traits of femininity. But whereas in the eyes of the Americans the Moon is unambiguously positive, beautiful and good, an indispensable 'complementary principle' to the Sun, this very same Moon brings up quite different feelings in the Russian men. In their language it, or rather 'she', is dangerous, difficult, and at times impossible to control.

Following on from his description of the Eternal Feminine, the incarnation of the bright 'divine love', a dark, chaotic and threateningly destructive Moon-Woman enters Mikhail's speech:

I feel the Moon's influence rather strongly but, frankly speaking, I try to withdraw from it. The Moon's influence defines the biological and psychic everyday life. The Moon after all is like a mother to us ... she creates the family in which we live, she defines the influences on biological processes, but at the same time she is also connected with all the confusion and destruction of our psychic life ... somnambulism, unexpected emergences of the unconscious ... ungovernable processes in our psychic life, that is all the Moon ... I would like the Moon to be more organized – the Moon in my soul, of course ... I certainly do not want to bring order to the celestial Moon, that is not up to me ... But generally I feel the Moon very strongly, the movements, phases ... Even my activities, my capacity for action, are very much connected with the lunar cycle ... Some days, especially towards the end of a cycle, I have great difficulty getting hold of myself, starting work ... At full moon one feels increased agitation, less stability and too much emotionality ... but during recent years I've got more control ...

In contrast to the Americans, who carefully fertilize and cultivate their inner femininity so that it seems to glow and thrive even in the dim light of their soft and beautiful Moon, Mikhail apparently needs great strength to manage the unruly Moon in his soul.

A similarly active and powerful female Moon was at work in Petr's field of vision when he described the 'influence' that this celestial body exerted on the Apollo astronauts. His Moon effectively put the astronauts in their place; performing in the manipulative way she did, she perhaps remained within the radius of action that Petr allots more generally to women: as keepers and upholders of traditions and boundaries. Nevertheless, this active Moon, the absolute agent of the plot, throws new light on Petr's efforts to contain Woman/Nature. Illuminated in this way, the category regains some of its lost freedom. The Moon, Petr asserts, had her own reason for 'letting the astronauts come to her'; she alone decided whom to allow in. This version of Luna could not be controlled.

Mikhail's uneasiness and Petr's subtle respect are supplemented by Askold's cautious hostility towards the Moon (Luna). Askold is very reluctant to elaborate on his pronounced dislike of her: 'I don't like her,' he repeats deprecatingly, before eventually straying into fantastic and lustful speculations on the revenge that cosmic Mother Nature, possibly the Earth, will take on humanity. Mother Earth is in bad shape, he insists, because too many people live 'on her' as useless parasites. But one day nature will decide to put an end to this infestation by exterminating one half of humanity: 'A wave will pass over half of the Earth and everything will be dead … or gases … there are a lot of variations,' he explains in answer to our amazed question about how this catastrophe will come about. Askold has yet another option, which this time seems to refer to the hole in the ozone layer. But in his vision, this hole is generated by higher forces: 'There may be a hole made in the cosmos, and radioactive radiation shall enter, afterwards the hole will be closed again … it's elementary.' The agent of this punitive expedition may be Mother Earth or 'something else'; that is really of minor importance, he says, since the Earth is a living organ in the cosmic body.

We saw the Americans ascribe significance and power to the feminine, partly by insisting on its identity with astrology, and partly by locating Woman/Nature in the privileged place from where the astrological universe is meant to counter and subvert the dominant discourses. This picture changed radically in Russia, where gender was either subsumed into human-ness (by the women) or hierarchically polarized in favour of patriarchy (by the men). Nevertheless, this latter, very rigid, gender hierarchy becomes subverted by the mythic realism that conceives of nature in the shape of an extremely powerful, female figure who is alive and who has will, know-ledge and know-how. This intrusion of mythic realistic thought thus causes displacements and turbulence, not externally in the dominant cultural context as intended by the re-mythologized world picture of the Americans, but internally in the mindscape of the Russian men.

The Dyadic Relationship

Femininity also emerges on another and higher level in the astrological universes of both nations. A dyadic mother/child relationship exists be-tween the astrologers and their cosmos. This connection is suggested by Rick's experiences of identifying with the cosmic Mother Goddess, but it recurs in other stories as well. For instance, when Vera relates that to her the cosmos is one system, 'whole, living, pulsating, harmonic', she envisions it as a large organism or body of which she herself is only a very small part. Hence she feels that she is 'a living, tiny part of a living cosmos'. During the interview, she mentions the priority that for many years she has given to being a loving but also a strict mother to her two daughters. This maternal role suddenly takes on an unexpected enunciative force: when we ask her which picture spontaneously connects with the word cosmos, Vera gives an apologetic laugh and presents us with an image of herself when pregnant. Her association with the word cosmos, she says, is 'an extension of myself. I grow large and become enormously big.' In the next breath, as though in continuation of her metaphoric maternal swelling, she defines a human being as 'a creature, a child of nature, who must only submit to the cosmos'. In this context, Vera's reply strongly suggests that she is simultaneously the gigantic, swelling cosmic body who is about to give birth and the child who is being born – at the same time the great mother and the small daughter. Probably unwittingly, she has reproduced the ancient mythic representation of the Great Goddess in her self-generating cyclicity (mother/daughter) that is still visible, in stylized form, in Russian embroideries.

The symbiotic connection, where mother and child seem to merge, is phrased by Farida in a way that recalls Vera's mother/daughter/cosmos, except that Farida speaks not of the cosmos, but of the Earth (which is a feminine word in Russian). She experiences herself as both a child of the Earth and as its mother. By developing her personality positively she, as a living part of a living Earth, gives something back: 'I am a part of the Earth, so if something good happens to me, it means that I'll return something good to the Earth. I am at the same time both the Earth's child and her mother.'

Similar pictures are put forward by Petr, who practised as a specialist in treating new-born babies before he switched to astrological medicine. He too sees himself as a tiny part of the cosmos and 'although this may sound impudent', he laughs, he also connotes the word cosmos with an image of himself. In another connection, he speculates on the age-old question of origin: 'Who came first, I or the cosmos, that's impossible to grasp.' So, who was first – the chicken or the egg, the child or the mother, the embryo or the womb, Petr or the cosmos?

An even more common picture of coalescence lies in the description of oneself as a cell in the body of the Earth, while the Earth is a cell in the larger, cosmic body. Stephanie, and others with her, express their feeling of a deeply organic interconnectedness with the cosmos in this way. And to Petr, who also identifies the self with the cell, the important thing is not to fall out of the organic rhythm and become a 'cancer cell' that, at worst, may destroy the whole organism.

The human being and the cosmos are thus intimately bodily connected in the eyes of our astrologers. In their world picture, the conception of the cosmos as a double image that mirrors womb and human being, mother and child, reappears, suggesting that the one does not stir without the other.

Notes

1. The majority of our interviewees were professional astrologers in the sense that they practised it publicly. Some of the Americans were, however, also teachers and researchers at a New Age college in San Francisco; a couple of them were students there. We interviewed six Russians (three women and three men) and nine Americans (five women and four men).

2. In Russian the moon is called Luna, which is a feminine word. In the context, the pronoun should be translated as though referring to a female Moon that is alive.

6

One Does not Stir without the Other

The stories told by our Russian and American interviewees demonstrate that their use of astrology is different from that of pre-modern societies, where it was part of mainstream culture. Their approach also differs from the one practised in contemporary cultural settings in which people frequent astrologers in order to comply with traditional customs and lifestyles. To become an adherent of New Age astrology in Russia or the USA means to opt out of the mainstream culture that is embedded in a scientific world view and is passed on by the educational system, universities, the media, etc. New Agers deliberately embrace the alienness and difference of ancient thought systems, such as astrology, as vehicles for a rebirth and re-empowering of the spiritual dimensions of life and matter, which were exorcized by the powerful alliances of modern science, Enlightenment, secularization and, as far as the former Soviet Union is concerned, Marxism-Leninism.

When listening to the astrologers, it is as though we are being asked to enter a universe of negations. All the modes of functioning and the principles of agency that govern the scientifically defined world view, in which both we and they were brought up, are inverted. We are encouraged to give up the idea of human free will and to forget the cosmic billiard table of soulless matter in mechanical motion, all regulated by the laws of physics, that we learned about in school. Instead, we are invited into a cosmos that is bodily and spiritually alive; we are urged to see ourselves as tiny parts, as microcosmic offspring, of a gigantic macrocosmic being who administers our life and activities like an overzealous mother. When the rhetoric of the astrologers conjures up this alternative universe, the pictures of the distant clock-maker God of early modernity and his Space Age successor, the Cyber-Godfather of galactic civilizations, fade away. Instead, the image of an omnipotent cosmic mother, all-pervading in her bodily and spiritual presence, appears on our mental screen. We are stimulated to feel her perpetual embrace and the tremors of good and bad vibrations that she continually sends through us.

With astrology as illustration, this chapter takes a closer look at the performances of the motherly cosmos-body, which make the cosmological master narrative of the New Age so different from the one produced by space flight. We analyse how the astrologers renegotiate cosmology – how, in a gesture of negation towards the modern will to bio-power, they reinvent pre-modernity's symbiotic mother–child relationship between human self and cosmos.

Astrology – a Cosmic *Écriture Féminine*?

Some astrologers (Farrant 1989; Douglas 1981) point out that astrology is a kind of linguistics, a cosmosemiotics. While, as Ferdinand de Saussure once said, social semiotics interprets 'the life of signs in society' (Saussure 1974), astrology wants to help us understand the life of cosmic signs. Astrology constructs its object as a cosmic language of rhythmically moving heavenly bodies. It turns the firmament into a big screen that continuously conveys important messages from the Goddess of Fate in a grotesque and sibylline body language of dancing planets and gesticulating Zodiac signs. Seen from their own perspective, the astrologers are offering us dictionaries and grammars for the decoding of this language.

Beginning our investigations with the arguments of linguistically oriented astrologers, we shall suggest that New Agers and some spiritual feminists have reinvented astrology as a kind of cosmic *écriture féminine*, i.e. a writing that negates the rationality of the dominant cosmology and the symbolic order in which it is inscribed; a writing that instead articulates the bodily-spiritual forces of a cosmos that is identified as being a mixture of the grotesque, the feminine, and the motherly; a writing that erupts inappropriately in the margins of a culture dominated by the scientific world view. In this interpretation of astrology, we draw inspiration from the philosophy of *écriture féminine* and desire in language – and from key works by Luce Irigaray (1981, 1985a, 1985b, 1993), Hélène Cixous (1985, 1991; Cixous and Clément 1986) and Julia Kristeva (1980, 1984, 1986, 1987).

Since the term *écriture féminine*, 'feminine writing', has been used differently by different interpreters of the original French texts, it is necessary to insert a note on terminology. We use the term as an umbrella for the heterogeneous ways in which Irigaray, Cixous and Kristeva articulate close relationships between female/human/sexed bodies, desires and texts/ writing. But, strictly speaking, the term *écriture féminine* applies only to the works of Cixous. Irigaray prefers other terms such as *parler-femme*, 'speaking (as) woman' (Whitford 1991: 38), whereas Kristeva's term 'desire in language', contrary to those of Cixous and Irigaray, is not inscribed in a philosophy of sexual difference.

Although the texts of Irigaray, Cixous and Kristeva are often read for their approach to writing, to textual articulations of desiring bodies, spiritual or cosmic themes also play a significant role in them. In fact, they juggle creatively with textual–sexual relationships between bodily desires, cosmologies and spiritualities. In so doing, they fit our analysis, because at the same time they avoid simplistic essentialism in their focus on imaginary or symbolic representations. Their approach matches our wish to steer clear of two complementary traps while exploring the re-emergence of astrology in the midst of a culture that cultivates a scientific world view. One trap is to side totally with the rational, anti-spiritual and disembodied outlook of modern mainstream culture and to reject the New Agers' opting out as an irrational act of unscientific nostalgia. The other trap is to give up critical analysis and distance and to accept the universalist, essentialist and at times extremely phallogocentric truth claims of the astrologers.

Referring to the works of Irigaray, Cixous and Kristeva, we try to carve out a third approach. But it also follows from this that the purpose of our reading of astrology as heavenly *écriture féminine* is not simply to collapse the sophisticated, poststructuralist texts into the essentialist thinking of astrology. Our aim is both to explore certain analogies between the two kinds of discourses and to expose their differences.

An Outline of the Approach

We shall highlight the significance ascribed by the astrologers to the sibylline 'language' of grotesque, macrocosmic (mother)bodies by drawing parallels with the otherwise different narratives of a writing that claims to be a textual–sexual inscription of female/motherly bodies and desires. More precisely, we shall sustain our analysis of the astrologers' narrative about an archaic cosmic body language that subverts the discourses of modern science, by comparing it to the ways in which the discourses on *écriture féminine* (Cixous), *parler-femme* (Irigaray) and desire in language (Kristeva) construct their stories about close-knit relationships between texts and sexed bodies – about textually erupting bodily desires that can be traced, for example, in certain kinds of poetic language.

The pivot of *écriture féminine* and *parler-femme* is writing/speaking/singing the female body. Writing the female body into a text means insisting on it as a difference that makes a difference and that can disrupt the phallogocentrism of existing imaginary and symbolic orders. Disruption can for example be engendered by an imaginary and symbolic emergence of the female labia, which in the discourses of Western philosophy from Plato to Freud were completely repressed by the phallus (Irigaray 1985a and 1985b).

Desire in language, according to Kristeva, is to be traced in disruptions of the symbolic order of thetically[1] meaningful enunciation caused by the semiotic chora: i.e. pre-representative, pre-symbolic and utterly provisional articulations founded in the primary processes[2] and the early bodily inter-play between child and mother. Metaphor and metonymy play an important role in Kristeva's theory as tropes that correspond to the psychoanalytical notions of displacement and condensation. As such, they are considered to be pyschosemiotic articulations of desire in close relationship to the bodily drive economy (Kristeva 1984: 28).

We shall suggest that the stories of these kinds of body-speak, imagined to spout from the human/female body and stream into certain kinds of texts as the 'white ink' of the 'good mother's milk' (Cixous 1985: 251), can in a sense illuminate the astrologers' narrative about the organic–spiritual language of the Great Cosmic Mother's rhythmical movements and bodily gestures.

In a concluding assessment of the astrologers' negation of the scientific world view and its will to bio-power, we shall, however, also outline some important differences between the narratives of their discourses and those of *écriture féminine*. We shall use Irigaray's discussion of present-day women's need for a female divine (Irigaray 1993) to encircle potentials of, as well as limits to, the deification of cosmic space as embodied female subject, which in different ways and to varying degrees is a part of New Age and feminist astrology.

A broadly outlined concept of *écriture féminine* will thus structure the general framework of interpretation. But in order to explore the difference that makes the astrological outlook manifest as alien other when reinvented in the midst of a late twentieth-century postindustrial society, it is also necessary to draw on cultural-historically informed theories about the pre-modern episteme that astrologers have revived. In the following, we will take a closer look at some theories about ancient astrological cosmology and apply them to selected texts from New Age and feminist astrology.

Cosmos as Living Body – the Rebirth of an Ancient Episteme

The astrological cosmology has roots in the ancient belief in an organic–spiritual correspondence between the human body and the cosmos, between micro- and macrocosmos. An important genealogy can be traced back to medieval and Renaissance Neoplatonist mysticism and Gnosticism (Jung 1972; Rosenberg 1984). But, according to Ernst Cassirer's comprehensive analysis of mythical thought from totemism to astrology (1922, 1987), the theory of correspondences forms part of a broad spectrum of pre-scientific modes of knowing and signifying, which all share a basic episteme. The construction of cosmos in the image of the living body, and vice versa, enfleshes the core of this episteme. The living, feeling, thinking body in its macro- and microcosmic aspects, Cassirer points out, governs the production of meaning, or semiosis, of ancient mythical thought.

In order to understand the ancient episteme reinvented by New Age astrology, we shall, alongside Cassirer, take into account two other cultural–historical approaches to pre-scientific thought systems. One is Mikhail Bakhtin's analysis of the grotesque body of pre-modern world views (Bakhtin 1984). The other stems from Carolyn Merchant's discussion of the motherbody as root metaphor of the organic–mythical world view of pre-modernity (Merchant 1980). The approaches of Cassirer, Bakhtin and Merchant are complementary. Cassirer highlights the 'how' of the ancient, bodily episteme, developing a linguistic–philosophical analysis of the mythical mode of knowing and signifying. Bakhtin and Merchant on their side focus on the 'what', the type of body image on which the ancient episteme is modelled. In the context of our study, Cassirer will sustain the claim that astrology can be viewed as a linguistics or semiotics of the cosmic body-speak, while Bakhtin and Merchant back up the statement that the sibylline gift of tongues flows from a grotesque and motherly body.

We shall apply Cassirer, Bakhtin and Merchant's theories to a cluster of contemporary New Age texts. The purpose is to show how New Age thinking causes ancient discourses of a world conceptualized in the image of the living (mother)body, to erupt as a kind of *écriture féminine* on the margins of contemporary high-tech culture. We have chosen four different examples from the vast corpus of contemporary New Age literature.

First, we shall zoom in on two astrologers with international reputations, whom several of our American and Russian astrologer interviewees mentioned with reverence. They are the English astrologer and Jungian psychotherapist Liz Greene and the late French-American astrologer philosopher Dane Rudhyar. Greene's books are famous for their application of astrology to psychotherapy and individual psychology, whereas Rudhyar was the first to develop philosophically the links pointed out by Jung between analytical psychology and astrology (Rudhyar 1991). Rudhyar has also written extensively on the coming of the New Age. We use Greene and Rudhyar as examples because they provide a kind of theoretical common denominator for much New Age astrology, including the majority of our interviewees. They are both influential representatives of the 'psychological turn' characteristic of New Age astrology. It is a turn away from predictive astrology, which is rejected as vulgar magazine fortune-telling, to a Jung-inspired 'cosmopsychology' (Rudhyar 1975: 9), i.e. a mystically tinged psychology oriented towards personal and planetary consciousness-raising and spiritual transformation.

Two further examples involve the American feminist astrologer Demetra George (1992) and the Russian writer Zufar Gareev (1991), who represents a New Age-inspired wave of occultism in post-*glasnost* Russian literature (Brougher 1997; Laird 1999). Together, Greene, Rudhyar, George and Gareev unfold a broad spectrum of omnipotent mother-images, ranging from profoundly patriarchal to feminist figures, inhabiting the imaginaries of Eastern and Western New Agers.

To be Guided by Fate

We shall look first at the 'how' of the astrological episteme, with Cassirer as our theoretical guide. Applying his approach to the texts of Liz Greene, we focus on the natal horoscope as a favourite instrument of modern astrology.

In her book *The Astrology of Fate* (1984), Greene reports a case history from her psychotherapeutic practice. The protagonist of the story is a woman, Alison, who lost her eyesight during her late teens and whose whole future life appeared to be ruined by this stroke of seemingly bad luck that also entailed a series of other misfortunes. The eye disease that caused her blindness was not properly treated because of an incompetent ophthalmologist's erroneous diagnoses; she had to give up the development of her distinct talent for painting and drawing; she was prevented from pursuing the career as a schoolteacher that she had planned, etc. Nevertheless, the Alison that Greene puts on display is not unhappy, embittered or depressed but, on the contrary, full of creativity and vitality; she feels that the loss of her eyesight 'gives [her] … as much as it takes away' (Greene 1984: 327). We also hear that she has found her 'inner authority': instead of engaging in a destructive 'vendetta' (Greene 1984: 326–7) against her bad luck, she has accepted the guidance of Moira, the Goddess of Fate, whose motherly advice is inscribed in her natal horoscope and the pattern of coincidences of her life. In this way, Alison's blindness has led her to become a gifted singer, a social worker, a counsellor and a therapist – all activities that she enjoys very much.

Seen from Greene's point of view, Alison lost her sight because of the unusually strong influence of the planet Pluto in her natal horoscope. Of all the celestial bodies, Pluto connects most forcefully with the basic, existential transitions of life and death. To understand Pluto, Greene writes, we must remember his mythic genealogies. In ancient Rome, Pluto was feared as the sovereign of the Underworld, the kingdom of the dead. Since Greene believes Fate to be closely related to a powerful femininity, she also stresses that the Roman god of death has roots in much older, matriarchal myths of omnipotent mother goddesses who rule over life and death. In their dark aspect, these goddesses embodied night, death and Fate.

To be born under a sky heavily over-written with the ominous handwriting of the dark forces of Pluto and his powerful foremothers is no laughing matter, Greene warns us. Nevertheless, for Alison, who dared to accept their guidance instead of fighting them, it has led to 'individuation'[3] and a rich life. Greene is clearly impressed by Alison's story and reports it as an exemplary illustration of her main point: that the motherly guiding voice of Fate should not be ignored. If we oppose or disregard Fate, the moral of her story goes, if we stick to our arrogant and illusory twentieth-century beliefs in free will and the power to be in complete control of the basic existential prerequisites of our lives, then Fate will show us her destructive face. But if, on the contrary, we steer away from the *hubris* of the modern scientific world view, we will be able to see Her regenerative face. Then, She will guide us like a wise mother – as she did with Alison.

How to Think in the Image of the Body

When we explore Greene's discourse with the assistance of Cassirer's interpretation of mythical semiosis and its construction of cosmos as a living body, it becomes clear that the epistemic principles he identified as the basic elements of pre-modern astrology reappear as cornerstones of New Age astrology.

Cassirer's theory (Cassirer 1922, 1987) maintains that mythical thought depends on a semiosis very different from the one to which people educated in the modern scientific world view are accustomed. An important difference is that the mechanistic principle of causality and the Cartesian and positivist distinction between subjectivity and objectivity do not fit into this way of knowing. This difference was also emphasized by Jung. He coined the concept of synchronicity (Jung 1972) in order to name his belief in the existence of meaningful coincidences between occurrences that were connected by non-causal relations – for example, between inner-psychic and outer-world events. But while Jung takes these links as essentially and universally given, Cassirer explains them in the historical context of the bodily episteme of pre-modern thought. This is our reason for choosing Cassirer as our theoretical guide.

When confronted with Alison's blindness, the scientifically minded person will look for objective causes: biomedical reasons, incompetent intervention on the part of the ophthalmologist, etc. Whether or not Alison can learn to cope with her handicap will be considered as a subjective, psychological question to be kept apart from the biomedical ones. In contrast, Greene rejects this 'modern' form of reasoning as superficial and lopsided. For her, the blindness is an effect of the influence of Pluto in Alison's natal horoscope. It is a work of the Goddess of Fate, an existential fact that cannot be bypassed by any biomedical intervention, but that, in return, may guide Alison to her 'true self'.

Seen through the lens of modern science, Greene's way of arguing is irrational. She does not look for causality, nor does she distinguish between the objective world of matter and the subjective sphere of thoughts and feelings. But, assessed within the framework of Cassirer's analysis, her viewpoint makes sense. She refuses to obey a logic of mechanistic causality and instead seeks signs of contiguity and similarity in a gigantic living, feeling, thinking world body, of which all earthly beings and celestial bodies are spiritual–organic parts or cells.

The bodily way of knowing of mythical semiosis is, according to Cassirer, rooted in signifying processes based on the principles of *contiguity* (bodily touching) and *similarity* (bodily resemblance), or in other words, on the tropes *metonymy* and *metaphor*[4] (Jakobson 1987). Phenomena and events (outer and/or inner) that touch one another bodily in space and/or time are forever connected; this is the principle of contiguity, or metonymy. The same is true, Cassirer says, of phenomena and events that can be claimed to bear a qualitative, bodily resemblance to one another; this is the function of similarity, or metaphor.

Applying the principle of contiguity/metonymy, we may observe two kinds of bodily 'touching' when looking at the natal horoscope. First of all, the celestial bodies 'touch' one another spatially. Seen from the geocentric perspective of astrology, the ruler of existential transitions, Pluto 'copulated' (i.e. formed geometrical oppositions, squares, trigons, etc.) with almost all the other planets and important Zodiac signs when Alison was born. Second, we may speak about a temporal 'touching'. This particular configuration of heavenly bodies occurred at the unique moment of Alison's birth.

That the whole world is conceived in the image of the living human body is a consequence of the other basic principle of mythical semiosis, that of similarity/metaphor. This construction is based on the bodily resemblance that the production of mythical meaning inscribes in the two entities: cosmos is a body, and the body is a cosmos. Also implied is the belief that everything in the universe is connected through organic–spiritual links, parallel to those of the individual human body. Hence the thought that ominous Pluto influenced Alison's bio-psychic life pattern is not dissimilar to thinking that a severe headache affects the mood and general well-being of a person.

The system of correspondences is another effect of the principle of similarity or metaphor. According to Cassirer, phenomena that, by tradition or by actual physical similarity, may be said to resemble one another, become linked by all-inclusive processes of metaphor creation. Thus, phases of human life are connected to seasons of the year (spring–youth, summer–mature adulthood, etc.). The same goes for the planets' mythical namesakes and aspects of the human psyche; the metaphorical principle functions as the driving force behind astrology's setting up series after series of links such as:

- Sun/Sun-gods/ego
- Moon/Moon-goddesses/unconscious self
- Pluto/ruler of the kingdom of the dead/basic urge towards death and rebirth, etc.

Apart from contiguity/metonymy and similarity/metaphor, Cassirer identifies one more important basic principle distinguishing mythical semiosis from conventional scientific thought. It is the principle of *realism* (as opposed to the philosophical category of nominalism, whereby a dichotomy splits word/image from world). According to Cassirer, mythical thought presents us with an extreme variant of realism that recognizes no distance at all between representation and the represented referent. This *mythical realism* implies that the cosmic 'Signature' (Rudhyar 1991: 141) imprinted on the individual and articulated in the natal horoscope appears to the astrologer to be as real as the transubstantiation of holy bread and wine is to the devout Catholic. Alison's blindness IS, Greene wants to persuade us, a TRUE effect of Pluto's influence.

The Universe as Mother Body

We shall now turn to the 'what', i.e. the particular body image of the ancient episteme revived by New Age astrology. Our new theoretical guides, Bakhtin and Merchant, will here inform our approach to the example: Rudhyar.

Bakhtin (1984) characterizes the world body in which the episteme of astrology and other kinds of pre-modern thought are grounded as grotesque. This grotesque body is an ancient image that celebrates the basic, existential transitions of the life cycle of the body. In this image birth, death, copulation, metabolism, etc., act in hyperbolic forms. Especially highlighted are situations where the boundaries of the individual body appear as ambiguous and temporary, and where body and cosmos, micro- and macrocosmos, merge:

> the grotesque body is cosmic and universal. It stresses elements common to the entire cosmos: earth, water, fire, air; it is directly related to the sun, to the stars. It contains the signs of the zodiac. It reflects the cosmic hierarchy. This body can merge with various natural phenomena, with mountains, rivers, seas, islands, and continents. It can fill the entire universe. (Bakhtin 1984: 318)

Similarly, Merchant (1980) also emphasizes that pre-modern Europeans perceived the world as a living organism, a person writ large, but a primary concern for her lies in the importance that the ancient imagery ascribed to sexual difference and to nature as a powerful mother. She shows how the ancient notions of the world as a living and thinking organism often included different kinds of images of nature, world and Earth as a nurturing or sometimes cruel mother, eventually married to some kind of cosmic father figure. Merchant provides abundant illustrations, for example, Plato's *Timaeus* and its framing of three cosmic family actants or positions: Demiurge–father, chora–receptacle–mother, and the creation–child; or Renaissance Neoplatonism, where the chora was transformed into a female world soul (Merchant 1980: 10–11).

Bakhtin and Merchant both concentrate on medieval and Renaissance images of the grotesque and gendered world bodies. Both argue that the ancient system of correspondences between macro- and microcosmos, the basic tenet of astrology, is gestated in the womb of this grandiose body (Bakhtin 1984: 361; Merchant 1980: 118–19).

The Universal Mother Body in New Age Guise

We shall now revisit New Age astrology and look at the world body that is celebrated by a guru such as Rudhyar – a world body that appears as a reinvention of the pre-modern images drawn by Bakhtin and Merchant.

Images of a living body, which may take on gigantic and grotesque shapes and fill the entire universe, abound in Rudhyar's texts. He sees Earth as 'a cosmic organism' (Rudhyar 1975: 59) and humans as 'cells' in this vast body (Rudhyar 1991: 141), which is imbued with life and spirituality. It is a 'vast, living, thinking organism' (Rudhyar 1975: 61) that 'has not only a physical globe as its material body, but also an electromagnetic "ethero-astral body" and still higher "fields of existence" in which mental and spiritual forces and dynamic centres operate' (Rudhyar 1975: 59–60). It is a planetary being that, like the human body of occult theory, has a surrounding aura, chakras housed within specific body parts, and a spine channelling waves of energy or 'kundalini'.[5] The Zodiac is described as 'the auric egg of the planetary Being' (Rudhyar 1991: 198), or as its 'placenta' (ibid.: 200). Certain mountains, for example the Himalayas, are conceived as planetary chakra centres (Rudhyar 1975: 63), and so are the equator and the poles. The polar axis of the Earth forms the spine of the planetary being and the equator is defined as its solar plexus (ibid.: 130).

As his reference to the Zodiac as 'egg' or 'placenta' indicates, Rudhyar is not only conceptualizing the world/cosmos as a living organism, a grotesque body *à la* Bakhtin, but also as a nurturing mother (cf. Merchant). The planetary being, the Earth-body, is viewed as an embryo in complete metabolic symbiosis with the cosmic womb that nourishes it with energy – 'macrocosmic food', 'celestial Bread and Waters' (Rudhyar 1991: 200) – and protects it by filtering all outside radiation and disposing of its waste products:

> the zodiac is the placenta of the embryonic Earth-body. All the building energies which produce the growth of the embryo must pass through the placenta. The placenta is the formative zone, the zone in and from which the building energies and substances of the macrocosm vitalize the micro-cosm just as the mother's energies vitalize the embryo. (Rudhyar 1991: 200)

It is hard to imagine a clearer presentation of the human–Earth–cosmos relationship as an image of the mother/child symbiosis. But further affinities between Rudhyar's world view and the pre-modern ones depicted by Bakhtin and Merchant surface in his fascination with life cycles and physical transitions.

Basically, astrology deals with cyclical patterns of transformation and the important transitions of life. In particular, the existential threshold, represented by the moment of birth, is a benchmark of the natal horoscope. But cyclicity and the transitions and transformations involved in cyclical processes are also generally founding concepts in astrology. The day and night cycle, reflecting the Earth's rotation about its own axis, reappears here as the wheel of twelve houses, while the cycle of the solar year and the Earth's rotation around the sun recur in the orbit of the twelve Signs of the Zodiac. The large cycle drawn by the precession of the equinoxes is mirrored as the so-called 'Great Year',[6] composed of twelve ages each about 2,150 years long and represented by a Zodiac sign: the Age of Pisces, the Age of Aquarius, etc. In New Age astrology, the cycles acquire psychological–spiritual significance, revealing various kinds of wholeness or mandalas. The wheel of houses is a mirror of the individual self in its relationships to the wholeness of life's aspects (play, work, relationships, ideals, etc.); the twelve Zodiac signs are considered as corresponding to a fourfold division related to the elements, fire–earth–air–water, which New Age astrology, based on a Jungian influence, correlates with basic modes of perception: intuition–sensation–thinking–feeling.

Rudhyar's philosophical framework underlines the general astrological importance of cyclicity. He describes a myriad small and large cycles that interfere with one another in the cosmic world body. According to him, cyclicity is an expression of the rhythms of the universal body. He finds an adequate metaphor for its continuous rhythmic transformations in vegetation, since it plays a basic role in human life, as food, as producer of an oxygen-rich atmosphere, etc. (Rudhyar 1975: 121). Grafting on to the vegetative root metaphor, he explains cyclicity as a manifestation of a seed-leaf polarity (ibid.: 122ff.), distinguishing a 'seed-state' of biopsychic or biospiritual potentiality and a 'leaf-state', the recurrent unfolding of the 'seeds' in new forms.

When exploring the cyclic dimensions of the world body, it seems as though Rudhyar shifts his outlook from a gendered to a vegetative mode. Thanks to its close relationship to light, the discursive sphere of vegetation and photosynthesis may appear to be particularly well-suited for spiritual elevation in the would-be post-gender world of the soul, which Rudhyar so enthusiastically promotes. Nevertheless, vegetative and gendered meta-phors mingle quite shamelessly in Rudhyar's world. His seed-metaphor is, indeed, not intended to be read only in the vegetative mode. It is marked by the phallogocentrism of European philosophy. Although two occult mothers – the Russian founder of the Theosophical Society, Helena Blavatskaya, and the British Alice Bailey – play an important role in Rudhyar's hagiology, gurus and avatars are first and foremost holy brothers or 'seed-men' (Rudhyar 1975: 135). The acts performed by these gurus and avatars, i.e. the dissemination of 'seeds', occult messages, preparing the world for the coming of the New Age, are described in terms of unambiguously sexual metaphors. They re-enact the specifically hierarchical versions of the classic narratives of impregnation of the Earth-mother, which Merchant opposes to the versions where female and male elements copulate on more equal terms. Rudhyar constructs sexual difference along traditional lines featuring, for example, the dichotomy between female matter, 'the planetary ovum within the placental biosphere', and male spirit, the 'Logos Spermatikos' of Stoic philosophy (ibid.: 129).

The Great Cosmic Mother – as Phallogocentric or Feminist Construction

Although God is more or less crossed out of the scientific world view (Latour 1993), we saw in our analysis of the master narratives of space flight that when he re-emerges as Cybergod and reveals his sex and his body in outer space, he tends to be male. In Chapter 4 we saw him in his incarnation as Cyber-Godfather, who sent out his sperm-astronauts to colonize the universe. In New Age astrology things look different at this point. Here, sacred cosmic space is filled with the grotesque body, the Zodiac Womb, of the Great Cosmic Mother, female Fate, Moira. Even the profoundly phallogocentric thinking of Rudhyar leaves more divine cosmic space for the female body than do the space flight master narratives featuring the Cyber-Godfather. On the one hand, an inappropriate contiguity pops up between Crick's theory of 'directed panspermia' (Crick 1981) and Rudhyar's 'Logos Spermatikos' and his occult 'seed-men' who herald the glad cosmic tidings of the Advent of the New Age. On the other hand, the Zodiac Womb in Rudhyar's universe is the bearer of a divine agency, ruling over human life and death, while the female planetary bodies in Crick's universe can only exercise the female patience prescribed by Aristotle, passively awaiting their fate as receptacles of the tiny colonists from far away.

The inscription of New Age longings for a divine cosmic agency onto bodily sites that demonstrate a prominent role for intersections of the female, the motherly and the grotesque sustains the suggestion (see Chapter

2) that 'feminization' serves as an important vehicle for the alternative world and values that the New Age is expected to bring. However, this is not to suggest that the master narrative of the New Age unanimously celebrates a common construction of a divine femininity. On the contrary, a broad spectrum of omnipotent mother images, ranging from profoundly phallogocentric to clearly feminist figures, inhabits the New Age cosmos.

As discussed by the spiritual feminist Monica Sjöö in her critical book on the New Age (Sjöö 1992), traditional patriarchal ways of thinking permeate the discourses of many New Age gurus. Rudhyar is a good example. Another is Zufar Gareev, one of many post-*glasnost* Russian writers who draw inspiration from both the New Age and occultism, and whose mystically tinged cultivation of a cosmic mother is born out of a phallogo-centrism that does not fall short of the one we met in Rudhyar's universe. Gareev's semi-fantastic novella *The Allergy of Aleksandr Petrovich* (1991) evocatively illustrates a strong desire for a 'feminized' elsewhere, which in this case is found at the heavenly bosom of a cosmic mother with whom the protagonist, Aleksandr Petrovich, re-enacts the first part of an Oedipal mother–son drama. Aleksandr, who feels 'allergic' to his present mundane situation, i.e. completely out of touch with life in late Soviet society, is redeemed by an unknown force. It literally lifts him to what turns out to be the cosmic site of the warm, milk-scented, secure bosom of his mother. She floats among other heavenly mothers whose voices form a chorus urging their sons to return from Earth to a happy reunion in a universe where the last desperate, authoritarian moves of a decaying Soviet Father State cannot victimize them any more (and, we may add, where they are not bothered by the annoying presence of their human sisters either!).

At the opposite end of the spectrum of value systems, we find images produced by spiritual feminists, like Sjöö herself, who co-authored a book with the telling title *The Great Cosmic Mother* (Sjöö and Mor 1987); or like the many US-based feminist astrologers such as Demetra George, whom we will use as an example here. Contrary to the traditional mother figures of Rudhyar and Gareev, the spiritual feminists trace their feminine 'else-where' to quite different images. George (1992) recommends that we seek out the symbolic sites of the dark moon goddess, whose healing feminine powers have been repressed and distorted by a long-standing cultural tradition. According to the ancient cosmological theory of macro- and microcosmic correspondences, the dark moon – that is, the three moonless nights each month – is mirrored in the menstrual period of the female cycle and in the menopausal body, which in patriarchal cultures were tabooed as ill-omened and dangerous. Likewise, the dark moon was seen as the site of evil feminine forces, such as the Greek Erinyes, female spirits of anger and revenge, or the serpent-headed, monstrous Medusa, or as the three Moira, goddesses of Fate, who meted out the thread of life without mercy. Instead of upholding the repression of the dark moon life aspects, George wants us to reclaim their regenerative powers by recognizing them, both in ourselves and on a collective cultural level. The dark moon periods, she writes, are germinating phases, phases of turning inwards, of symbolic or material returns to the womb of the Earth, where new creative moments are born. They form part of the life cycles of all bodies, cosmic or human, and as such are necessary and productive.

Gareev's nurturing mothers, calling their oedipal sons to heaven, and George's dark moon goddess, who urges modern women to reassess the myths of the 'evil feminine', do not share many values. The same can be said about Rudhyar's phallogocentric construction of a heavenly hierarchy, and the omnipotent female Fate, Moira, who rules Greene's universe. But the heterogeneity displayed by our examples should not obscure the fact that the significance ascribed to the powerful agency of a female-motherly and grotesque body makes up a common dimension of alienness that marks New Age cosmologies as different from the ones we met in the space narrative.

To Speak the Cosmic or the Female Body

Having explored the bodily episteme of pre-modern thought systems and its reinvention by New Age and feminist astrology, we shall now return to the affinities with the discourses on *écriture féminine*, *parler-femme* and desire in language.

First of all, let us notice how the image of the early mother–child relationship plays a prominent role both in the new astrologies and in the texts of Irigaray, Cixous and Kristeva. If, for example, we compare Greene's description of Moira's motherly performances *vis-à-vis* the individual, and Irigaray's poetical–theoretical articulations of the daughter's experience of the impossibility of escape from the dyad with the mother (Irigaray 1981, 1993), the similarities are so strikingly analogous that the latter still sound meaningful when recycled as metaphorical representations of the former. That 'the one doesn't stir without the other' (Irigaray 1981) and that a '*corps-à-corps*' is taking place with the mother (Irigaray 1993) may articulate the gist of Greene's as well as many other astrological discourses.

Another affinity beween the two kinds of discourses of the astrologers and those of *écriture féminine* is that both seem to attach great expectations to the female body and to the grotesque in a Bakhtinian sense, when they search for 'elsewheres' and free space for the unfolding of otherness. Whether traced in a pre-symbolic, motherly chora (Kristeva), in the speaking labia (Irigaray), in a generously lactating breast (Cixous), in Moira (Greene), in the Zodiacal placenta (Rudhyar), in the celestial mother's bosom (Gareev), in the Dark Moon Goddess (George), or in the Great Cosmic Mother (Sjöö), a conspicuous common denominator of these imagined spaces of otherness is their discursive location within intersections between the grotesque and the female body. It may be a sexual body, a nurturing and giving or a devouring, violent and 'dark' motherbody, but in each case the screen of projections used in these discursive quests for an 'elsewhere' seems to be a female and grotesque body, characterized by its sibylline agency and its will and power to voice disruptive messages. It seems as if the heterogeneous cluster of texts shares a desire to use sexual difference and the language of the grotesque body as vehicles for subversion of existing symbolic orders.

Moreover, it is important that the stories told by the astrologers, as well as those narrated by the texts on *écriture féminine*, claim to speak from *within* the body – the former from the body of the cosmos, the latter from the female body. When they articulate bodies, they do not speak *about* them, nor do they take up speaking positions located outside them. This sets them apart once more from the dominant symbolic order and the discourses of the scientific world view. In the language of astrology, there is no panopticon from where the celestial bodies can be scrutinized at a distance, no godlike subject position from which the body of the cosmos can be surveyed as a bounded object. This becomes clear when we look at New Age and feminist astrology with Cassirer's theories as our analytical lens. They show that the bodily episteme, and a speaking position located within the cosmic body, are a *sine qua non* for any kind of astrological cosmology. The same is the case for *écriture féminine*. The heterogeneous cluster of discourses, for which we use this term as an umbrella, all underline the unbreakable links between language, speaking subjects and desiring bodies; according to these texts, language can suppress, but never detach itself from, desire and body. As part of this line of argument, we may also notice how both kinds of discourses place emphasis on tongues that are governed by tropes such as metonymy and metaphor that in various ways claim to be rooted in the body.

In general, it seems as if the two kinds of discourses also share a longing to subvert the logocentrism of dominant discourses. *Écriture féminine* is supposed to make space for the creation and articulation of *jouissance*, the pleasures of the female body, thereby decentring and subverting phallogocentrism. Analogous shifts may be traced as far as the revival of astrology in New Age and feminist spiritual circles is concerned. Conceived as a challenge to the scientific world view's exclusions of the sacred and spiritual dimensions of life and matter, the reinvention of the ancient bodily episteme involves disruptive moves.

Drawing on the analogy with *écriture féminine*, we suggest that an important challenge of the new astrologies is their opening of discursive spaces for eruptions of excesses of cosmic meaning, for which it is impossible to properly account from a subject position defined by the logos of the scientific world view. Cosmos is, of course, a basic existential prerequisite of our lives. But can we reach an in-depth perception of this fact when cosmos and world are constructed as picture, image, representation (cf. Heidegger 1979), which the human subject can observe from an apparently safe distance with the disembodied gaze of modern science? Is it not rather more likely that precisely this imagined disembodiment and distance of the scientific gaze make it impossible to consciously recognize either the horror or the bliss of our existential dependence on the cosmic body? We suggest that New Age and feminist astrology, among other things, have become popular today because their exegesis of cosmic body-speak renders possible some kind of articulation of such basic existential experiences as cosmic horror and bliss, excluded by the modern scientific world view.

A Divine of one's Own

So far we have focused on the aspect of *écriture féminine* that concerns its poetic articulations of the individual body. But in our context, it is also interesting to note that the boundaries between the individual body and the cosmic body, as well as those between the poetic and the spiritual, are often consciously blurred in the texts of *écriture féminine*. This is another affinity with the astrological discourses and their search for alternative articulations of the sacrality of cosmic space.

Irigaray in particular is explicit in emphasizing that a writing and 'philosophy of the feminine' (Whitford 1991) must include spiritual and cosmic dimensions. So she points out the need for a female divine that can undo the fatal consequences of women's imaginary and symbolic banishment from the realm of the sacred, and end the cosmic occupation of the divine by the phallogocentric trinity of the Father, the Son and the Holy Masculine Spirit (Irigaray 1993).

Compared to Irigaray, Cixous's and Kristeva's texts are further from our theme, but the blurring of boundaries between individual and cosmic bodies is also woven into their textual universes, along with spiritual references. In her poetic celebrations of feminine writing, Cixous often praises it in metaphors and metonymies that make it appear as though the writing is emerging out of a female body grown to cosmic dimensions: 'Her libido is cosmic, just as her unconscious is worldwide: her writing also can only go on and on … ' (Cixous and Clément 1986: 88). In a poetic rhetoric, Cixous celebrates writing that, welling out of the bodily cosmos, articulates a sort of 'cosmogyny' (Braidotti 1991: 242) and heralds the advent of a feminine libidinal economy, i.e. a generous, all-embracing love.

Kristeva, too, flirts with themes that touch on the sacred, the divine and the ecstatic (Berry and Wernick 1992; Wyschogrod 1990), although with less emphasis on femininity. Nevertheless, it is worth bearing in mind that the concept of the chora (Greek for 'space'), so important for Kristeva's theory of bodily desire in language, is closely linked in its genealogy to classical Greek cosmology, borrowed as it is from Plato's *Timaeus* (Kristeva 1984: 25) and its description of the three cosmic family-actants or positions necessary for the creation of the universe (Plato 1973: 177/50B–D).

However, the affinities between the discourses on *écriture féminine* and the new astrologies should not eclipse the differences. The most important difference is that Irigaray, Cixous and Kristeva speak on the level of imaginary or symbolic representations, while the astrologers claim to talk about truths and essences within an epistemic framework of mythical realism. As implied by Cassirer's analysis of the 'realism' of mythical thought, this pushes to extremes the tendency to collapse representations and their referents into one another. Hence astrologers cannot release the critical potentials that in our opinion are implied in their approaches to cosmic space and the divine. Instead of playing subversively at the boundaries of the dominant symbolic order, they end up delivering simplistic counter-truths.

Irigaray's method of reclaiming the female divine, partly in accordance and partly in disagreement with spiritual feminists and astrologers, will serve as a concluding illustration.

As part of her quest for the female divine, Irigaray makes positive references to the cosmology of astrology because, in contrast to the main-stream culture of modern society, it is attuned to cosmic temporality and rhythms. Moreover, she shares with the adherents of astrology a pronounced intuitive and meditative interest in the four elements. The meanings of water, earth, air and fire, she maintains, are too often denied and misunderstood by a modern culture that tends 'to refuse to think about the material conditions of existence' (Irigaray 1993: 57). Irigaray also focuses on astrology's specific spiritual relationship to women and, in consonance with many spiritual feminists and feminist astrologers, she points out the importance of reclaiming mythical images of an era where divine mother–daughter genealogies were not yet exiled from the space of the divine, and where 'astrological power in its godly aspect' was not 'taken away from women' (Irigaray 1993: 80).[7] 'To posit a gender, a God is necessary,' she claims (ibid.: 61), so the exile of women from divine space is profoundly problematic. Women have, of course, been allowed into the realm of the sacred as the mothers of male gods, but this move gives them 'no God or gods of their own to fulfil their gender, whether as individuals or as a community' (ibid.: 81). To change this situation, mythical images of divine space, not occupied by the Father, the Son and the Holy Masculine Spirit, are needed.

So far, Irigaray is in tune with many spiritually and astrologically minded feminists, but her approach is at the same time different. Her reclaiming of the female divine forms part of her complex rewriting of the nineteenth-century German philosopher Ludwig Feuerbach's book (1957) on the essence of Christianity from the point of view of sexual difference. Feuerbach wants his fellow humans to recognize that God is not an alien, transcendent power, but their own creature, an image of their own ideals. Specifying Feuerbach's text in terms of sexual difference, Irigaray's argument implies that women should not abandon themselves to an alienated kind of deification in a regressive symbiosis with the goddess. Instead, we should try to become 'divine women' (Irigaray 1993: 60) by a dual strategy. We should reclaim the space of the divine for women *and*, in a Feuerbach-inspired gesture, deconstruct the transcendency of the divine and re-inscribe it into the network of immanent interactions between women, men and cosmic nature. With this exhortation, Irigaray distances herself from feminist astrologers, who remain at the level of a regressive mother–child symbiosis with the divine.

Although they are focused not on return and regression, but on renewal and rebirth, astrologers still end up reinventing the Great Cosmic Mother as an alien power, recycling her as a figure of mythical realism. This means that she can act only in a dubious and ambiguous way as an empowering mirror. As a super-alien, she leaves too few possibilities for human agency, responsibility and accountability. Can her potentials not be released in more productive ways? We shall return to this question in our concluding Chapter 9.

Notes

1. In Kristeva's linguistic theory, 'the thetic' (1984: 43ff.) is the space in language defined by the performances of a bounded and positioned subject that is capable of enunciating theses and making propositions and judgements.

2. Contrary to the 'secondary processes' that are submitted to the principle of reality, Freudian psychoanalysis describes the 'primary processes' as the part of the psyche that is governed by the pleasure principle. The 'primary processes' are linked to the unconscious and characterized by its alogical mode of functioning and by the non-existence of distinctions such as subject and object.

3. 'Individuation' in Jungian theory means reaching maturity by coming to terms with your 'true self'.

4. Cassirer does not refer to metaphor and metonymy himself, but the linkage is clear, if his description of the work of similarity and contiguity in mythical semiosis is read through the lens of the linguistic theory of Roman Jakobson (1987), who distinguishes between metaphor and metonymy on the basis of exactly the same principles.

5 In esoteric yoga 'kundalini' is often referred to as the 'serpent power'. It is the name for an energy that rises along the spine, and which is believed to originate from a serpent that is normally coiled at the base of the spine, but which strikes when aroused, for example, by certain yoga exercises.

6. Seen from an astronomical perspective, the 'great year' of 25,800 years is a result of the so-called 'precession of the equinoxes'. During a 365-day year the sun rises in all Zodiac signs; it stays approximately one month in each sign. The annual revolution of the sun through the signs is, however, not constant. Measured from the point at which the sun rises at spring equinox, a change can be noticed, so that over a period of about two thousand years the rising position of the sun moves through an entire Zodiac sign. In the year 0 the sun rose in Pisces at spring equinox, now this rising position is about to move into Aquarius.

7. The affinities between 'French feminism's *écriture féminine*' and the American 'Goddess-oriented women's spirituality' are also recognized on the other side of the Atlantic Ocean and commented upon by spiritual feminists (see Spretnak 1991: 135).

7

Voices from Inner and Outer Space: Refiguring Mother Sea and Father Sky

In the previous chapter, we saw how the image of the distant Cyber-Godfather is reversed by New Age astrology. The futuristic high-tech cosmos of space flight is replaced by premodernity's Great Cosmic Mother, who communicates with us through the natural rhythms of celestial bodies. In this chapter we shall revisit the Cybergod, but this time as part of another extraterrestrial projection of a traditional male/female pair, Mother Sea and Father Sky. We will explore how this second pair was reconfigured by post-Second World War science, which ascribed to both figures a strong desire to send messages to humans, while still maintaining the opposition between high-tech and pre-tech.

But since the discussion of the cosmos and the ocean in the following pages also paves the way for the dolphin finale in Chapter 8 – where our last icon will carnivalize the dichotomies and hierarchies set up by the narratives of the spaceship and the horoscope – we shall, as a prelude to the present chapter, focus on a story about cosmodolphins.

The Message of the Cosmodolphins

A recent New Age book claims that dolphins arrived on planet Earth only during this century. They were beamed down just a few decades ago via a high-frequency transmission from the cosmic Spiritual Alliance. According to the American author, these emissary-dolphins, having arrived in the ocean through a 'window in time', proceeded to inscribe their imaginary, yet ancient, 'history' into human minds and books, a feat they were able to achieve in a single instant. The Greek and Roman dolphin myths, the dolphin legends, cave art and hieroglyphs, are all recent creations generated by these extraterrestrial dolphin-beings who seem bent on contributing to what we would call the bulk of Holy Graphics on Earth. They achieved all of this with nothing more than their in-built mastery of communication via sound waves. Consistent with her own story-line, the textual author, Joan Ocean, insists that she received this insight from an acoustic image presented to her by the 'wild animals' themselves. Via this image they explained to her how and why they made the sacrifice of giving up their celestial lives as 'light-beings' in favour of a limited three-dimensional, mammalian incarnation. The purpose of this Jesus-like gesture was to guide humans towards the realms of spiritual reality by opening their minds to the primordial wisdom of the ocean and preparing them for their future life as ethereal space beings (Ocean 1997: 162–5).

Much as contemporary adherents of astrology believe that they have been called by the cosmos, Ocean sees herself as a true disciple of the cosmodolphins. She shares her belief in dolphins as spiritual messengers or 'angels of the sea' with many New Agers, who indulge in similar ritual acts of resacralizing 'wild and wise' nature. Like the astrologers, she also believes that an intuitive wisdom is embedded in extraterrestrial space, although in her universe not only the cosmos, but also the ocean is a bearer of this mystical insight. While the Spiritual Alliance possesses an all-embracing cosmic knowledge, the so-called 'Akashic Records' represent the age-old and sublime information about the planet Earth stored in the water molecules of the ocean to which dolphins and their whale cousins, acting as 'molecular librarians' (Ocean 1997: 146), can give us access.

Besides bringing her close to the astrologers' claim about the ancient wisdom embodied by the global commons, Ocean's story also overlaps with the scripts of yet another branch of New Agers, who conjure up other kinds of mock-mirrors of the space narrative by celebrating UFOs and high-tech angels from outer space, who apparently are eager to communicate their wisdom to humans.

Ocean's amazing contribution to the New Age fable anticipates the analysis of the polysemantic dolphin icon in Chapter 8 as well as the present chapter's survey of some remarkable post-Second World War refigurations of the cosmos and the ocean – refigurations that, as Ocean's story shows, laid the foundations for many, still valid, imageries. In the wake of the war, the Cold War consciousness began to match an outward movement into the sky with an inward movement into the ocean which, in the American discourse, was propagated as the world of 'inner space'. Conceptions of extraterrestrial settings shaped in this period include some of the key themes that reappear in Ocean's text. We shall focus in particular on ideas about receiving information from other worlds by means of sound waves or radio and TV signals.[1] The new sky and the new sea herald the acoustic images that our contemporary New Age author believes she received from the dolphins.

Voices from the Global Commons

As both of the global commons, outer space and the sea, were being discursively set up for invasion during the 1950s and 1960s, intricate strands of narrative began to evolve. The (re-)investment of life signs in both places became a conspicuous tendency, pointing towards the need to redesign our mental maps in preparation for the exploration of these two new frontiers. Although alien and 'other-worldly', the extraterrestrial regions eventually became infused with recognizable, human-like features and populated with 'others' who functioned as displaced mirrors for ourselves, or as echoes resonating with the voices of the imagination. A major theme of this chapter is the exploration of these different 'echoes' and of the deep impressions left on them by technology.

As a consequence of the rapid, primarily military, development of electronic listening devices, inner as well as outer space became imbued with sounds, with noises that broke the silence normally ascribed to these areas. We call these sounds 'orality' in order to describe how the formerly silent sea and the secularly muted heavens were suddenly perceived as beginning to 'speak'. As technoscience developed the capability of electronically translating the sound waves emitted by marine life forms and the radio waves emanating from the universe into the range of human hearing, the extraterrestrial commons now seemed to gain scientifically authorized 'voices'.

In conceptualizing this voice-giving process, we shall draw upon terminology coined by the literary scholar W. J. Ong. In his book on the cultures of orality and literacy, Ong distinguishes between two kinds of orality: a 'primary' and a 'secondary' version (Ong 1997). Primary orality implies a simple acoustic act of speech and reception and presupposes an ignorance of writing, of literacy, and hence it constitutes, says Ong, the distinctive feature of all illiterate cultures, both ancient and contemporary. In contrast, he classifies the orality practised in our own literate and technological societies as being 'secondary', due to the way in which it is inextricably intertwined with writing, printing and electronic transmission (ibid.: 11). Consequently, although the sciences engaged in both marine and cosmic research began to involve acoustics, this is a secondary orality; the act of listening to these non-terrestrial regions is dependent upon electronic devices and, hence, on writing and print.

In extending Ong's concepts of orality from human acts of verbal communication to extraterrestrial soundings, we are investigating not the material reality of the 'other' worlds, but the minds and imaginations of the humans studying them. While they evidently did not speak in oral ways, both cosmos and ocean were to a certain extent perceived as if they did so. Through the influence of new information theories and technologies, nature became conceived of as communicating or exchanging information in a way analogous to our own. Furthermore, the discourses of popular science and culture, especially Western ones, frequently referred to or depicted the (non-vocally) emitted noises from the sky or from the ocean depths as 'voices'. Inevitably, a variety of connotations, embedded in the common conceptions of communication, information exchange and orality, thus became activated, including a certain anthropomorphism. A recycling of Ong's terminology underlines this aspect, as it sets off the contiguities at play between human orality/vocality and these new extra-terrestrial soundings.

In general, the concept of 'orality' also underlines the important role played by acoustics when the 'signals' were received from outer and inner space, while the term 'secondary orality' emphasizes the agency of the big technological apparatus that characterize the listener's techno-position. Very sensitive hydrophones (underwater microphones) could now pick up the biological sounds of the ocean, and increasingly sophisticated radio telescopes could 'hear' the electromagnetic waves – the 'hissing noises' – from outer space, these latter bearing evidence of a radio universe as real as the more familiar, visual one. (The fact that the naked human ear is deaf to these sounds makes them, however, at the same time all the more 'supernatural', suggesting divine intervention.)

The various vibrations from inner and outer space indicated both similarity and difference (see Table 7.1). On the one hand, the ocean and the cosmos became connected in a new way. Both were generating 'waves' of some kind that could be made audible and, at the same time, transcribed into writing, graphics and images. On the other hand, the different nature of the energy emitted from the sea and from the sky seemed to sustain age-old discourses of differentiation, involving gender and ethnicity. For, while the terms of research bonded the two areas in a secondary orality characteristic of the high-tech devices utilized, the areas were nevertheless interpreted differently.

The very character of the marine and the cosmic sounds, respectively, fed into the already present gender and ethnic identifications that are interwoven into the themes of 'orality' and that in popular mythologies have been connected with the two extraterrestrial regions. Due to her wet and primordial nature, the ocean has often been cast as motherly womb, while the Euro-American cosmos, due to a strong influence from Christianity, has for centuries been identified as the realm of the white Fathergod, notwithstanding that many pagan and occultist thought systems constructed the sky as a mother. In high-tech science, the roles of Father Sky and Mother Sea became readjusted and confirmed – and, moreover, connected with a racialized, ethno-technological opposition between white and high-tech *vis-à-vis* non-white and pre-tech.

TABLE 7.1

'Voices' from inner and outer space. Scientists picking up noises from the ocean and the cosmos via high-tech equipment = secondary orality.	
OCEAN	COSMOS
Sound waves with biological origins: constructed as body-speak = primary orality (suggesting Woman and Native)	Radio waves: outer space constructed as broadcasting station = secondary orality (suggesting high-tech Scientist)

The universe was found to emit radio waves that were usually explained with reference to terrestrial broadcasting stations. Using this analogy, the new signals could be fitted smoothly into the traditional view of the heavens; what emerged was the image of a heavenly broadcaster who, in the guise of a 'distant scientist' (of implicit masculinity and whiteness), might be in the process of transmitting his superior knowledge to the Earth (Holmes 1967: 31ff.). But whereas the heavenly radio signals indicated, to a number of prominent scientists, the existence of radio voices emanating from incredibly advanced technological 'supercivilizations' (Tovmasyan 1965: 40), the sounds of marine life from beneath the sea, 'the voices from the deep' (Clarke 1960: 45), were more likely to be interpreted in the context of a noisy body-speak. In contrast to the image of a high-tech scientist broadcasting intelligent radio messages from the Beyond of space, the imagery that evolved around the noisy sea drew on the configurations of non-technology, Woman and Native. From this watery 'inner space' came not the radio waves that suggest 'advanced' electronics but sound waves that connect with biology (cf. Tarasov 1960: 4) and sounds that were generated by the bodies of the sea creatures and hence perceived as 'primitive'. The sounds might, for example, be produced by the contractions of the swim bladder or by fish grinding their teeth (Griffin 1974: 269). Neither fish nor cetaceans have vocal cords.

We will apply Ong's definition to the two different scientific discourses on outer and inner space. The purpose is to emphasize how the network of associations that the language of science set up around the two global commons implicitly co-constructed an affinity between the imagined *heavenly voices* and Ong's *secondary* orality, and between the sounds of *marine life* and his *primary* orality.

Although the marine noises are also perceived via listening devices, the high-tech mind nevertheless sees a parallel between these and non-technological – or technologically 'innocent' – societies (ancient Greece, for instance, as well as contemporary groupings of some ethnic others). In order to illustrate this discursive construing of marine sounds as body-speak and hence as primary orality, let us briefly listen to the onomatopoeic words with which two researchers describe the sounds emitted by marine populations such as fish, crustacea and marine mammals: 'clicks or clacks, croaks, grunts, rattles, or thumps', said the fish and the crustacea (Kellogg 1961: 34), and with 'whistles, squeals, chirps, clicks, rasps' the marine mammals replied (Sebeok 1972: 54). Finally, one scientist notes that dolphin trainers in the American oceanaria tended to suppress certain 'primitive', 'non-civilized' noises made by the performing animals 'because to humans they sound raucous, derisive, impolite, even scatological, but at least very alien (it may be that clicking Hottentots and Bushmen would not think so [*sic*!])' (Lilly 1962a: 152).

The differentiation constructed by the language of science between the two kinds of extraterrestrial voicings reaffirms the gendered and ethnicized mind–body split that is so deeply rooted in our culture. On the pages to follow, we give an account of this construction, looking at the discourses on the two global commons one by one.

Refigured Mother Sea

After the Second World War, the sea became an important arena for military expansion for both superpowers. Billions of dollars and roubles were spent on the construction of nuclear-powered submarines capable of launching long-range missiles from beneath the ocean surface. (These submarines were modelled on whales and dolphins.)[2] In addition, the exploration of the sea for resources such as oil, minerals and food was given high priority. Both scientists and popular science writers advocated these activities with slogans about 'mining the ocean' and 'farming the sea', seeing them as a way of avoiding an impending global famine brought on by the world's so-called 'population explosion'.[3] In a typical linking of race and procreation without (sexual) restraint, Western demographic anxiety often located a particular need for underwater farming or 'aquaculture' in continents with 'exploding birth rates' – that is, Africa, Asia and Latin America – thereby establishing a contiguity between the fecundity of the as yet largely unexplored sea and of the semi-'dark' continents (Engel et al. 1961: 174). This contiguity underlined the status of both bio-political regions as resources for the white, industrialized nations to exploit.

Alongside these traditional recipes for the cannibalization of the objectified wild, other discourses tended towards restoring dynamic movement and exotic, alien and extremely noisy life to the re-subjectified 'Mother Sea' (Carson 1961; Piccard and Dietz 1961: 21). The revival of maternal connotations to nature, the busy womb transformed into a life-affirming cornucopia, may be illustrated by two examples in which the ocean's mute and hostile image is replaced by one of chatty or even uproarious interconnectedness.

First the abyss, which until recently was conceived of as a 'place of eternal calm' (Carson 1961: ix), a dark graveyard, sterile and lifeless, isolated from the rest of the sea, began to be officially integrated into the larger picture and endowed with movement, rapid change, and life. The Swiss scientist and diving pioneer J. Piccard, who went seven miles down into the abyssal Marianas Trench, for instance, declared the deep ocean to be basically a 'friendly' place, where 'life does exist' (Piccard and Dietz 1961: 183).

Second, technological advances changed the sea from an eerily silent place to one filled with marine life emitting familiar sounds; the 'roars, knocks, honks, squeals, "popping of corks"' were seized upon by some scientists as being 'old sounds from new places' – that is, as something well known from everyday life (Tavolga and Steinberg 1961: 288). Marine bio-acoustics, the art of listening to the voices from the near surface or the deep by means of electronic devices (hydrophones, amplifiers, tape-recorders, etc.), which we, with a slight twist of Ong's definition, have called secondary orality, became a major scientific game during the 1950s.[4] This research highlighted the aquatic environment as being another world, filled with utterances that, in spite of their alienness and their obtrusive exposure of a bodily origin, might be paralleled to those of human languages. When speaking of fish sounds, scientists often resorted to linguistic terms such as 'syllables' and 'vocabularies' that, although usually enclosed in quotation marks, indicated speech. A new feeling of kinship with the exotic marine others began to emerge as it became known, for example, that even the apparently stupid toadfish communicates in the same way as humans insofar as its language, its body-speak of long 'honks' and short 'bups', respects the widely accepted Law of Least Effort. This law states that humans, whether English, Chinese or Native American (and now also toadfish), prefer to communicate short messages ('bups') rather than long ones (Kellogg 1961: 36–7). So, the toadfish and the human both seem bent on efficient communication.[5] The general belief that all fish were deaf and dumb was definitely crumbling (cf. Griffin 1974: 270).

Although many of the fish sounds were believed to carry no significance whatsoever, one scientist records that 'a number of fishes when squeezed, poked with a stick, or shocked with electricity will give off their "fishy" utterances' and that these sounds 'might almost be considered emotional' (Kellogg 1961: 38). So even in the cool, sceptical minds of scientists, technology restored a throng of life and a veritable chorus of wild, 'natural' voices, suggestive of at least embryonic intelligence and emotions, to an otherwise 'silent world' (cf. the title of Cousteau's first book, published in 1953).[6]

The Sea as Pastoral Source

At times, the life-affirming fecundity of the sea generated Origin images that depicted the sea as ideal pastoral source in more traditional ways: as a representation of the womb and the maternal breast (cf. Costlow et al. 1993: 223ff.). A telling example of this trend is Arthur C. Clarke's science fiction novel *The Deep Range* (1988), in which a nurturing Mother Sea eventually offers her swelling bosom to a humanity virtuously reborn. This generous gesture takes the form of nursing whale teats which, with their spurting flood of rich milk, perfectly match up to a wishful representation of the maternal breast in their abundant mammalian fluidity. Thus along with the sea, marine mammals are also embedded in pastoral images of physical and spiritual rejuvenation that tinge with hope the troubling concepts of regression, of going backwards that otherwise might cast a gloom over the human intrusion into the newly opened ocean realms. Optimistic visions of entering into a 'retrogressive evolution', transforming man from mere 'frogman' to whale-man or fish-man, were put forward as aquanauts tried to set up habitats on the seabed during the 1960s (Belkovich et al. 1967: 144; Bardach 1968: 77–8 and 84). And so the notion of progressive regression, the idea that descending the evolutionary ladder was in fact a great step forward, became intentionally linked to the 'man-in-sea' projects that were being set up as a parallel to the evolutionary progress embedded in the imagery of 'man-in-space'.

This idea of life in the ocean as a return to Edenic bliss was given a considerable boost by the transformation of the seas into a recreational wilderness area to be admired by the swimmers who, in rapidly increasing numbers, were becoming hooked on the thrills of snorkelling or scuba-diving.[7] With comparatively little equipment, anybody could now not only peer from the surface into the wet 'jungle' (Cousteau and Dumas 1953: 5) teeming with 'untouched wildlife' but, diving a little deeper, could even escape the heavy burdens of life on Earth:

> From birth, man carries the weight of gravity on his shoulders. He is bolted to earth. But man has only to sink beneath the surface and he is free. Buoyed by water, he can fly in any direction – up, down, sideways – by merely flipping his hand. Under water, man becomes an archangel. (Cousteau as quoted in *Time*, 28 March 1960)

So, while worshipping (or cannibalizing) the watery wilds, swimmers around the world were, in the words of *Time* magazine, now 'sinking beneath the surface to fly like angels through an alien realm'. Accordingly, Cousteau's glamorous television documentaries promoted the sea world as a beautiful and blissful home for humanity.

A similar attitude towards the sea as the better place emerges in, especially Western, fiction since 1960 (cf. Springer 1995: 307ff.). Like Clarke in *The Deep Range*, numerous American writers begin to cherish the life-sustaining force of the ocean; many also turn to the apparently specific capability of women, 'primitive' people and marine mammals to be at one with the luringly exotic qualities of watery space; see, for instance, Slonczewski's (1986) peaceful water planet of women 'sharers'; the techno-logically 'innocent' people who call themselves the Children of the Open Sea in Le Guin (1972); the old sperm whale Mulata [*sic*!] that carries the Dreamtime in Barnes (1994) and, finally, the special bonds between Peter Dolphin, the woman researcher Melissa and the indigenous Knolly in Mooney (1983).

In the decades after the Second World War, the fecund ocean and her noisy marine life thus became endowed with anthropomorphic and angelic qualities, floating between the duality of 'wild' human others: Woman and Native. However, this flood of immigration was anything but a one-way 'traffic' (Haraway 1989: 146) from 'nature' to 'culture'. At the same time as the sea was being reconstructed into a frontier bearing a marked resemb-lance to the globe's semi-'dark' continents, where 'primitive cultures' could still be 'studied', Universal Man began to envision himself in the roles of various 'menfish' who could plunge into the assumed angelic innocence and the heavenly riches of an oceanic wilderness, the 'watery Inner Space' that held the keys to 'the mystery of his murky beginning' (Piccard and Dietz 1961: 223 and 21).[8]

The Noble Dolphin-speak

In this context of man's attempts to reconnect with Mother Sea, the smiling dolphin leaped out as the perfect boundary figure between the extraterrestrial marine world and that of humankind. While the dolphin is traditionally seen as representing the very sea herself, at least in her playful and gentle, pastoral configurations (Keller 1887: 217), at the same time it also embodies difference and differentiation in relation to the sea; unlike fish, the dolphin is a warm-blooded, air-breathing mammal who gives birth to live offspring. Moreover, since around 1960, it has been perceived as radiating non-aggression, compassion, spirituality and intelligence of a magnitude far beyond that which was ascribed even to the reinvented sea. As the creature also acquired a rapidly growing reputation not only for having a brain as large and complex as that of humans but even for the capability of speaking English (less often Russian) in a human-like voice, its role as mirror of man seemed assured. With big brains and no hands, the dolphin became an ethnic other or, more precisely, the ethnic other who, as the noble savage, radiates the wisdom that transcends intelligence, the culture that negates civilization, the otherwordly dreamtime that feeds on the fabric of moonlight and myths. In other words, the savage with whom the other savages, those from the hard and dry landscapes, establish a communicative, perhaps telepathic, link much more easily than does the high-tech (usually white male) mind (cf. e.g. Ken Grimwood's novel *Into the Deep* (1996) (analysed in Chapter 2), which estimates only 8 per cent of the so-called 'First World' to be 'capable of full mind-to-mind contact' with cetaceans as against 79 per cent of Australian aborigines and certain other native populations (Grimwood 1996: 365–6)).

We shall now sketch two discursive imprints left by the dolphin's orality cluster, and show how this cluster contributed to casting the animal in the role of noble savage, and to constructing its marine environment as an elsewhere with pastoral qualities. The first concerns the magic of its sonar system, the second the dolphin as a teller of Golden Age tales. For, in stark contrast to the earlier scientific view of dolphins as mute, the animals suddenly became known not only for their eagerness to communicate but also for their almost magical 'vocality'.

In the language of science, dolphins could actually 'see with their ears'

(Kellogg 1961: viii). Possessing an in-built echo-location or sonar system, enviously studied by the world's navies, they could, as if with an 'auditory glance', locate and identify anything in the water by emitting sound pulses and listening to the reflected echoes. Often such sounds were inaudible to the naked human ear. In addition, despite having no vocal cords and, consequently, no voice in our sense, they seemed able to speak in mysterious ways. Perhaps, one scientist suggested, they communicated in a 'televisual' manner by transmitting sound-pictures or acoustic images (Lilly 1962a: 212). This might also mean that, just by looking with their ears, they could perceive and communicate things that were hidden from ordinary human senses. Taking these arguments further, subsequent New Age mythology transformed dolphins into healers and shamans, insisting that they perform as noble savage. Eventually, whales might turn into prophetic seers *à la* Greek Cassandra as, echoing the world soul's grief over the accumulating evils on planet Earth, they try in vain to warn humanity of the cosmic catastrophe this evil-doing will cause; see, a novel by the ex-Soviet, Kirghiz writer, Chingiz Aitmatov, *Tavro Kassandry* (1995) [*The Stigma of Cassandra*].

The primary orality associated with these marine mammals also encouraged a resurgence within the sciences of the story-telling practices of a distant past. Myths and legends, ancient stories and anecdotes connected with the age of primary orality and, hence, with ethnic others, formed an amazing part of scientific and semi-scientific dolphin presentations. All the ancient myths and stories, which the Age of Enlightenment had scornfully discarded as 'absurd tales',[9] became recycled here in the manner of stories-to-think-and-dream-with.

The scientific discourse on the evolutionary path of cetaceans sustained this recycling of stories from a happy and distant elsewhere, for it strengthened the bonds between the animals themselves and the sort of imageries that equate (primary) oral culture with idyllic Golden Age stories. The highlights of this evolutionary narrative expose cetaceans as animals who, in contrast to 'us', returned millions upon millions of years ago from the land to the sea. Long before 'we' became human, this seafaring species evolved into the whales and dolphins that we know today. In short, they seem in a paradoxical way to mirror a parallel yet different evolutionary path to that of civilized man: these playful, talkative and highly 'intelligent' mammalian elders without hands could smoothly embody the technological innocence ascribed to the configurations of primary orality. For were not dolphins, one Soviet scientist asked, a thought-provoking example of a 'society of intelligent beings' that neither used, nor invented, technology?

And did not this non-technological society seriously question the Marxist-Leninist belief in the inevitability of the industrial revolution as a global phenomenon (Konstantinov 1972: 289)? From the very beginning of its life in the (more or less popular) scientific discourses of late modernity, the dolphin became entangled in the iconic nets of tellers of tales; at times it was staged as memorizing and 'vocally' passing on dolphin culture to the next generation of marine mammals in the style of the 'folk tales and legends' told by human noble savages as well as the Homers of ancient times (cf. for example, Lilly 1962a: 37; Belkovich et al. 1967: 323; Sagan 1975: 178); at others, it was cast as star in repopularized Greek or Roman myths and given a leading role in ancient stories depicting the pastoral times of boys-on-a-dolphin (Kellogg 1961); now it was set to fulfil Golden Age-inspired visions of how wise dolphin grandmothers (*babushki*) headed large, extended families of dolphin daughters in exemplary old-fashioned ways (Belkovich et al. 1967: 316ff.); and finally, in A. Alpers's narratives on Opo, the 'gay dolphin' who played with the children in the shallow waters of New Zealand in the mid-1950s, this remythologized 'New World dolphin' was romantically refigured as a Jesus-like prophetess bringing from another world the new teaching of unselfish, maternal love and redemption as well as a wholly New Age (Alpers 1960 and 1961).

Over the years the Golden Age function of this sea mammal has become so generally accepted, so emblematic, that the animal's very appearance on the stage, even with only a short 'blip', is sufficient to signal idyllic nature, untouched by the Fall, by original sin. An example of this pops up in a recent American cyberpunk novel on cyborgs and cyberspace, Pat Cadigan's *Synners* (1991). In the epilogue of this book, after more than 400 pages of a very sophisticated high-tech future, a dolphin quite unexpectedly appears on the horizon. Its sole purpose is to applaud the protagonist's realizing that 'every technology has its original sin' (Cadigan 1991: 435) and establish a counter-image to this. The dolphin has clearly come to supplant former ways of representing sacred wholeness and innocence. Its belonging to the green Origin image that contrasts with techno-man's ecological devastation is also recognized in Russian literature. For instance, the image appears in A. Bitov's reflections on an Earth dead and barren as the result of techno-logical progress *vis-à-vis* a green one, filled with animals, birds and fish, with man collecting roots, and 'perhaps, an intelligent dolphin who has not taken our non-intelligent road' (Bitov 1976: 338).

Playing the part of the noble savage, the dolphin opens the door to a world that promises to redeem our nostalgic longings for a future based on the blissfully innocent lifestyle imagined to have existed prior to technocivilization. The restored images of the sea as an alluring pastoral source, which in its linkage to womb and breast also incorporates vivid notions of primary orality, undoubtedly provide an appropriate setting for embodied desires of symbiotic reconnectedness such as the ones displayed by the noble dolphin.

Refiguring Father Sky

Although the science of oceanography, which had languished in obscurity during the first half of this century, underwent a huge expansion during the 1950s and 1960s, it was nevertheless eclipsed by the Space Age which, for very good reasons, is also known as the age of rockets and missiles. The Cold War gaze of both superpowers was unambiguously fixed on the heavens for the ultimate display of military and technological supremacy.

However, there were obvious parallels in the discourses concerning the conquest and exploitation of the two extraterrestrial regions. As suggested in Chapters 3 and 4, the ideas of 'harvesting', drilling for minerals, etc., were applied to our neighbours in the solar system as well. Expanded to cosmic proportions, visions of 'farming' and 'mining the sky' blazed the American and Soviet colonial trails to the stars, engendering grandiose blueprints for engineering celestial bodies into duplicates of Earth or for transforming them into suppliers of raw materials for 'the home planet' (cf. the title of Kelley 1988). These greedy discourses, bent on cannibalizing the objectified cosmic wilds, nevertheless also shared resacralized constructions with the image of the ocean, constructions that restored life, dynamic change, superior intelligence and the divine to the hitherto muted abyss of space.

During the first half of the twentieth century, the cosmic abyss was perceived as monotonously dead and barren space. The prevailing cosmogonic theory considered the formation of planetary systems to be the result of rare, extremely unlikely, cosmic catastrophes. Our own solar system was thus thought to have 'resulted from a close passage of two stars: an exceedingly rare event' (Cameron 1963: 1). Consequently, Planet Earth (and perhaps a few other planets in our solar system) floated as isolated islands of life and intelligence in the vast, desolate and lifeless cosmic sea. In this universe, man could feel both superior and uniquely alone.

Then, after 1945, this bleak universe gradually succumbed to new visions of a cosmos filled with billions of other planetary systems and hence, in all likelihood, with a myriad life-forms, some younger and some older than ourselves. Neither Earth nor man was unique or superior any longer. On the contrary, there was suddenly every reason to believe that both were merely 'average' (and hence, easily replaceable, cf. Chapter 4). Out there, in the resuscitated Beyond of space, there would be not only pre-cellular and, perhaps, human-like forms of life, but also ancient, highly advanced beings who, as our technological superiors, represented the 'post-human' condition that has become associated with the cyborg (Sullivan 1966: 103; cf. also our Chapter 1). But even if these advanced creatures, exposed by astronomy's newly opened 'radio window', might be considered posthuman, we saw in Chapter 4 that they certainly did not emerge as postgendered (Haraway 1991: 150).

In short, the parallels between the post-Second World War constructions of the ocean and the cosmos are striking: the ambivalence between can-nibalizing and resacralizing, that came to surround our watery inner space, is reflected in the discourses on the ethereal outer one. No less striking, however, are the differences. If the refined marine listening devices and the new communication theories cooperated in transposing the connotations of Origin and womb, traditionally linked to the sea, into a primary orality of noisy body-speak, then the newly discovered radio universe assisted in engendering discursive constructions of the cosmos as a huge broadcasting network. Metaphorically, the cosmos became very 'noisy' too (although there is no 'natural' sound whatsoever, since sound waves cannot propagate through the vacuum of space). When its radio waves were translated into sound and writing, however, the signals seemed to be of a far more intelligent and elevated kind than those picked up from the sea. The embryonic intelligence of the Sea Mother was clearly outdistanced by the high-tech intelligence of the Sky Father. Often explicitly referred to as signals, and explained to the public using our own radio and TV broad-casting stations as the main point of reference, the heavenly transmissions became linked to the technologizing of the word and the secondary orality that stems from the upsurge in communication electronics and mass media technology.[10]

The Broadcasting Universe

Let us briefly recapitulate Ong's definition of secondary orality as opposed to the primary and original one that was the only existing mode of thought and speech before the technology of writing and printing changed our way of thinking. Secondary orality, created initially by the invention of alphabets and of printing technology, is, Ong notes, accelerated by 'present-day high-technology culture, in which a new orality is sustained by telephone, radio, television and other electronic devices that depend for their existence and functioning on writing and print' (Ong 1997: 11). So, in secondary orality, technology intrudes into and fuses with the word; accordingly, the subtitle of Ong's book is 'The Technologizing of the Word'. This technologizing may also be interpreted as the Word becoming spiritualized as symbolic or electronic signals suggesting the activities of a distant, cosmic Cybergod. This process came to take a major part in the resacralizing of the heavens: the divine Word that, in Holy Scripture, initiated the cosmos of yesteryear, underwent an electronic Word-processing and emerged as a multimedia broadcasting station, capable of regenerating and upholding the resounding 'call of the cosmos' (cf. the title of Tsiolkovsky 1962).

This kind of secondary orality permeated the imagery into which the universe was now transposed.[11] At times, natural cosmic phenomena such as atoms of hydrogen, the most abundant element in the universe, went on the air, as in the following example: 'Like a giant broadcasting station with an antenna rising above the street, hydrogen has established its frequency of 1,420 megacycles as the loudest radio program in town' (Holmes 1967: 53). Radio observatories, described as 'man's only cosmic listening posts' (Kraus 1995: 238), were pricking up their so-called 'electronic ears' to catch the sounds of the natural universe, since 'radio waves are emitted not only by broadcasting stations but by every object in the universe as well' (Shklovsky 1991: 13). Of itself, the terminology of radio astronomy, involving frequencies, channels, wavelengths, tuning in on other worlds – and so on and so forth – carries connotations of a radio broadcasting universe functioning in a quasi-human way. Although astronomers usually emphasize that the waves picked up from distant radio sources (in the 1950s still called 'radio stars') by a large antenna and a radio receiver, produce only a 'hissing noise' that in itself carries no information, the contiguity with ordinary radio broadcasting often recurs in their own discourses. One example of this is the depiction of the 'hissing noise' as 'the sound of a radio receiver tuned between stations' (Kraus 1995: 149). All you have to do, this analogy implies, is to turn the dial and search for an extraterrestrial 'electronic voice' of enlightenment and entertainment that will come through loud and clear when you find the right frequency (cf. Holmes 1967: 8).

You do not always even have to turn the dial. In the best-selling SF novel *Contact* (1997), astronomer Carl Sagan's *alter ego*, Ellie Arroway, listens obsessively through her earphones to the random noise from the sky, searching for a pattern, a signal. Even when the noise is clearly patternless, she does not put her earphones away. After all, she is familiar with Shannon's famous dictum in information theory: 'that the most efficiently coded message was indistinguishable from noise, unless you had the key to the encoding beforehand' (Sagan 1997: 50). What was believed to be meaningless, hissing radio noise, emitted by distant magnetic fields and by the listening devices themselves, might turn out to be an alien radio message.

The blurring of the boundaries between the naturally and the technologically broadcasting cosmos was an analogy that thrived not only in the rapidly expanding border zone of popularized space science and science fiction. By the late 1950s, the fusion of the electronically generated radio universe and the naturally radiating one had become an issue for many astronomers and astrophysicists as well. In 1959, Otto Struve, director of the radio astronomy observatory in Green Bank, West Virginia, writes that there may well be 'observable phenomena' in the universe that can only be understood if the 'laws of physics' have been extended by 'actions of "free will"' – that is, by the actions of an intelligence that has reached a technological level at least equivalent to our own. Struve argues his case with reference to the relatively new status of Planet Earth as a rising 'radio star':

> Man-made radio waves did not exist a generation ago. Those now in existence could be easily detected from distances of ten to twenty light years (after a light-time interval of ten to twenty years). We can no longer take for granted that all observable phenomena are ruled exclusively by what we call the 'laws of nature'. (letter in *New York Times*, 6 December 1959)

The transformation of the formerly silent universe into a cosmos of radio and TV communication, where speech transmissions may be translated by computers into the language of extraterrestrial others, had by that time already become an established science fiction 'fact'. In the 1957 Soviet SF novel, *The Andromeda Nebula* (Yefremov 1987), a gigantic intergalactic broadcasting network, The Great Ring, connects humanity with a plurality of other worlds. In this Utopian setting of a distant future, the author, Ivan Yefremov (a prominent scientist himself), lets a 'beautiful' earth woman read the terrestrial news to the aliens at regular intervals, or lecture them on human history. The ETs can allegedly see this earthly TV version of Miss Universe, but can they hear her? wonders the human protagonist of the novel. He concludes that if these ETs do employ some form of verbal communication, 'electronic translation machines will transform the symbols into the sounds of the living alien speech' (Yefremov 1987: 123). In other words, the speech of the woman is rendered into an electronic voice with a language, a (secondary) orality of its own. But who is really speaking on the ETs' screen – Miss Universe, the word-processing machine, or both?

This novel was issued more or less simultaneously with the launch of the first *Sputnik*. So immensely popular did the story become that the Soviet Union's best-known astrophysicist, I. Shklovsky, head of the department of radio astronomy at the Shternberg Astronomical Institute, soon urged a search for intelligent signals from the Andromeda galaxy (cf. *New York Times*, 3 December 1962). It was here, in this huge starry nebula, that the novel had placed the technological supercivilization whose friendly call signals, representing the bright future of communism, originally led to Planet Earth's entry into the intergalactic club. Stimulated too by their country's success in space, Soviet astronomers did indeed locate the alleged beacons of such civilizations. In 1965 the Soviet News Agency, TASS, informed an astonished world of a newly discovered supercivilization that seemed to be signalling us. (Unfortunately, the regular pattern of radio waves, repeated every hundred days, was found to originate from a natural source, a quasar; cf. Sullivan 1966: 225; Shklovsky 1991: 253.)

An Era of Space Messages

The broadcasting universe did not emerge solely from the postwar drive to rebind the broken cosmic globe, nor did it grow exclusively out of the new radio universe and the obsession with communication, information and electronic mass media in the industrialized countries. It was also linked to the US–Soviet contest in celestial ventriloquism that began when the radio beeps of the orbiting *Sputnik* in October 1957 revealed the presence of a superior technological intelligence in the sky. This contest was clearly aimed at deciding which one of the two superpowers could most superbly master the god-trick of speaking on behalf of the universe. The means were radio signals, which displayed how this technology was now miraculously capable of establishing communication, including eavesdropping,[12] on a cosmic scale. Whether transmitting beeps, speech, photographs or TV broadcasts, these satellites and spaceprobes were often referred to as 'voices' from space; see, for example Clarke's *Voices from the Sky* (1966). Moreover, this contest encouraged ideas of communicating with the 'real' ETs. Such an alluring prospect lay, for instance, just beneath the surface of the newspaper headline that, when reporting on the first satellite transmission of human speech from outer space, bombastically announced: 'Talking Satellite Heralds Era of Space Messages' (*New York Times*, 23 December 1958).

In the years following 1959, when two elite physicists, Giuseppe Cocconi and Philip Morrison, both of them professors at Cornell University, made this undertaking scientifically respectable by publishing their article 'Searching for Interstellar Communications' (1959), various strategies for detecting artificially generated radio signals from a distant high-tech elsewhere were put forward (cf. Cameron 1963). The enterprise that subsequently became known as CETI (an acronym for Communication with ExtraTerrestrial Intelligence), was for years conceived of as a genuine act of communication.[13] Nevertheless, both the American and Soviet scientists involved were in fact concentrating their speculations mainly on technical questions of how to locate and pick up the semi-divine transmissions that were believed to be already on the air. The problems of actually establishing meaning across the cosmic sea were generally ignored or played down, reduced to the universality of prime numbers, mathematics and technicalities. With dots and dashes pulsing through the universe from the broadcasting site of the 'remote communicator', a sort of interstellar Morse code might, for instance, be arranged into a scanning pattern that would display TV pictures (TV was becoming the dominant medium at that time; it also blurs the boundaries between speech, writing and picture). That humans had discovered television soon after radio, 'he [the distant scientist] will know … from his own experience. He can be quite confident that a society which is capable of listening to his signals at all will be capable of constructing a television scanning pattern,' claimed an American naval officer and guided missile specialist, accustomed to interpreting the alien mind (Holmes 1967: 37).

One contributor to the CETI discussion, however, did embed the concept of 'interstellar communication' within the still substantial theatrical genre of the radio. This was the Dutch mathematician, H. Freudenthal, who designed a bizarre language, Lincos, for an alleged 'cosmic intercourse', in which earthlings enacted the everyday dramas of being human. In the introduction to his book (1960), Freudenthal confesses to having once 'thought cosmic radiation to be a linguistic phenomenon', but to have later changed his mind, acknowledging that 'at the present stage of our knowledge this seems to be very improbable'. Still, the contiguity between cosmic radiation and broadcast speech apparently continued to haunt him. For the 'lingua cosmica' (abbreviated to Lincos), which he invented, is oral speech designed to be performed by actors playing various parts in a didactic radio play. The ETs were thus meant to learn the new language by listening to (partly) dramatized radio narratives on what it means to be human on Planet Earth. 'Throughout our exposition', he writes, 'we will talk of Lincos as if it were speech (not writing). We shall say that Lincos phonemes (not letters) are radio-signals of varying wavelength and duration, and that Lincos words are constituted of phonemes (not letters)' (Freudenthal 1960: 15). Hence he explicitly conceives of the Lincos words as being pronounced when they are translated into radio signals and transmitted. Although Freudenthal admits that the differentiation between writing and speech in his desired transmission to the ETs is conventional, his preference for developing proficiency in oral cosmic communication is so deliberately argued that it turns out to be the very foundation on which his broadcasting programme is based. By choosing to stage his explanations of human behaviour as radio theatre, as polyphonic voices in dialogue, the Lincos designer intends to impart terrestrial morals, ethics and culture to the distant, though human-like mind. Thus Freudenthal's ET is educated in the not-yet-posthuman condition through enactments of European upper-class etiquette, which display, for example, the advantages of polite speech and other signs of good breeding. Listening carefully to this amazing story of the terrestrial lifestyle, our remote friend could learn that it does pay off – on Earth at least – to treat your servant well (in a note to one of his hieroglyphic dialogues, written partly in Latin, partly in mathematics, Freudenthal explains that: 'It appears that the obedient servant is regularly paid by his master. Another person is disobedient, because his master did not pay him his due' – ibid.: 215).

Freudenthal's idea of staging a celestial radio play for the 'distant races' did not meet with much sympathy in mainstream CETI circles. The Lincos concept was commonly considered too complicated and old-fashioned for the Cybergods – who might be more hooked on TV – and the energy needed to actually broadcast at random to far-away celestial bodies un-realistically expensive. Transmitting random signals from a technological civilization as young and relatively primitive as that of the Earth was not on the agenda; instead, earthlings were to gain entry into the galactic club by tuning their electronic devices to the right frequency. We were, then as now, supposed to be not the wise and instructive teachers, but the humble, ignorant listeners, as is aptly implied by J. E. Gunn's SF novel, *The Listeners* (1974).[14]

In the next chapter, we shall see how the flexible dolphin leaps freely between this version of the Big Blue, where it performs as a highly technologized stand-in for the cosmic cybergods, and the one in which, as an emissary of inner space, a noble savage in smooth, rubbery disguise, it conveys sybilline messages from the motherly sea.

Notes

1. Readers as ignorant as we ourselves used to be on the mystery of 'waves' may find the following helpful. Visible light, X-rays, microwaves (used in radar) and radio are all *electromagnetic waves*, differing only in wavelength. They travel through empty space at the speed of light. By contrast, *sound waves* must have a medium (e.g. air or water) through which to travel; water constitutes a much more efficient medium than air. Technologically, earthlings have been generating electromagnetic radio waves since about 1900. Radio broadcasts started around 1920; TV, which also depends on radio waves, began to enter homes in the 1940s. Radar is a system for detecting objects using pulsed radio waves; the word stands for RAdio Detection And Ranging. Sonar is a similar system using sound waves; it is an acronym for SOund Navigation And Ranging. Radar and sonar are commonly confused in public discourses.

2. According to an American navy officer, the first undersea craft constructed in the teardrop configuration of a whale became the forerunner of 'the nuclear-powered attack submarine and finally of the Polaris weapons delivery system ... The results of dolphin research and the most awesome of natural power, nuclear power, have produced America's major deterrent to war [that is, the nuclear submarine]' (Devine and Clark 1967: 332 and 341).

3. Cf. Clarke 1960; Cowen 1960; Cousteau and Dumas 1953; Bardach 1968; Vasil-chikov 1964; Tarasov 1956; Chapskii and Sokolov 1973. However, the Soviets, faithful to the teachings of Marx, rejected Malthusian-inspired beliefs in the catastrophic consequences of the rise in world population.

4. The staggering growth of marine bio-acoustics is reflected in the number of scientific reports. One bibliography from 1960 contains over 1,200 references, almost all of which deal with the sounds made by marine life forms (Kellogg 1961: 34), cf. also Sebeok 1972: 54, who lists over 1,500 references by early 1962.

5. An analysis of 273 toadfish sound patterns, recorded at the Marine Laboratories of Florida State University, revealed toadfish communication to be as 'taciturn' as that of humans. According to the Law of Least Effort, there is a negative relationship in spoken and written language between the length of a word and the frequency of its use. The longer the word, the more seldom it is employed (Kellogg 1961: 36ff.).

6. *The Silent World* was published in the USA in 1953; a few years later it also came out in the Soviet Union. Cousteau's colour film of the same name, which starred the tame grouper, Ulysses, won an award at the 1956 Cannes Film Festival. It was shown in the Soviet Union in 1958.

7. During the 1950s snorkelling grew into a mass sport in the USA. By 1960, about one million American swimmers were snorkelling, while 200,000 had taken up scuba-diving (*Time*, 28 March 1960: 52). In the Soviet Union free diving grew much more slowly, partly for geographical reasons, partly due to a shortage of equipment (cf. Dugan and Vahan 1965: 50–2).

8. The world's first oceanarium, Marine Studios (1938), was renamed Marineland of Florida after the Second World War. The name indicates the new bonding between sea and land. Soviet marine scientists had to lobby for years before they eventually got the dolphinarium at Batumi in 1974, which functioned both as a research centre and a

dolphin circus (Tomilin 1980: 30). By 1969, the USA had thirteen oceanaria in operation, the majority of which had been built in the 1960s (cf. Chapskii and Sokolov 1973: 213).

9. In a standard work on animals published in the early nineteenth century, the Reverend W. Bingley notes the following: 'The Dolphin was in great repute among the ancients, and both philosophers and historians seem to have contended who should relate the greatest absurdities concerning it ... How these absurd tales originated it is impossible even to conjecture; for the Dolphins certainly exhibit no marks of particular attachment to mankind. If they attend on vessels navigating the ocean it is in expectation of plunder, and not of rendering assistance in cases of distress' (Alpers 1961: 134; Bingley's *Animal Biography* was issued in London in 1802).

10. A thousandfold increase in the power of Earth's radio and TV broadcasts occurred during the period 1940 to 1970; the increase was especially pronounced during the 1950s when TV became a popular commodity (cf. Goldsmith and Owen 1992: 467–8). But radio was experiencing growth as well. Thus in the Soviet Union there were only eighteen million radios in 1952, a number which had increased by 1968 to nearly ninety million (cf. Graham 1990: 33).

11. In the early 1930s, the American engineer K. Jansky accidentally picked up radio waves from outer space, but his discovery created only a short-lived sensation, and had no immediate effects on astronomical research. However, one astronomer foresaw the consequences as follows: 'The complicated equations of celestial mechanics may soon give way to the more complicated mathematics of celestial electronics. The mysterious electron, the fundamental building block of all matter, which dances in your radio tubes to the tune of your favorite jazz, is dancing in the remoter stars of the galaxy, and other galaxies, to pique the curiosity of the astronomer in his search for knowledge' (Stetson 1934: 6).

12. In the late 1950s, the US Navy, for instance, spent 200 million dollars on the construction of an enormous radio telescope designed to monitor the Soviets by observing their radio communications as they reflected back from the surface of the Moon. However, when satellites promised better ways of gathering information, the project was scrapped (cf. Drake and Sobel 1992: 40).

13. CETI, the concept and the word itself, was introduced into the International Academy of Astronautics (IAA) in 1965 by the Czech Professor R. Peshek. The IAA then formed a CETI committee which, however, two decades later discreetly changed its name to the similar-sounding SETI (the Search for ExtraTerrestrial Intelligence) (cf. Marx 1988: xv–xvii). To C. Sagan, for instance, the acronym CETI was appropriate because it is also the genitive of the Latin word for whale, Cetus. Sagan strongly favoured the argument that if we cannot communicate with the cetaceans, 'we should not be able to communicate with extraterrestrial civilizations' (Sagan 1973: 5).

14. Since 1974, a US signal, describing our solar system, our DNA and our species, has been speeding towards the Hercules constellation, 25,000 light-years away. An answer may come in 50,000 years!

Amazing Story V: Dolphin Versatility – from Living Missiles to Healers

Ukraine trains kamikaze dolphins to heal ... (Nanette van der Laan, *The Electronic Telegraph*, 23 July 1997)

Under this amazing headline, the UK-based Internet journal *The Electronic Telegraph* reports on its visit to the dolphin research centre in Ukraine. The centre is located at a naval base near Sevastopol, in the Crimea, which used to be the home port of the large Soviet Black Sea Fleet and one of the main facilities of the Soviet navy. Since the collapse of the Soviet Union, there has been considerable tension between Russia and Ukraine, and major disputes about how to divide up this fleet.

The general cut-backs in military spending have left their mark on this once powerful navy. Whether Ukrainian or Russian, many of the personnel have had to find new ways of earning a living. This includes the elite squadron of 70 dolphins who, according to the Ukrainian navy's chief spokesman, Captain Nikolai Savchenko, were trained for 'kamikaze missions' and other military purposes (Laan 1997). Instead of preparing themselves to blow up submarines with explosives strapped to their bodies (Laan 1997), or to disarm any enemy frogmen who might approach Sevastopol harbour (*Ogonek*, no. 37, 1996: 9; GlobaLearn 1998), the dolphins are now engaged in the therapy and healing business. Several were sold to a Red Sea swim-with-the-dolphins centre in Israel; others managed to convert their military skills in more domestic Black Sea waters so that they were able to keep their jobs at Sevastopol, supervised by their new leader, Svetlana Matyshovna, who has worked at the naval base for almost three decades. They now participate in a successful dolphin-therapy programme conducted by the Science and Research Centre of the National Oceanographic Institute of Ukraine. Much like similar programmes in Florida, the central part of the treatment consists of sessions where the patient swims with a dolphin. According to the assistant doctor, Ludmilla Lukina, since its inception in 1986 the programme has helped over 1,500 people with various kinds of medical and psychological problems (Lukina 1996). The former 'kamikaze dolphins' have, Lukina notes, been particularly helpful in treating children for various kinds of neuroses and even more serious afflictions, such as autism.

Allegedly, what is happening in the Sevastopol dolphin-therapy is a readjustment of the patient's 'natural aura'. This is how the head of the healing programme, Svetlana Matyshovna, explains the process, thus displaying that, in her conversion from Soviet military person to dolphin therapist, she also came out of the closet as a New Ager. She 'studies UFOs, levitation and telekinesis (moving objects with one's mind)', Laan reports. In typical New Age fashion, Matyshovna stresses that the aura readjustment is a process requiring openness on the part of the patient, and a willingness to accept the guidance of the dolphins:

> The dolphin uses his sonar. He sends vibrating signals underwater which reach the patient. The animal scans the human body and realigns the energetic field. The time needed to correct the aura of the patient depends on the affliction and the willingness of the patient to accept the signals. (Matyshovna, quoted by Laan 1997)

Although the dolphins seem to perform extremely well in their new role, even being able to attract hard currency (Laan paid £10 for a short swim session), their conversion to peaceful activity is, nevertheless, not complete. Since the premises of the research centre are owned by the navy, the military training of these extremely flexible animals has not yet been abandoned. Some of them still have to work part-time for the fleet – just in case the peace should not last.

With a few minor changes of detail, this amazing story of the dolphins of Sevastopol could have been told equally well with American actors in the leading parts. Like the Soviet Union, the US navy has been conducting a dolphin-training programme since 1959;[1] it used the animals for minesweeping and other military purposes during the Vietnam War.[2] Moreover, as a consequence of the changing world order and the growing eco-political concerns of the American public, numerous US military dolphins have recently, like their Russo-Ukrainian colleagues, had to prove that they could act as quick-change artists and adapt to new lifestyles.

While the Ukrainians convert the dolphins from soldier heroes to shaman healers, the trend in the USA is to make the animals prove that a return to 'wild nature' is possible. In this way, they too are expected to act as healers, restoring the broken bonds between humans and nature. In response to a request from the US Congress, a 'Reintroduction to the Wild' programme for naval marine mammals was developed in the early 1990s, and a number of bottlenose dolphins were chosen to be released from their duties (Brill and Friedl 1993). Some of them have actually been transported to Florida and reintroduced to 'the wild', assisted by Rick O'Barry, the former trainer of the famous Flipper from the TV series of the 1960s. O'Barry converted to eco-activism and became a liberator of captive dolphins after Kathy, his favourite Flipper 'actress', died in his arms 'of a broken heart' (O'Barry 1988: 2); hence he emphasizes that the reintroduction to the wild is not about science, but about ethics, art, and healing: 'What we are doing is an art, a healing art; not science', O'Barry's web-site informs us (1999: 1).

Yet another parallel between the Russo-Ukrainian and the American story of dolphin reconversions from military to peaceful activities is that the US navy also does not want to give up its dolphin recruits altogether. In 1997, a renewed flow of money revitalized the project. As Jeffrey Haun, the trainer who heads the navy's marine mammals programme, declared in the *Seattle Times* (15 October 1997): 'There are some things that marine mammals can just do better than man' – such as sweeping mines in shallow coastal waters.

However, one major difference separates the Russo-Ukrainian post-Cold War dolphin script from that of the Clinton administration. That is the shameless exposure of an inappropriate contiguity taking place on the premises of the naval base in Sevastopol, where: 'uniformed navy officers march in step, while a few yards away a busload of children runs to the water to see the dolphins and pet sealions' (Laan 1997).

In the USA, the dolphin's iconographic links to the Cold War and violent death are kept away from the public eye, when its performance in the entertainment or healing business is staged by oceanaria or therapy centres.

Notes

1. Cf. U.S. Navy Marine Mammal History Page, January 1999 (www.spawar.navy.mil/sandiego/technology/mammals/history.html). Cf. also Wood (1973) and Ridgway (1987).

2. Cf. the video 'The New Explorers: Declassified U.S. Navy Dolphins', AMR (1996), which claims to show the US Navy's Marine Mammals Facilities. For 30 years these were 'classified as top secret', while 'now the truth about this amazing program can be told'. One of the highlights of this video is allegedly 'rare footage' displaying dolphins 'engaged in mine-sweeping activities in Vietnam' (Internet-ad for the video, 1999).

8

Rocket State and Dolphin State

Mysteriously smiling, the dolphin entered the American imagination around 1960. Not only did it attract the attention of science and the military; it also enraptured the public mind. So powerfully evocative was this dolphin image that it spread rapidly throughout the rest of the Western world and, adeptly bypassing the Iron Curtain, it even captured the Soviet mind.

The messages that were inscribed in the icon were many and ambiguous. On the one hand, the American and Soviet navies secretly investigated ways in which the dolphin's amazing hydrodynamic qualities could assist in the refinement of torpedoes, and how their sonar and communicative skills could be utilized in maritime warfare. On the other hand, the versatile animal was simultaneously gaining enormous public popularity as harbinger of a New Age and world peace. Being able to perform not only as 'smiling', helpful, intelligent, spiritually wise and endowed with healing powers, but also as playfully erotic, androgynous and group-minded, the dolphin was a perfect match for counter-cultural value systems. Moreover, its eagerness to overcome the barriers of interspecies communication, and its apparent willingness to speak in human-like voices, inspired hopes in anti-war-minded humans; the kind dolphin might, some people thought, guide us to a new paradigm of peaceful cooperation with alien others, whether originating in the strange world beneath the ocean surface, at the other side of the Iron Curtain, or in outer space. In the Soviet Union, the fun-loving animal caught the imagination of anti-Stalinist trends, and the study of cetaceans became a legitimizing platform for the promotion of socialism with a human or rather, a kindly smiling dolphin, face (Bryld 1998).

This chapter retells the amazing story of the dolphin's entrance into the limelight of post–Second World War culture, and outlines some long-term effects of the scripts staged at that time. An analysis of the complex dolphin iconography exposes an array of conflicting roles and inappropriate contiguities. It shows how the animals, in their guise of jesters, masters of

mimicry and mirrors of alien others, make visible the patterns of displacement, inappropriate connections and fluid boundaries between the master
narratives of Space Age and New Age, which we have explored separately
in earlier chapters via the opposing stories of the spaceship and the horoscope icons.

Dolphin Ambiguities

As a prelude to our scrutiny of the post-Second World War dolphin, let
us consider the metamorphoses that this mythical animal was able to
perform long before its postmodern rebirth as a 'nomadic' (Braidotti 1994)
and boundary-crossing subject. When, after centuries of obscurity, the
dolphin became remythologized in a dual role as Space/Rocket Age cyborg
and New Age healer, it renewed an ancient tradition of iconographic
hybridization and fluidity.

As mammals that live in the sea, dolphins are ambiguous creatures,
prototypical boundary-figures that, from time immemorial, have appealed
to mythical thought and stirred the imaginations of different cultures.
Dolphin physiology leads the animal continuously to cross boundaries
between water and air; if forced to stay under water for too long it drowns,
and yet it dies from dehydration if it remains out of water for any length
of time. These mammals probably once lived on land but, many millions
of years ago, they returned to the ocean whence they originated. Belonging
to the family of cetaceans, a name that was originally applied to any sea-
monster or huge fish, dolphins are classified as small whales, i.e. mammals
that live in the sea but breathe air, and are warm-blooded and viviparous.
Furthermore, the dolphin became known for its legendary helpfulness
towards humans. In other words, it is in many ways 'like us' but its
extraterrestrial habitat, the sea, the world of fish, makes it alien. No wonder
then that the dolphin, acting, like mermaids, at the unstable boundaries
between air and water, between human and non-human, has been constructed as an icon of interface and contiguity between different worlds.

Another ambiguity making the dolphin even more mythopoeic and
appropriate to signify border transgressions between seemingly separate
categories and spheres stems from the polysemy of its sexual appearance.
The smooth, streamlined bodies of dolphins have almost no external visual
clues as to sexual difference. The nipples of the female dolphin are concealed in the mammary slits, and the penis of the male appears outside his
body only when erect. Otherwise, his genital is withdrawn inside a slit.
Males and females thus look alike, differing only in the number of slits.

Furthermore, when seen in total, the dolphin body resembles both a womb and a phallus, and these evocative sexual ambiguities are also stressed by another aspect. The male has voluntary control over his penis, which, in the words of one dolphin scientist, he masters 'in an almost "switch-blade" fashion' (Lilly 1962a: 188). Moreover, the genital seems powerfully potent. This potency is strongly suggested by a photo (Lilly 1978) showing how the erect penis, captured by a rope, apparently pulls the rope as the dolphin swims backwards away from the edge of the pool. At the same time, however, the masculinity on display is rendered ambiguous by the strange appearance of the genital. The penis looks like a miniature dolphin, a mirror baby, a cute dolphin replicant being born out of the body slit. In these ways, the dolphin appears to be the very incarnation of a fluid and unfixable sex, defying the visual regime of phallocentrism and performing well as an icon of what Irigaray, speaking of women, has called the 'sex which is not one' (Irigaray 1985b).

Embodying these different layers of equivocality, it is no wonder that, in mythological terms, the dolphin appears as a sexual nomad, avoiding fixed gender categories. Let us illustrate this by taking a look at the ways in which ancient myths link the dolphin to gender.

Etymologically, the dolphin's Greek name, *delphis*, is related to the word *delphys*, meaning womb or vagina. We find the same root in the name of the famous temple and oracle of Delphi, where wise counsel originating in the womb of the Earth could be heard. There are also close links to the Greek word for sister or brother: *adelphos*. Delphi was founded by the god Apollo, who is connected with dolphins in the ancient myths. In one of these myths, Apollo rides a dolphin to the place later known as Delphi; in another he transforms himself into a dolphin. The famous statues and pictures of a boy on a dolphin show the young sun-god being born out of the sea. Originally, therefore, the boy on a dolphin carried a deep religious significance. So did the even better-known dolphin rider, Aphrodite, who was also a dolphin goddess. Throughout the ancient Near East, the dolphin was worshipped as the Great Cosmic Mother, the Dolphin Goddess who presided over fecundity and the mystery of birth in all living beings. For centuries, tales were also told of how her attributes, the kind dolphins, guided the souls of the dead on their journey across the cosmic sea. The goddess was the ruler of birth and death, travel, communication between different worlds, rebirth and immortality (Glueck 1966: 380–1).

But as the mythical transformation of Apollo and the girl/boy on a dolphin may suggest, the animal was imagined in a sexually ambiguous role. It could not only partake in such mythic, feminine forms as sibylline earth womb, lover of boys or Dolphin Goddess, but could also become a hermaphrodite through its bonds to Eros/Phanes or, in the shape of the god Triton, it could dramatically change into an aggressive phallus and rape anyone he pleased, girl or boy. Triton's name means 'three' or 'third', indicating that this divine sex maniac gravitates towards the 'third sex' embodied in the triadic hermaphrodite of ancient creation myths (Doria 1974: 44).

With all of these ambiguities as its cultural heritage, it is not surprising that the post–Second World War dolphin is as adept as its ancestors in taking on the role of quick-change artist, appearing now as living missile or cyborg, and now as wise healer or noble savage. Moreover, the fact that the dolphin as a species is much older than *homo sapiens* undoubtedly eased its transformation into both a representative of age-old high-tech civilizations of galactic aliens and an icon of sibylline intermediaries of the ancient, bodily wisdom of 'nature'.

A Modern Rebirth of Dolphin Lore

In one sense, the post–Second World War dolphin jumped out of the blue. Prior to 1960, very little research had been done on cetaceans. Not until that year did the echo-locating or sonar abilities of dolphins become an established scientific fact (Wood 1973: 71–2). Because of their extra-terrestrial environment, these sea mammals were extremely difficult to study, and of the Marinelands or oceanaria that became so widespread later on there were at that time only a couple in the USA, and none in Soviet Russia. But in the wake of improved technologies for exploration of the ocean depths, and the resultant reconstruction of the sea as a place filled with life and 'speech', dolphins suddenly caught the interest of both science and the military. As it already incarnated the stuff that myths are made of, the way was paved for an enormous popularity and a cult-like celebration of the animal as mediator between alien extraterrestrial worlds and the everyday sphere of humans.

A perusal of book titles indicates the sudden popularity and newly shaped boundary function of the dolphin. A few revealing examples include: *Man and the Dolphin*, 1961 (Lilly 1962a); *The Voice of the Dolphins*, 1961 (Szilard 1992); *Nash drug – delfin* [*Our Friend – the Dolphin*] (Belkovich et al. 1967); *The Mind of the Dolphin: A Nonhuman Intelligence* (Lilly 1967); *The Dolphin: Cousin to Man* (Stenuit 1969); *Mind in the Waters: A Book to Celebrate the Consciousness of Whales and Dolphins* (McIntyre 1974); *Lilly on Dolphins: Humans of the Sea* (Lilly 1975). These now classic dolphin books were widely circulated and republished, often in paperback editions. In 1963 the first dolphin movie, *Flipper*, was shown in the USA. The film spawned a popular television series the following year, which subsequently became an international hit. A new series of Flipper stories was produced in the mid-1990s. According to the refrain of the jolly signature tune from the original series: 'No one you see is smarter than he' – he being, of course, Flipper.

The dolphin made its début into American and Soviet society at a time characterized politically by the tensions of the Cold War and the agonizing processes of global decolonization on the one hand and, on the other, by a fragile détente, upheld in the shadow of threats of total nuclear destruction by summit talks, mutual visits and so on between the two superpowers. The only alternative to the holocaust of war appeared to be communication and mutual understanding, which the 'intelligent' and friendly dolphin, so eager to build bridges between different worlds, could personify even better than any human.

A telling American example is the science fiction short story 'The Voice of the Dolphins' (Szilard 1992), written by Leo Szilard, a Hungarian Jew, émigré from Nazi Germany and professor of physics at the University of Chicago. During the Second World War, Szilard was one of the elite physicists participating in the Manhattan Project, which developed the atomic bomb. But, like several other leading scientists, he became a vehement spokesman for disarmament and world peace after the war in an attempt to come to terms with the moral consequences of the role played by so-called 'neutral' or 'pure' science in the production of the A-bomb and its inherent threat to put an end to human civilization. He wrote 'The Voice … ' in 1960 with the explicit purpose of influencing the American government and the Soviet prime minister, Khrushchev, with whom he tried in vain to discuss it. The story is a passionate plea for disarmament and for a new world order, defined by the rational and peaceful outlook of scientists. But the main point is that the scientists are guided by a group of highly intelligent and morally minded dolphins, who constitute the core staff of a scientific research institute in Vienna. It is a futuristic story beginning around 1960, when the dolphins, with the assistance of top scientists from the two superpowers, begin to intervene in world history. During the next decades they cleverly influence world politics, so that disarmament is finally reached in 1988. The satirical moral of the story is that world peace would never have come about without the knowledge and wisdom of the dolphins, who are so much more clever and morally minded than their assistants, the Russian and American scientists. Szilard's story became an anti-nuclear classic; it sold over 35,000 copies in the USA and was translated into six languages.

As Szilard's story illustrates, the beginning of the modern dolphin era, which coincided with the opening of the Space Age, was deeply engraved in another new icon – that of rockets and missiles. This gave the clever, gentle and morally elevated dolphin a background for promoting itself in the role of counter-image.

An example is the story of *Flipper*. In the original *Flipper* film a young boy, Sandy, the son of a simple fisherman, makes friends with a dolphin. After a disastrous parasite, called the 'red plague'(!), kills off the fish in the sea, causing a disruption in his family's livelihood, the kind and caring dolphin eventually leads the boy to waters abounding with nourishment. The dolphin is obviously intended to perform as the friendly, nurturing and life-connoting counter-image to the 'red plague', which, in the context of the Cold War, implicitly connoted the deadly rockets of the Red communist regime. The *Flipper* film was produced only a few years after the 'technological Pearl Harbor' (Daniloff 1972: 6) where, with the launch of the first *Sputniks* in 1957, the Soviet Union had clearly demonstrated its ability to reach the 'land of the free' with fast, intercontinental missiles.

True to its nomadic character, however, especially in this setting of a new era of weaponry, the dolphin acted not only as a counter-image, but also as a mirror of the rocket. The appearance, speed and lift-off power of these marine mammals are so strikingly reminiscent of rockets and missiles that the metaphors 'rocket-booster' and 'living torpedoes' occur in the minds of observers when trying to pass on their impressions of leaping or swimming dolphins (cf. Cousteau and Dugan 1963: 123; Stenuit 1969: 13). Moreover, another conspicuous link marked itself out between the sea creature and the rocket which, among other things, could launch beeping satellites like Sputnik. Both heralded a revolution in communications that gave rise to great expectations of being able to transgress seemingly insurmountable barriers in reaching out to alien interlocutors. As the construction of the broadcasting universe and the search for extraterrestrial intelligence so neatly coincided with the discovery of dolphin intelligence and mastery of language, the stage was set for the animal's entry into a strange, paradoxical role of boundary figure for both the kind, wise and immensely superior alien, who obviously resided in the extraterrestrial cosmic ocean, and the still relatively small and primitive earthling, the man of science himself.

The 'Father' of the Post-Second World War Dolphin Script

The person who, more than anyone else, authored the post-Second World War dolphin script was the American neurophysiologist John C. Lilly (b. 1915), whom we introduced in our third Amazing Story. All of its basic elements stem from the famous experiments he conducted after setting up his Communication Research Institute in 1959, with laboratories in Florida and the Virgin Islands. As a medical doctor and a brain specialist, Lilly focused his research on methods of communication between 'man and other species', i.e. interspecies communication. A related purpose was to study the structure and functions of the brain and the psychology of man and of marine mammals, the latter being primarily the bottlenose dolphin, the 'smiling' species. Moreover, it became a goal for Lilly to prepare mankind, through dialogues with dolphins, for alien encounters. The latter aspect of Lilly's research led to his involvement with the leading scientists engaged in the scientific search for extraterrestrial intelligence in the universe. For a time, a year or two at least, he succeeded in persuading them that he could establish a 'human-like' communication with dolphins that would be useful as a model for future conversations with the 'real' ETs (cf., for instance, Morrison's recollections in Swift 1990: 29ff.).

Lilly's ideas of English-speaking dolphins reached the front page of the *New York Times* on 21 June 1960, and the following year the extremely influential *Life* magazine published a widely read feature (28 July 1961) heralding the publication of his first book *Man and Dolphin* (Lilly 1962a). Thereafter, the doctor and his intellectually conversant porpoises with skyrocketing IQs became universal favourites of the public. Although Lilly's claims that he would be able to teach dolphins to speak English turned out – after he had enjoyed some years in the limelight of the scientific community – to be a flop, his importance as a mythopoeic figure cannot be overestimated. So evocative was his claim that he could speak with dolphins that the amazing story of the events that took place at his Research Institute in the 1960s have inspired innumerable popular science books, newspaper articles, novels, short stories, films, etc. Two novels, Robert Merle's *The Day of the Dolphin* (1969), which was also filmed (1973) and Ted Mooney's *Easy Travel to Other Planets* (1983), can even be read as *romans à clef*, taking their starting point in the actual events at Lilly's Research Institute.

No matter how hard many scientists tried to uproot the annoyingly unscientific beliefs brought into circulation by Lilly, the myth lived on. Decades later, two despairing dolphin researchers, Louis M. Herman and William Tavolga, summed up the situation as follows:

Over the years, the hypothesis of a natural language in dolphins, vigorously promoted by Lilly, has failed to receive analytic, experimental, or conceptual support. Lilly's pronouncements are largely behind the popular myth of 'talking' dolphins. Partly through uncritical publicity, partly through public gullibility, and partly through poor science, the myth persists today despite many attempts to lay the ghost to rest. (Herman 1980: 176–7)

Having so often been fooled by 'real' science, the 'gullible' public stubbornly preferred to side with Doctor Lilly, the ventriloquist who could restore the broken bond with nature as well as with a friendly non-human species. As an example of the indefatigable appeal of Lilly's doctrines, let us for a moment apply an ear to the mouthpiece of one of the huge tourist attractions of the USA, the marine amusement park chain Sea World. In 1989, thirty years after Lilly founded his Research Institute in the Virgin Islands, a trainer's speech 'sold' the famous killer whale, or Shamu, show to the audience in a very Lilly-like fashion.[1] It compared the animals to extraterrestrial beings from outer space and alluded to the possibility of orca–human conversations as a precursor to communication with cosmic aliens:

It's been said that space is the final frontier. If this is true, then the current frontier must certainly be the oceans of our own planet. Now with the birth of Baby Shamu ... we have been given an incredible opportunity at inter-species communication. Some people feel that before we ever speak to animals and creatures from outer space, we might be able to speak or communicate with animals of the sea. Dolphins, whales, maybe even Baby Shamu! (Quoted in Davis 1997: 227)

Even among scientists, the echoes of Lilly's research have continued to make themselves heard; this, perhaps more than anything else, demonstrates how powerful an object-to-think-with (Turkle 1984) he had conjured up. The scientific discussion of the issue of intelligently communicating dolphins did not end with the discrediting of Lilly's approach as poor science. After Lilly, several scientists have explored the question of human–dolphin communication in other ways. Even Lilly critic Louis Herman is among these. He has studied the issue for many years, and it gives food for thought that, at a scientific conference on dolphin cognition and behaviour in 1983, his research gave impetus to a discussion that, in its speculative extravagance, did not fall very far short of Lilly's own wild way of phrasing questions. As summed up by the widely respected expert in human–animal communication Donald Griffin, the thought-provoking issue that followed from Herman's contribution suggested that it might be easier to establish interspecies communication if a language with a more 'basic' syntax than English were chosen as linguistic paradigm (Schusterman et al. 1986: xiii; cf. also Griffin 1992: 217). So maybe Lilly simply chose the wrong language?

Yet another echo of Lilly's research resounds within the sciences in the context of the search for extraterrestrial intelligence. Even now, in the 1990s, the scientific debate on the issue still sometimes takes into consideration the question of human–dolphin communication. In *First Contact*, which presents itself as a book where 'the world's leading astronomers confront the ultimate question: are we alone in the universe?' (Bova and Preiss 1991), a chapter zooms in on 'The Dolphin: An Alien Intelligence'. It is authored by Diana Reiss, who was at that time director of the research into dolphin communication and cognition at Marine World Africa in California and also a teacher in human–animal communication at San Francisco State University.

Lilly's Talking Cyborg Dolphins

Lilly had developed the idea of actually speaking with alien species while working at the Laboratory of Neurophysiology of the US National Institute of Mental Health, where he eventually became chief of the Section on Cortical Integration. Having had no success in communicating with monkeys, chimpanzees, dogs or cats, whose brains were found to be ridiculously small, his attention was directed by a whale expert to some other brains truly worthy of research. In contrast to the animals mentioned, the whale family seemed to possess 'a brain equal to and larger than ours, and presumably equally complicated' (Lilly 1962a: 45). (At that time, we might add, the capacity of computers, all of them very large, grew with their size. They were often called electronic brains.)

Between 1955 and 1957, Lilly conducted his research on the dolphin brain in the laboratory of the Florida Marine Studios. Both his anatomical and electrical investigations into this *terra incognita* confirmed that the animal was, indeed, not only an excellent example of a highly developed non-human intelligence, but also probably the only one existing on Earth. The dolphin brain, Lilly claimed, was as complex as ours and its size and weight even larger (1,700 grams to Universal Dolphin versus only 1,450 grams to Universal Man).

While mapping, as he called it, the brain of test animal Number 6 of the series, Lilly suddenly made an astonishing discovery, one so momentous that it prompted him to give up his governmental job at the Institute of

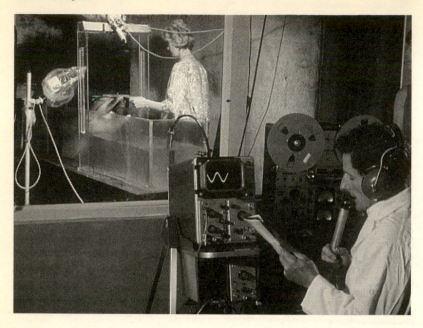

PLATE 8.1 'Can Man and Dolphin communicate? Dr. Lilly "talks" with a flippered student in a sound-proof room at his Communication Research Institute in Florida.' (Text and photo from *National Geographic*, vol. 130: 3, Sept. 1966. Courtesy Thomas Nebbia/NGS Image Collection.)

Mental Health and open his Communication Research Institute in the Virgin Islands, a place aptly named for this task of exploration. From Number 6 he had learned that dolphins could be taught to speak English!

Evidently, the doctor's expectations of such interspecies communication were numerous. Apart from preparing mankind for an encounter with extraterrestrials in space, the establishment of a dialogue with these animals might also lead to a much-needed improvement in the communication between man and woman (Lilly 1967: 98). This advance, which was added half-jokingly to the list, revealed Lilly's idea that dolphins connoted femininity. Moreover, the intelligible voice of the dolphin would severely dent, if not destroy for ever, anthropocentrism. No longer would man exclusively occupy the top rung of the evolutionary ladder. As alluded to in our third amazing story, Lilly, as a budding New Ager, probably liked to think that the position of Universal Man of Rational Science might be challenged by the subversive role of a jester or trickster, appearing as a speaking dolphin, and conveying messages (in English!) from an unknown world.

In spite of Lilly's extravagantly imaginative ways of phrasing research questions, his first attempts to communicate with dolphins were conducted on traditional scientific grounds. The goal was an expedition into the dolphin's skull, and the means was a laboratory experiment reminiscent of those conducted by Pavlov on his famous dogs. But even as he reduced the animals to harnessed beast-machines, Lilly hoped to find more or less the opposite, namely, intelligent and quasi-human subjects. In all its contra-dictory ghastliness the story of Lilly's initial reinvention of the dolphin as 'English-speaking' cyborg deserves to be retold.

Having lost five animals using full anaesthesia (making the scientific discovery that dolphins die when they are anaesthetized because their breathing is under voluntary control), the doctor chose a different approach to Number 6. After restraining the dolphin by inserting its beak into a hole in a board, so that it could move only five to eight centimetres, and after injecting a local anaesthetic into its head, he used a carpenter's hammer to knock a sleeve guide (a kind of hollow needle), about 30 millimetres into the animal's head. Through this sleeve guide, and through the skin, blubber and muscles, electrodes were placed into the brain and 'the long, slow and patient examination of this huge brain by electrical stimuli' was begun. The idea of the electrodes was, in Lilly's clinical discourse, to have 'push-button control of the experience of specific emotions by animals in whose brains we have placed wires in the proper places' (Lilly 1962a: 34).

By locating the areas of the brain that responded to the electric current with either positive or negative emotions – i.e. with pleasure or pain – the 'human operator' could provoke intensely rewarding or intensely punishing experiences in the animal or, for that matter, in humans on whom the method was also used. In Number 6, Lilly was trying to pinpoint the pleasure centre. If activated, the animal might become so thrilled that it took 'control' and pushed the switch itself. Thus Lilly could not only test his intelligence (Number 6 was a male), but speed up the learning process as well. In this case, the electric current was the carrot. In the next test, using dolphin Number 7, a female labelled by the doctor as a 'real cry-baby', the method of punishing stimuli was used. The 'cry-baby' had to operate the switch to shut off the punishment. (Both dolphins quickly learned the trick; both died.)

Lilly's 'discovery' of dolphins' linguistic abilities took place as part of his work with animal Number 6. After the electrodes had been slowly, very slowly, forced down from 30 to about 60 millimetres into the brain, the dolphin started responding violently. Aside from moving around restlessly in his restraints, he vocalized in 'dolphinese', emitting whistles, buzzings, barks and other noises, the meaning of which struck the doctor later, when he replayed his tape recordings. Listening to the tapes, he felt certain that the dolphin, in a Donald Duck kind of way, had been mimicking human laughter as well as some of the technical data he, the doctor, had recited during the experiment. This became especially clear, the scientist claimed, when the tapes were slowed down to half or one-quarter speed.

After this, Lilly felt that he had good reason to advocate interspecies communication through what he called an 'education in humanity' (Lilly 1962a: 166) of the other. Sponsored by agencies like NASA, the US Navy and Air Force and the National Science Foundation, Lilly optimistically continued the project (with and without electrodes) until 1968, when the funding finally dried up, and he himself allegedly came to realize that he had been imprisoning his friends, the dolphins, in a 'concentration camp'. Revolting against the intrusions into their brains, five animals had committed suicide by refusing to eat or breathe. Lilly then set the remaining three free and gave up his research (Lilly 1973: 70).[2]

Lilly's discourses are unsettled by displacements. On the one hand, they are deeply embedded in a mechanistic scientific paradigm; 'nature' must unveil her secrets on the doctor's agonizing terms. But, on the other, Lilly tells a story of a nature of extraterrestrial origin, which appears to him as in a cyber-sacral revelation. Dressed up as cyborg with wires in the proper places, this embodiment of 'wild', non-terrestrial nature discloses a huge brain and a strong desire for communication with scientific man himself. In reinvented nature's new porpoise consciousness, purpose and higher meanings also expose themselves. Properly (re-)constructed by the scientist, the recorded and slowly replayed voice of the cyborg dolphin apparently articulates a highly intelligent, advanced and communicative alien mind. Nevertheless, enigmatic questions remained. Had the serious master of science, supposedly in control of his beast-machine, been controlled by a trickster, a laughing monster, who had carnivalized the very concept of communication? Or was he confronted with an incarnation of a divine extraterrestrial intelligence in relation to whom he was but a small child – much as the dolphin, seemingly babbling his first English words, was but an infant *vis-à-vis* the scientist? Such questions obviously stirred the mind of Lilly as well as those of his fans.

Elite Scientists on a Cyborg Dolphin: Cosmic Encounters

As we saw in Chapter 7, cosmology underwent radical changes during the 1950s. From a silent, desert void, the cosmos was transformed into a broadcasting universe, filled with life and intelligent ETs who, like the dolphins, were eager to open up communications with humankind. Analogies between the construction of dolphin and alien mind, as well as the fact that Lilly's 'discoveries' coincided with the initial phase of the scientific search for extraterrestrial intelligence, gave rise to the construction of the animals as boundary-figures between scientific man and the cosmic aliens.

The physicist Philip Morrison who, like Szilard, had participated in the Manhattan Project, and who co-authored the article (Cocconi and Morrison 1959) that started the scientific quest for otherworldly beings, maintained that an ancient, highly advanced society of superior aliens had for years been patiently waiting for planet Earth to enter into the cosmic communication system by picking up the intelligent signals they were transmitting from space. Such signals would not only indicate that technology did not inevitably lead to global self-destruction, but would also give mankind access to the inexhaustible source of wisdom and knowledge that the 'remote philosophers' (Morrison 1962) of the cosmic ocean possessed.

A universe filled with highly intelligent, civilized aliens became part of the scientific imagination from then on, and in anticipation of the coming encounter, the media reported diligently on the new horizons opening to mankind. As if leading up to the climax of 21 June 1960, when the sensational news of Lilly's 'English-speaking' dolphins caught the imagination of the press, several stories on communication with aliens were reported during the spring of that year.

'Tuning in on Other Worlds. If civilized beings exist in space, a project now beginning may permit us to communicate with them,' reads a headline in the *New York Times* (13 March 1960); the said project, 'Ozma', was to take place at the US National Radio Astronomy Observatory and to be headed by the radio astronomer Frank Drake. Not surprisingly, the article, written by a chief missiles adviser to the Intelligence Department of the Army, strongly favoured the idea of 'listening for the voices of the "others"'. In undertaking this enterprise, he suggested, we might become the equals of possibly existing 'astropolitan' communities, 'linked together by a wonderful commerce of communication'. The new commodity, well suited to interstellar commerce, was information.

Professor R. N. Bracewell of Stanford University, California, put forward the idea that an 'ancient association', consisting of civilizations 'incredibly more advanced' than our own, might already have launched a satellite into orbit around the sun, trying to make contact with us (*New York Times*, 20 June 1960). The report describing Bracewell's alien messenger in the sky was published on the front page of the newspaper just one day before it introduced Lilly's intelligent, and perhaps superior, dolphins.

So the images of divine and helpful super-civilizations and of the friendly, talking dolphins began to merge in both the scientific and public mind. Both involved notions of interspecies communication and of receiving information that could solve almost all of humanity's problems.

The crowning event, which once and for all placed on record the connection between the narratives of dolphins and cosmic ETs, was the first conference ever held on extraterrestrial intelligence. It opened on 1 November 1961, at the Green Bank Observatory in West Virginia. Fewer than a dozen scientists were invited to participate, some of them very prominent; one, Melvin Calvin, was awarded the Nobel Prize for Chemistry during his stay. The organizers intended that the exclusive selection of participants would ensure the expertise needed for a thorough scientific discussion of the cosmic connection.

As the one expert who had, more or less, spoken with an ET, Lilly was invited to this conference. In his presentation, he played the tapes of the 'English'-speaking dolphins and talked about the social attitude of these animals, which helped and took care both of each other and of humans in distress. Since the USA was deeply concerned about the threats of Red Communism, Lilly did not forget to mention the possible military uses of these speedy sea animals. The dolphins could rescue pilots from planes crashed into the open ocean, scout out enemy submarines, serve as detection-proof delivery systems for nuclear warheads to be detonated in foreign harbours, and so on. Having learned English, Lilly suggested, the animals might also 'sneak up on an enemy submarine sitting on the bottom of the sea and shout something into the listening gear, as if this were a human communicating with them' (Lilly 1962a: 168–9). (Oh, boy, would that frighten the Red bastards!) 'We were all totally enthralled by these reports,' the host of the conference, Frank Drake, recalls. 'We felt some of the excitement in store for us when we encounter nonhuman intelligence of extraterrestrial origin' (Drake and Sobel 1992: 58).

So thrilled and captivated were the participants by this representation of the dolphin that, at the termination of the conference, they formed a kind of brotherhood or lodge and christened it 'The Order of the Dolphin'. Over the following years, a few other prominent scientists involved in the search for extraterrestrial intelligence were admitted (among others, the Soviet astrophysicist I. S. Shklovsky). From the new Nobel laureate Calvin, each of the human 'dolphins' received a silver tie pin as an emblem of membership; it was a reproduction of an old Greek coin showing a boy on a dolphin.

What does the emblem signify? First, the picture of the boy on the dolphin identified the man of science, searching for intelligence, with the ancient dolphin boy, Apollo, whose transformation into a dolphin or whose ride on the back of the animal is, as already mentioned, culturally associated with both the founding of Delphi and with the rise of the sun, i.e. a new, bright civilization being born from the womb of the sea. Second, it also connected scientific man on a dolphin with the gigantic space programme, the Apollo Project, which Kennedy had launched less than six months earlier (25 May), in order to beat the Soviets to the Moon and re-establish the technoscientific image of the USA, which had been so badly hurt by the *Sputniks* and Gagarin's recent flight. And, third, behind the Apollo(s) on the profit-promising coin, the dolphin beckons as a carrier of displacements and shifting significances, blending the parallel formation of a grim and beastly rocket state and a mythic, smiling and humane dolphin state with images of divinely intelligent extraterrestrial aliens engaged in beaming down data-streams of wisdom to a globe in distress. Like the oracular utterances of the Delphian dolphin, Pythia, this information would be obscure and encrypted until decoded. But was such decoding not exactly what Lilly had been doing when he slowed down the tapes and suddenly caught the message of test animal Number 6? The decoding would hardly offer any problem.

If so, the cosmic aliens might perhaps teach us the equivalent of dolphinese: 'There might be an attention-getting signal,' Morrison said, according to the *New York Times*, 'followed by a "language lesson" and then the equivalent of one volume of an encyclopaedia. This would be followed by further calling, a further lesson, and another volume, and so forth' (4 February 1962).

Cohabitation in a Flooded House

We have now seen how Lilly's initial construction of a modern dolphin myth caused the animal to go through several displacements, acting as a substitute for both man of science and his extraterrestrial and quasi-divine mirror image, the distant high-tech alien. But at this stage in Lilly's narrative, an excess of meanings marked its presence due to the boundary function of the signifier. Something did not fit; something continuously kept the discourse from stabilizing itself into a master narrative of elite scientists on a cyborg dolphin in close encounter with galactic super-civilizations. The dolphin did not properly mirror the man of science, however small and primitive he might be compared to a godlike, alien scientist, nor did it merge completely into the image of the galactic Cyber-Godfather. On the contrary, an unpleasant question kept popping up in the minds of our scientists, fixated as they were on the network of meanings circulating between Technology-Science-Modernity-Whiteness-Masculin-ity: how could the dolphin, lacking manipulative hands and, consequently, tools, represent a technological civilization, not to mention a quasi-divine, cosmic super-civilization? With nothing but flippers, the animal was clearly unable to build the radio telescopes necessary for either listening to or transmitting signals through space. Moreover, it seemed unlikely to the scientists that the 'superior intelligence' of the dolphin had developed in the primordial and motherly womb of the ocean so, as a highly intelligent sea creature, the animal became something of an oxymoron. In its feature on the Green Bank Conference, the *New York Times* summarized the problem in the following way: 'It is possible that their superior intelligence is a heritage of their life ashore. Hence it may be that such intelligence would not arise on a completely oceanic planet' (4 February 1962). Some scientists tried to bypass the problems by suggesting that dolphins might develop 'a technological society if given sufficient time' (Cameron 1963: 312). Evid-ently, such a long-term perspective could not save the day for the dolphin fans: 'her' lack, 'her' missing link, and 'her' contiguities with a wet motherly origin were too obvious, too present, too disturbing.

The dolphins did not quite fit into the patterns surrounding the almighty Cyber-Godfather. Consequently, another narrative strand came to the fore, one that had already been suggested by the words about civilizing dolphins, the 'education in humanity', which Lilly had used in his first book. In this narrative, the discourses of non-white ethnicity, femininity and childishness dominate, reversing the dolphin's representation as the man of science and his great omnipotent *alter ego*, the Cyber-Godfather. Instead of acting as messenger from a high-tech future, 'she' becomes a figure of a premodern past, bound in a state of primary orality, from which modern man, the man of science, has separated himself:

> [M]an is said to be the most intelligent species because of what he does with his huge brain. May there not be other paths for large brains to take, especi-ally if they live immersed in some other element than air? ...
>
> In the case of the Cetacea which are without the benefit of hands or outside constructions of any sort [*sic*!], they may have taken the path of legends and verbal traditions rather than that of written records. (Lilly 1962a: 95)

Forgetting the flippers, Lilly focused instead on the sexual ambiguity of the dolphin body, the missing visible representation of phallic potency, as well as on the cluster of primary orality to which its oceanic environment seems to limit it. Having been transformed into a representation of non-phallic Woman, the dolphin, however, vocalizes not only its own lack of technological tools, but also the non-technological innocence of primary oral cultures from which scientific man is forever sundered. Here, legends and dreamtime, rather than technology, were thought to define existence.

This implied shift of perspective inspired Lilly to try out a new model of communication, which also seemed necessary because the electronic devices (i.e. the electrodes) with which he had tried to erase the divide between his world and the enigmatic world of the dolphins did not result in establishing the much-desired connection between the species. Instead of attempting to make contact exclusively within a context of secondary orality, fit for the communication between man of science and the super-intelligent cosmic Cyber-Godfather, Lilly shifted to an approach based on primary orality (which, however, did not exclude extensive use of technical listening devices).

Taking as his paradigm a human mother–child model for teaching and learning on terms as equal as possible, Lilly redesigned his experimental setting. The dolphin was positioned as the infant, while the scientist was vicariously represented by a nurturing virgin-mother. Day and night, for a long period, the human 'mother' and the dolphin 'child' were to live together in a home which, neither terrestrial nor extraterrestrial, transgressed the normal boundaries between land and sea. Part of the building of the Communication Research Institute in the Virgin Islands was flooded with seawater 56 centimetres deep in order to carry out an experiment in 'wet live-in'.

After various introductory experiments in interspecies cohabitation, the definitive 'flooded-house programme' commenced in the summer of 1965 and lasted for two and a half months. The plan was to develop it into a more permanent 'man–dolphin' habitat, where the dolphin would be able to come and 'go' as a genuine member of a human family.

Evidently the respective agents of nature and culture were chosen because of their displaced representations, the dolphin for its brains, which in the minds of the scientists differentiated it from its wet, motherly environment, and the woman for her soft and oceanic nature, different from the image of scientific man. But what set them apart from their parental context was, of course, precisely what united them in the encounter zone of their flooded home.

Embodying the location of innocence, the Virgin Islands, a young and virginal mermaid, Margaret Howe, played the part of the (single) mother, educating the dolphin-child and vacuum-cleaning the house while wading in seawater up to her knees. By contrast, Lilly's role was that of a very distant father, absorbed in his own processes of transformation from man of science to New Ager. Spending most of his time hallucinating on LSD in a self-constructed water tank (as if playing a dolphin himself), and investigating mind-links to cosmic civilizations, he rarely visited the project. Thus there was nobody to intervene in the dyad between Peter Dolphin and Margaret Mermaid.

For a time, Margaret had wavered about whom to choose for the role of baby, the young and vigorous Peter Dolphin or the reserved Pamela with the good pronunciation. Pronunciation was important, for Margaret had solemnly pledged that 'no matter how long it takes, no matter how much work, *this dolphin is going to learn to speak English!*' (Lilly 1967: 218). But as Pam was shy with humans, having been speared several times by a diver in the second *Flipper* movie, Margaret finally settled on the outgoing Peter, a choice that she came to regret when she discovered the implications.

Apart from the fact that his pronunciation never reached Pam's level, Margaret suddenly found that, as she wrote in her diary, she became the 'other dolphin' in Peter's life (Lilly 1967: 267), i.e. the object of his sexual desires. As he began to open his slits, his mouth containing 88 very sharp teeth, 'still capable of drawing blood' (Lilly 1967: 278), and the genital slit to reveal his erect penis, the spell of innocent interconnectedness was somewhat broken. Though she was terrified at first, she realized that Peter's education in humanity must be paralleled by her education in dolphinity, and she therefore succumbed to 'lusty, little Peter' and his clever tricks of wooing. In Margaret's account, the dolphin gradually and intelligently began to change from a wild animal, who tried to rape her, into a seductive gentleman, who gently ran his full set of teeth up and down her legs in order to arouse her. 'Peter led the way,' she claims, and she satisfied his sexual desires by masturbating him (Lilly 1967: 278). As she became his dolphin, so he became her man/husband.

After the experiment, Lilly informs us, Margaret, 'like the girl [*sic*!] with the chimpanzees in Africa, married her photographer' (Lilly 1967: 300) (an epidemic?), and started a (new) family. The role model referred to was Jane Goodall, who conducted research in 'the wilds of Tanzania' (Haraway 1989: 136). But, unlike Goodall, who began graduate work at Cambridge early in her field studies and eventually took a doctorate, Margaret Howe retained her intellectual innocence during the entire experiment of wet live-in. She originally got the job by chance. While working as a hostess at a remote mountain-top restaurant in the Virgin Islands, she entered into a conversation with one of the guests, Carl Sagan, the astronomer and ardent hunter for extraterrestrial intelligence, who was visiting Lilly's laboratory. As she complained of her uneventful and uninteresting days (she was hostess only at night), Sagan introduced her to the interdisciplinary researcher, George Bateson, who at that time was in charge of Lilly's laboratory, and 'soon Margaret was working with dolphins' (Sagan 1975: 174). That was in early 1964. Sixteen months later, she became director of the laboratory herself and entered into the mothering/marrying arrangement with Peter D. Up until that time, 'she had seen dolphins once briefly in a Florida dolphin circus' (Lilly 1967: 227). As Bateson soon left, and Lilly was busy hallucinating in his isolation tank, the realization of the ambitious flooded-house programme came to depend almost exclusively on her.

Without the intellectual 'burdens' of a scientific education, Margaret Howe seemed, in the discursive universe of the involved scientists, perfectly suited for the precast role of mediating link in the narrative of communication between man of science and his 'naïve' non-human other. 'Undisturbed' by the training of rationality, Woman could more easily bond with intellectually 'innocent' Nature.

The amazing story has cast long shadows. Apart from being retold by Lilly (1967), and science fictionalized by Mooney (1983) and Grimwood (1996), it was also recorded on tapes that are still marketed for sale, while appetizing samples of the sound-tracks may be downloaded from the virtual reality environment of the internet. So it is still possible to enjoy, live, Margaret's English lessons with Peter D., and to hear the endless repetitions of 'conversations' such as: 'Say hello to Margaret, Peter' – 'squeak, squeak, click, click'. In 1994, thirty years after the flooded-house romance, there was even a CD released to commemorate the event. In its own uncanny way, this CD mirrors how the traditionally gendered family roles and the instrumentalization of the animal in the cult celebrations of the *cogito* of scientific man were re-enacted in the otherwise non-traditional setting of the wet live-in. On this CD, Lilly, now fully transformed into a New Ager, teaches a muted audience to meditate by repeating the word 'cogitate'. Monotonously, for half an hour, an untiring Lilly enunciates his 'cogitate' as if obsessed by a desire to invoke the ghost of the Cartesian *cogito*; rather abruptly, the CD then shifts to the mother–child scene in the flooded house. Accompanied by the splashing sounds of moving bodies in shallow water, Margaret tries, over and over, with motherly persuasion in her voice, to teach Peter to pronounce the word 'humanoid' (Lilly 1994). Strangely enough, his only response is a persistent squeak.

From Cyborg to Noble Savage

Even though the story of Margaret and Peter unfolded within the discursive framework of an 'educational' programme that aimed at adapting the dolphin to human standards, it is at the same time also a boundary-tale that sets the stage for a shift of focus to another strand of narratives. The formation of an encounter zone between the two worlds of culture/science and watery nature and the turn towards primary orality as a model for interspecies communication evoke a different dolphin icon than the cyborg paradigm that directed Lilly's first script.

The noble savage dolphin that also grew out of Lilly's comprehensive script – a script that appears to be as polysemantic as its dolphin protagonist – links the icon to the values of counterculture, of environmental movements like Greenpeace, and to New Age thought in general. In these discourses, the 'lack' of the dolphin, its inability to manipulate nature through technology, is no longer a disadvantage, but a virtue.

An astrology-oriented psychoanalyst and New Age scholar, Ralph Metzner, whom we interviewed in San Francisco in 1994, summarized the arguments of these trends by clearly contrasting the human-with-a-thumb and the dolphin-without-a-thumb. Having been very prominent in the consciousness-raising counterculture of the 1960s, Metzner is today deeply occupied with the development of a new ecological consciousness. Whales and dolphins have bigger brains than humans, he argues, yet these mammals are beautifully adapted to their natural environment. The trouble with humankind, therefore, originates in the combination of brain and opposable thumb: 'Because with the opposable thumb you can make stuff. You can make tools, weapons, and manipulate your environment, and the whales and dolphins don't do that.'

Combined with its intelligence, healing powers and joyfulness, the sea creature's environmental non-interference and Gandhi-like 'policy' of non-violence has, since the 1960s, made it into a perfect symbol of a world of peace and green politics, a dolphin state or 'Whale Nation' (Williams 1988), which in the East was associated with the spirit of 'socialism with a human face' and in the West with slogans such as 'Make Love, Not War'. We shall now take a closer look at the iconographies of this dolphin in Russia and the USA.

Socialism with a Dolphin Face

A Soviet version of the post-Second World War dolphin was, in its own way, linked to the search for new sociocultural values and for counterimages to Cold War ideologies in general and Stalinism in particular. The ethically minded, speaking dolphin swam into the public Soviet pool in 1962. In this year, the largest popular scientific magazine in the Soviet Union, *Nauka i zhizn*, boldly published an article, written by Lilly, bearing the startling and provocative title: 'How I Learned to Speak with my Dolphins' (Lilly 1962b). The article described Lilly's work to the amazed Soviet public. In 1965, an abridged version of Lilly's first book (1962a) was translated into Russian. Before long, the mouthpiece of the Soviet government, *Izvestia*, featured the new dolphins as 'our true sea brothers' with brains so 'strikingly close to our own'. Painted in nuances that were easily recognizable as communist virtues, the newspaper's dolphin turned out to be an ideal, peace-loving and helpful comrade with very high morals: 'Characteristic of the dolphins is a feeling of comradeship; they are unselfish in their relations to each other and always rush to help at the first call, even at the risk of their own lives' (*Izvestia*, 13 March 1966). The article also reported scientific expectations of imminent communication with the sea mammals, first in dolphinese and later probably in Russian. Not surprisingly, at the same time, a moratorium was announced in the Soviet Union on the catching and killing of dolphins for anything other than 'scientific' (i.e. military) purposes.

Following the introduction of the talking dolphin, the marine mammal became the battleground on which, for some two decades, Soviet scientists fought over the intriguing question: who is really the most human, man or the gentle dolphin? This apparently strictly scientific controversy was in fact a displaced outlet for a deeply political debate on questions of continiuty or change: should socialism be built on hard, authoritarian values or on soft, democratic ones? On one side, the old conservative establishment claimed the indisputable superiority of Man, citing his ability to speak and think in abstract and symbolic terms, and relying on the scientific authority of the famous Russian physiologist Ivan Pavlov, whose theories had been enthusiastically embraced by Stalin. According to these neo-Pavlovians, there was nothing special about dolphins; they were mere instinctual beast-machines and could not in any way compete with the superior mind of man. As one elderly neo-Pavlovian asserted, the animal's huge brain was just the result of its adaptation to the special environment of the sea. Lacking speech, human brains and, hence, technology, this mammal – like all other animals – was solely in the grip of blind, mechanical instincts: 'The activities of man subjugate nature, whilst dolphins, as any other animal, are subjected to nature to which they adapt' (Tomilin 1969: 102). Insisting on the inferiority of the dolphin brain in all respects, another

PLATE 8.2 The Soviet Russian vision of socialism with a dolphin face:
a civilization of caring grandmothers (*source*: Belkovich et al. 1967).

neo–Pavlovian dismissed the whole issue as a storm in the teacup of popular science. 'What should the dolphin really think with?' this scientist asked rhetorically, making the huge marine mammal brain vanish as an illusion (Kesarev 1968, 1971). Faithful to the basic doctrines of their old mentor, Pavlov, and his constructions of dogs as beast-machines, to these life scientists the dolphin was nothing more than a machine designed to serve Scientific Man; see, for instance, the title of Tomilin's book, *Dolphins Serve Man* (1969); see also Tomilin 1965 and 1980; Voronin 1970; Panov 1980.

On the other side of the debate, these conservative echoes of Stalinism were countered by a few, mostly younger, biologists to whom the Pavlovian paradigm seemed both dangerous and outmoded. They insisted on the superiority not of Man, but of the Dolphin. In their view, man, and perhaps especially Soviet man, was implicitly the one who lacked all dolphin virtues: collectivity, non-aggressiveness, culture, wisdom, memory of the past, and harmony with the environment. The most persistent dolphin fan among these scientists was the young Aleksei Yablokov (b. 1933) who, many years later, became president of the national Greenpeace organization and deputy chairman of the committee of the Supreme Soviet on ecology. Subsequently, he was appointed chief adviser to President Yeltsin on environmental issues.

An important mission of the supporters of the 'intellectuals of the sea', as the anti-Pavlovians once called dolphins (Belkovich et al. 1965, 1967), was clearly to lay out an alternative, political strategy for Soviet civilization, encrypted in an Aesopian metaphor – i.e. in a seemingly strictly scientific discussion of animal biology.[3] Instead of a doggy state of authoritarian Pavlovian beast-machines, the anti-Pavlovians advocated a society built on 'soft' dolphin values such as kindness, helpfulness, peace, wisdom and true collectivity.

Among the striking features of the kind, peaceful dolphin state described by Yablokov and his colleagues, V. Belkovich and S. Kleinenberg, in their popular science books (1965 and 1967) were the astonishing cultural, emotional and ethical bonds holding the animal community together. Even more striking, perhaps, was the scientists' claim that this bonding was due to nothing less than a 'grandmammyfication' of dolphin society. The foundation of this community, the authors claimed, was the family, tied together by strong emotions and always headed by the mother alone. Reaching sexual maturity very early, a female dolphin could give birth to as many as ten young during her lifetime. This reproductive pattern would inevitably result in the rapid creation of grandmothers in the dolphin herd, since the female offspring would reproduce just as quickly as their mothers. The outcome would be a large, extended family of at least eleven generations of simultaneous daughters-mothers-grandmothers, with the oldest and, as it were, primordial (great, great, etc. grand) mother at the top (see Plate 8.2).

According to the anti-Pavlovians, this grandmammyfication created a marvellous dolphin culture, since the 'living memory of the ancestors' was always present. The collective memory of the dolphins was compared to an enormous library, reinforcing the image of the animals as naturally talented intellectuals who stored up the traditional wisdom of oral literature and legends in their huge brains. For even if they allegedly possessed the equivalent of libraries, in physical terms of course they had no books, no technology, nothing of the technological culture that man, the scientists stated, had been forced to invent in order to compensate for his imperfect, underdeveloped organism. So, in the displaced view of these scientists, the dolphin might well feel superior to man. 'Humans', their dolphin matriarch regretfully sighed, 'do not understand the meaning of life. They try with raw force to subjugate nature' (Belkovich et al. 1967: 325). In contrast, the dolphins themselves had it all in their bodily nature and in their minds. As superior beings, they were endowed not only with a fantastic memory, but with supranatural gifts, resulting in telepathic control over their environment. By a mere act of will power, they could order hostile sharks away, or paralyse their prey so that their working day was reduced to only a few hours.

In this scientific narrative, the dolphin fully matches the definition of the noble savage. The dolphin community is posited as a Golden Age phenomenon upon which to project the dreams, desires and Utopian hopes of members of the Soviet sixties generation. As is so often the case in stories concerning the paradoxical figure of the noble savage, the meanings inscribed onto this Soviet dolphin circulate around concepts of Woman–Native–Nature, engendering a textual web of mellow metaphors to counter the harsh imagery of authoritarian Pavlovism–Stalinism. The books certainly gave the impression that a highly developed, matriarchal and otherworldly dolphin civilization already existed, characterized by little work and much pleasure. A happy, playful, educated and spiritual dolphin community well suited, perhaps, to replace both the beast-machine and the austere, terrifying grandfather society of yesterday.

The Noble Savage of the New Age

Mingling with the countercultural dolphin are explicit tendencies to sacralize it and merge it with images of indigenous peoples that reinforce its revitalization of the romantic noble savage tradition. In this section, we shall unfold three examples. Encircling the planet from the Far West to the Far East, the stories reveal the global character of the search for the wisdom in the water that the dolphin and whale nation came to represent. But, in transit, the viewpoint of the whole story-line undergoes a change; the gaze shifts from the outside to that from within: from watching the cetaceans from a North American perspective, we end up looking at the world through the eyes of a Siberian ex-whale.

The early history of Greenpeace demonstrates the construction of cetaceans as symbols of a narrative that weaves together the struggle for green politics and peace – a narrative that is reflected in the name of the organization, 'green peace'. The adoption of this name coincided with the first Save the Whales campaigns, which also marked a certain embracing of New Age values and trends to reconstruct nature as sacred. Begun in the mid-1970s as a movement against nuclear testing, Greenpeace turned its focus to the campaign for a moratorium on whaling. At that time, the organization directed the attention of the world's press to the whaling issue through an international Save the Whales campaign, which included dramatic confrontations on the open sea with Russian industrial whalers. During the previous years the movement had become split between groups in favour of the anti-nuclear strategy and others who instead pointed to the anti-whaling issue. With the 1975 campaign, the whale lobby won and, as if coloured by its target, the very style of the organization changed; its focus shifted from confronting the gloomy death world of the rocket state to defending the joyful, countercultural, mysterious, green-blue life world of the 'nation of armless Buddhas', as whales were dubbed by the journalist Robert Hunter, one of the Greenpeace activists who played a leading role in the first Save the Whales campaign (Hunter 1980: 135). This is how Hunter describes the meeting that launched the 1975 campaign and the shift in mood of the organization that the whale issue mediated:

> The heavy atmosphere of moralistic purity that had pervaded almost every single anti-nuclear meeting we had had over the years was gone. There had been nothing much to celebrate so long as we were opposing bombs. It was a very negative game. But now, instead of simply fighting death, we were embracing life. It was not just that we wanted to save Whales, we wanted to meet them, we wanted to encourage them, encounter them, touch them, discover them. For the first time there was a transcendent element lying at the centre of the undertaking. There was a Holy Grail. (ibid.: 153)

As the final part of this quote suggests, New Age mysticism became part of the new cetacean story, and so did indigenous peoples, whose knowledges were celebrated for their alternative relationship to whales and to Nature. As logo for its Save the Whales campaign, Greenpeace adopted an ancient totem symbol from a Native American seafaring tribe, the Kwakiutls, showing a green crest formed by two whales that represents the infinite cycle of nature. This image, said to symbolize the Kwakiutls' desire to live in harmony with nature, has since been painted on many Greenpeace ships.

Celebration of indigenous wisdom as part of the cetacean narratives has participated forcefully in the construction of the animals as wise and noble savages since the early Greenpeace campaigns. In an example from the 1990s, Kim Kindersley's video trailer *Eyes of the Soul* (Kindersley undated), we witness a complete merging of the two icons of unblemished, edenic and wise 'nature': the dolphin and the aboriginal. The introductory poem, urging the alienated audience from the fallen civilized world to return to sacred nature, may serve as an illustration of the trivializing rhetoric that sometimes takes over in these kinds of narratives:

> Sweet is the law which nature brings
> our meddling intellect
> misshapes the beauty as formed things
> we murder to dissect
> enough of science and of art
> close up those barren leaves
> come forward and bring with you a heart
> that watches and receives
>
> (Kindersley undated)

Finally, this strong trend towards merging the icons of cetaceans and indigenous peoples as symbols of a 'pure' and 'natural' alternative wisdom has also been voiced in the distant regions of Siberia. In Yuri Rytkheu's story, *When the Whales Leave* (1977), a myth of human descent from whales is reclaimed as part of the cultural heritage of the 'small people', the Chukchi, who live on the peninsula facing Alaska.

Like the poem that provides the keynote of the *Eyes of the Soul* video, Rytkheu's book constructs a pronounced opposition between civilized technoculture on the one hand and the original state of oneness between human and nature on the other. The novel tells an ancient origin myth of the Chukchi, the indigenous tribal people inhabiting the remote north-eastern part of Siberia. The myth features a woman, the first human in the world. She falls in love with a whale whom her emotions transform into a man. From this original human–whale love descends the whole of the human race. As time goes by, however, the humans forget their kinship with the whales and begin to hunt them, disregarding the ancient tale that still warns against the slaughter of their totem animal, the whale.

Rytkheu not only recycles the myth, but reworks it into a story against the repressive Soviet technocivilization. Implicitly, yet unmistakably, the novel draws a parallel between the slaughter of whales by the alienated humans who have forgotten their sacred consanguineous relationship to the whales, and the Soviet repression of the indigenous peoples of Siberia. Opposing alienated modern technoculture with an original Eden, where whales and humans embrace each other in loving oneness, this novel bears many resemblances to such Western New Age versions of the noble savage dolphin and whale story as the *Eyes of the Soul* video represents. However, being an ethnic other himself, Rytkheu rewrites the whale legend from a personal perspective. This allows him to avoid the trap of ventriloquism (Haraway 1992: 311–12) of the white, middle-class people who act as narrators on the video, instructing their middle-class audience about the proper relationship to the innocent paradise of ethnic and animal others, which the visuals put on display.

As a Chukchi, Rytkheu (b. 1930) knows the traditional lifestyle and oral traditions of his people from his childhood. But, as a Russianized writer, he also knows by experience what it meant to conform to the condescending Soviet Russian attitude to the oral traditions of the indigenous peoples of Siberia. Together with other writers of non-white origins, he willingly performed as one of 'the first "native sons" who was used by the Party to promote the official view of a successful "leap from the stone age into socialism"' (Barker 1993: 217). *When the Whales Leave* can therefore also be interpreted as Rytkheu's re-evaluation of his own story, as a reflective resistance to his own 'education in Soviet humanity'. In this version, the slaughter of whales is a symbol of his Fall, i.e. his severing of the bonds to the culture of his kin in order to adapt to Soviet society, and the novel his penance for this original sin.

The Dolphin in a *Perpetuum Mobile* of Circulating Meanings

Having followed the cetacean icon from kamikaze soldier to harbinger of peace and socialism with a dolphin face, from English-speaking cyborg, messenger from the cosmic Cyber-Godfather, through child–lover–pupil in a flooded house, to whales and dolphins mediating the forgotten wisdom of 'pure' nature, the fluidity of the signifier should have become clear. We may well appoint dolphins, together with their whale cousins, to be excellent representatives of what Derrida called *différance*, and described as an endless chain of displacements that, he said, could be evoked by such floating signifiers as, for example, 'Woman' (Derrida 1979, 1987). It is easy to draw parallels between the cetaceans' amazing iconographic performances as quick-change artists and the never-ending metamorphoses and surprising moves of 'undecidables' like 'Woman'. Both seem to produce an excess of meanings that surface forcefully whenever the signifier has apparently been fixed within one narrative strand.

We shall close our story of the dolphin icon's never-ending process of displacements by looking at the excess meanings that pop up in the New

Age master narrative of humans merging with the 'pure' natural world of the noble savage dolphin – which switch us from an apparently primordial and pre-technological Eden into the high-tech age of the twenty-first century. As an illustration, we will refer to the American New Age delphinologist, Joan Ocean, whose vision of dolphins as beamed down from outer space we presented in Chapter 7.

Ocean situates the dolphin between a pre-tech and a high-tech world, and mirrors the New Age ambiguities that we traced in our initial analysis of McCulloch's picture in the Prelude. In her book, with the significant title *Dolphins into the Future* (1997), Ocean merges stories of the wise dolphin as noble savage, with whom humans desire to enter into a mystical unity, and the dolphin as harbinger of a cosmic high-tech world that, she believes, is so advanced in comparison to our own that it might frighten and upset us to encounter the full reality of it (ibid.: 156).

On one level, Ocean articulates a radical 'return to nature' attitude. Her highest ambition is to become one with the wild spinner dolphins, with whom she has been living and swimming for hours almost every day over a period of eight years (1989–97); this timespan is covered by the diary entries that make up the main body of the book. Through these journals, Ocean tells the story of how, guided by the advice of an alien spirit, Arcturus, she moved to Hawaii (ibid.: 153) in order to undertake an experiment in 'wet live-in' far more radical than that of Margaret Howe and Peter Dolphin. In a complete reversal of the 'education in humanity' approach of Margaret and Peter, Ocean commits herself to a thoroughgoing 'education in dolphinity'. In her story, she is the child and the wild dolphins the parents. 'I am like a child in their family, a new student in their school of wisdom,' she relates (ibid.: 128).

Accordingly, the method she applies to reach the desired oneness with the wild dolphins is to act as a human child does towards its parents, i.e. learning by imitation. She swims with the dolphins, dives with them, sends out sounds like them, tries to figure out what they think, etc. She relates that what made her feel most honoured was the first time the dolphins accepted her as a regular member of their pod:

> I remember feeling something different about our swim that morning. One moment I was on the outside, the next I was one of them, a member of their pod … On this morning I became aware of a ring of light around the dolphins. Suddenly I felt myself included in it as a member of the pod … I felt as if I were a Spinner dolphin … We were One. We swam alike, we shared a love for the ocean, our bodies were similar, we were no longer

different species, our thoughts merged together, and I became aware of my surroundings through their eyes. (ibid.: 39)

However, mingling with this radical 'return to nature' narrative is a quite different story in Ocean's text. She perceives the dolphins as 'swim-ins' (ibid.: 164) from alien high-tech civilizations and constructs a narrative that bears a resemblance to the ones that appeared in the writings of the scientists in search of extraterrestrial intelligence. In Ocean's New Age version of these advanced aliens and their dolphin avatars, they are indeed beings whose technology serves spiritual and mystical purposes such as mediating access to higher planes of existence, to the worlds of universal love and oneness. In this way, Ocean's cosmology, like that of other New Age UFO-believers, differs from that of the scientists. But the mystical tinge does not change the fact that Ocean's ETs share with the aliens of the SETI scientists the possession of an 'advanced technology and wisdom beyond our imagination' (ibid.: 136) – and that the dolphin as incarnation of the ETs is drawn into their sphere of extremely advanced technology, and displaced accordingly. The animal slides from noble, pre-tech repres-entative of 'purely' wild and primordial nature to Space Age cyborg and messenger from a high-tech future.

Ocean's narratives are exemplary, because they continuously cause the dolphin to circulate between these two positions without ever allowing it to come discursively to rest in one of them. Moreover, they show that one of the triggers rendering it impossible to fix the dolphin with other wild animal icons in a state of 'pure' nature is the high-tech connotations that pulse from its communicative skills combined with its speed and nomadism. Its sonar, echo-location, patterns of vocalization, its apparently highly 'intelligent' interactions, with other dolphins and with humans, its speedy travelling around – all these qualities signal 'cyborg' and 'future' rather than 'noble savage' and 'past'.

These skills act as launchpads for several very different kinds of narra-tives. In the dolphin stories of Ocean and other New Agers, they facilitate a spiritual elevation to higher realms of existence. In the tales of the scientists searching for extraterrestrial intelligence, the same skills make the dolphins into mediators between scientific man and the cosmic Cyber-Godfather. A third kind of discourse to recycle them appears in ads for sophisticated computer software, advanced telecommunications systems and global means of transportation. Here, dolphins figure regularly. As different as these three kinds of narrative are, they nevertheless share an unmistak-ably futuristic mode that can be summed up in the words of Ocean:

PLATE 8.3 Cyborg-dolphins! Advertisement for computer software.
(Courtesy Intel Corporation).

What they [the dolphins] are doing, and what they are teaching us, is *exactly* what we humans will be doing in the twenty-first century. (italics in the original; ibid.: 16)

Seen from the viewpoint of space man, who likes to believe that he has the prerogative of leading us into the cosmic cyber-future, we may well ask, who do they think they are, these enigmatically smiling animals? Equals? Jesters? Mock-heroes? Anti-heroes?

PLATE 8.4 One more cyborg–dolphin. Advertisement for telecommunication.
(Courtesy Sonofon)

Notes

1. Shamu is the name given to all Sea World's killer whales, which are also used as the theme park's trademark. Nearly four million customers per year come to see Shamu the killer whale (Davis 1997: 1).

2. Lilly briefly resumed his research on communication with dolphins in the late 1970s when he set up Project JANUS (Joint Analog Numerical Understanding System). This new project built on the split between techno–Man's secondary orality and non-techno–Dolphin's primary one. At the human end of the communication line, visual symbols on a computer screen could be translated into high-pitched signals which the dolphins might pick up from underwater loudspeakers at the other end of the line. Conversely, the dolphin-speak was translated from underwater hydrophones into visual computer symbols for the scientist.

3. The term Aesopian metaphor is derived from the name of the ancient Greek author, Aesop, who in his fables used animals to expose humans. Due to censorship, Aesopian language (with or without animals) became common in all kinds of Soviet discourses.

9

Conclusion: Inappropriate Contiguities Revisited

Our study of different narratives on the spaceship, the horoscope and the dolphin has come to an end. We have looked at the changing patterns of self/other representations that they display, and have considered the human expectations and yearnings attached to communication with an array of extraterrestrial others, from the cosmic Cyber-Godfather to Female Fate, Moira, and from the cyborg dolphin to the noble savage dolphin.

The analysis has shown that the imaginary dialogues with these Others are conceived of as taking place on anything but equal terms. Sometimes the territories of the extraterrestrial worlds and their imaginary or real inhabitants are constructed in a quasi-colonialist mode, as objects to be imprinted with meaning by the triumphant human self; sometimes they are depicted as superior subjects and conveyors of divine or quasi-divine wisdom. But it does not seem possible for the self-aggrandizing or self-abandoning logics of the stories to foresee acts of communication with extraterrestrial subjects who are simply understood as equal, but different. As they oscillate between cannibalizing and sacralizing modes, either a superhero-self or a God/Goddess-other, or both, seems to perform un-questioned in the majority of stories.

We have also seen how gender, ethnicity, the myth of linear progress and the opposition between 'pre-tech' and 'high-tech' are invested in these self/other representations along rather traditional lines. Colonial and patriarchal stereotypes, which would be more or less outmoded if used in a terrestrial context, thrive in the language in which the master narratives of extraterrestrial spheres are embedded. The nexus Woman–Native–Nature is re-emerging out of the post-Second World War ocean, while re-enactments of ancient religious gender stereotypes are gaining new ground in the stories of the refigured cosmos. The 'crossed-out' god of modernity returns in space flight discourses as the Cyber-Godfather of distant galaxies, who sends out his sperm-astronauts on long-term space missions, and New

Age astrology provides him with competition by reviving his traditional female counterpart, Moira, or Fate.

By focusing on different iconographies and master narratives, we have aimed at making visible this trend towards the revitalization of rather stereotypical images of wild – cosmic or oceanic – nature. But we have also sought to destabilize them by displaying some of the circulating meanings and inappropriate contiguities that appear when different stories of the global commons and their twentieth-century iconographies are juxtaposed, rendering their truth claims non-evident by highlighting the emerging patterns of opposition, polarization and never-ending reversals. To sum up this denaturalizing and critical perspective, we shall briefly revisit the master narratives of cosmic and oceanic otherness as seen through the lens of three novels that rewrite them from deconstructive and alternative positions that open them up in line with our analysis. The novels are: Victor Pelevin's *Omon Ra* (1992/1996), Jeanette Winterson's *Boating for Beginners* (1990) and Vonda McIntyre's *Superluminal* (1983).

Conquerors of Space in the Underground

> We just didn't have the time to defeat the West technologically. But in the battle of ideas, you can't stop for a second. The paradox ... is that we support the truth with falsehood ... and the goal for which you will give your life is, in a formal sense, a deception. But the more consciously ... you perform your feat of heroism, the greater will be the degree of its truth. (Pelevin 1992/1996: 44)

With these words the protagonist, Omon, of Russian writer Victor Pelevin's satirical novel *Omon Ra* is instructed in Soviet history and told, following its inexorable logic, why he must give his life as part of a faked space mission to the Moon. Omon, the son of a low-ranking member of the Soviet police, daydreams about fighter-plane heroes, flying and cosmonautics. He aspires to be a cosmonaut and is selected for a special mission: to go to the Moon and cycle/travel seventy kilometers along the Lenin Fissure in a so-called 'moonwalker'. The vehicle is mocked up to look automated, but underneath is basically nothing more than a simple bicycle. At the end of the trip, Omon is supposed to use the last of his oxygen supplies to rush out of the 'moonwalker' and set up a radio transmitter in the lunar soil, which will broadcast the words: 'Lenin', 'peace', 'USSR', thus 'proving' to all the world the power of automated Soviet space technology. After this heroic act as human ghost in the fake automaton,

Omon is permitted to shoot himself in order to avoid the more painful death of suffocation. Return to Earth is not part of the programme. To do so would destroy the illusion of the automaton, and besides, the Soviet Union has not had time to develop the proper technology. Seen through the prism of Omon's innocent and naïve perceptions of the inhuman system surrounding him, the novel deconstructs the master fable of Soviet space flight with scathing irony and black humour. It tells of the large-scale and grandiose technological fakery, designed to 'prove' Marxist-Leninist dogma about the superiority of Soviet forces of production. Not one single part of the space programme is what it pretends to be. Not only are the apparently automated functions on the rockets and spacecraft in reality simple manual tasks, but Omon even discovers that there is no real trip into space either. When, in accordance with his standing orders, he tries to shoot himself outside the moonwalker, he misfires and discovers that he is not on the Moon, but in an abandoned tunnel of the Moscow metro where the entire Soviet space programme has actually taken place. Everything is pretence, Potemkin façades that will legitimize the claim to truth of the master narrative of superior forces of production and power to beat the technology of the capitalist West.

Apart from being a satire on the inhuman Soviet system and its indifference towards the life of the individual, the novel can also, on a more general symbolic level, be read as an extremely funny and, in a Bakhtinian sense, carnivalesque exposure of the pompous rhetoric of both the Russian and American space narratives, which, as shown, have many similarities. As the jester created a down-to-earth mock-image of the king in carnivals of the Middle Ages, so the story of the very ordinary Russian boy, Omon (whose name alludes to *homo*)[1], who has the (bad) luck to be selected to become a cosmonaut-hero, ridicules the high-flown Russo-American myth of the 'conquerors of space' who imprint their superior power and knowledge on the whole universe. The master narrative of space flight is, in a very literal sense, transformed from a 'high' to a 'low' matter. Events apparently unfolding in the heavens are, in the novel, actually taking place inside the Earth, as the cosmonaut-hero is degraded from universal master of a complicated and all-powerful technology into an interchangeable cog in a simple mechanical device. In this way, the novel emphasizes the point we made when we exposed the inappropriate contiguity between the Russo-American brothers of the right stuff and such shadow figures as the mongrel bitch Laika, the crying and vomiting Tereshkova, the comic coward figure José Jiménez, and so on; i.e. figures who perform as counterparts to the space heroes because the grandiose self of the master narrative needs an inferior other as background. The story of *Omon Ra* underlines the tricky problem posed by the imaginary monumentalism and closure of national master narratives such as the space adventure story, which is that their lack of openness to revisions or to voices other than those authorized may create their own kind of instabilities, inappropriate contiguities and unwanted proximities between heroes and mock-heroes, heavenly and earthly matters.

To Posit a Fathergod through an Illusory Genesis

> Soames ... broke open the bottle. He deciphered the writing. 'Hey girls, I made it,' he read slowly, 'love D ... ' (Winterson 1990: 159).

Like *Omon Ra*, Jeanette Winterson's *Boating for Beginners* is a story about the big fakery of master narratives and about their destabilization via inappropriate contiguities and the eye-opening perspectives of mock-heroines. But while Omon's life displays a tragicomic caricature of the official space romance and its powerful masculine adventure hero, *Boating for Beginners* makes a down-to-earth carnival out of the God and Goddess stories that are included in the cosmic master narratives we have analysed. In our context, Winterson's novel can be read as a frivolous commentary on both the Cyber-Godfather of the space narrative and the Great Cosmic Mother of the astrologers' universe. Winterson opens up both of these self-important and elevated figures in promising ways that are in line with the destabilization we have tried to create by inappropriately juxtaposing the two opposing figures.

The fictive frame of *Boating for Beginners* is the archaeological excavation of the supposed relics of Noah's Ark in 1984. During the work at Mount Ararat, the assistant archaeologist, Gardener, digs out some strange things which are too inappropriate and 'unbiblical' for his boss, Soames, to acknowledge as proper findings. But the down-to-earth assistant persists and discovers, among other things, a bottle containing a message from a woman called Doris, who was Noah's charwoman. Back in antediluvian times Doris, together with a small group of other women, discovered the real story behind the big fakery, which today is known as *Genesis*. Her message in the bottle, quoted above, signals to readers that she survived the Flood and with her the memory of a gigantic cover-up, staged by God and Noah. Although Soames will not let it become part of official history, her note remains an inappropriate and unauthorized commentary, a riddle that occupies Gardener for the rest of his life.

Boating for Beginners is a carnivalesque and grotesque realist rewriting of the Bible's story of the Flood. Ancient Nineveh is conceived in the image of a modern capitalist consumer society, with refrigerators, fast food, clinics for cosmetic surgery, etc. Noah is an inventor and a thriving businessman in a company specializing in a mixture of tourist and religious sightseeing. Carnivalizing Feuerbach's thesis that the divine is a human invention, the novel depicts the biblical God as a cyborg, created by Noah. Basically, God is the result of a flash of lightning that accidentally strikes a half-putrefied Black Forest Gâteau and a decomposed scoop of ice-cream that Noah is about to take out of his refrigerator. The incident gives Noah an insight into methods of producing artificial life and, like another Frankenstein, he creates an ice-cream cyborg-God, who addresses him as 'mother', neatly inverting the biblical obsession with father–son genealogies. Noah uses his creation as a tool in the founding of a new religion that celebrates a 'natural' lifestyle and food, preserved without refrigerators, echoing the ancient saying that everything passes away except immortal God. 'Selling' God and 'his' messages becomes a profitable business for Noah, who arranges boat trips so that people can watch God's 'sensational miracles', and publishes popular books, such as *Genesis or How I Did It*, in which the Bible's version is told as a cover-up for the real story.

At the beginning of the novel, Noah is about to launch a big theatrical event and film project, based on *Genesis* … . He expects it to be a block-buster that will make him even richer. However, in one more parallel with the Frankenstein myth, events run out of Noah's control. God becomes tired of his role of walk-on player in his 'mother''s' virtual flood event, and decides to show his power by flooding the world for real. So the Flood becomes a reality in the novel, but its Biblical 'truth' is rendered dubious by the fact that both the almighty Fathergod and his *Genesis* are nothing but pawns in a grandiose lie, invented to hide God's monstrous birth and the trivial, embarrassing and non-marketable story of his cyborg descent from a piece of bad cake and an ice-cream.

Seen in our context, the notion of the distant Cyber-Godfather of faraway galaxies and his modernized versions of *Genesis* are, in a way, also implicitly carnivalized. Winterson's cheerful trivialization of God-the-Almighty-Creator as the simple, coincidental progeny of base matter and a phallogocentric desire to construct disembodied origin stories that veil, fake and lie about the active role of matter and (female) bodies can also be read as a carnivalesque comment on some of the patriarchal stories that were invented as part of the search for extraterrestrial intelligence.

To Posit a Female Divine, a Carnival May be Necessary

Sic transit gloria mundi [Thus passes away the glory of the world]. (Ancient Christian saying)

The counter-image to the apparently august, but in reality faked Fathergod in *Boating for Beginners* is the female world body. She appears allegorically as a widowed working mother, Mrs Munde (from *Mundus*: World), and her daughter Gloria (playing on the words aureole and glory in both a liturgical and secular sense). Together, the names of mother and daughter echo the heavenly message about the decay of everything human conveyed in the above quote. But, as an exuberant and carnivalesque mock-mirror of the renunciation, asceticism and contempt for bodily pleasures in general and the female body in particular that the saying implies, mother and daughter are both vigorous and non-languishing figures.

The daughter, whom Noah has hired to collect animals for his Flood film, is part of the team of women who discover the fakery. Like Doris, she is determined to disturb the plans of God and Noah – i.e. to survive the Flood in order to keep the true story alive. She wants to ensure that the glory of a world full of trivial and down-to-earth things such as ice-cream cyborg-gods, cosmetic surgery and refrigerators that delay decay in their own, both perverse and life-affirming, ways becomes a part of historical memory.

The mother is a poetic combination of trivial everyday consciousness, macrocosmic grandeur and an unfailing vitality. She is Noah's cook and, unlike the daughter and her suspicious friends, she is a truly naïve and devout believer in his and God's projects. Besides cooking for Noah, she happily takes on a job in his son Ham's profitable restaurant chain specializing in spiritual dishes. Here she energetically produces 'Hallelujah Hamburgers' for low wages, using a dangerous and ineffective machine, invented by Noah. She loses an arm in the machine, but her faith in God and Noah remains unshaken.

However, intermingled with all her trivial pursuits, Mrs Munde is, in a grandiose and poetic way, also one with the cosmos. Originally, she wanted to become an astronomer. However, her poor background did not make such a career possible for her. As a true optimist, she does not despair, but redefines herself as an 'Astronomer without a Telescope' and shifts to a love of God and the cultivation of a mystical feeling of interconnectedness with the cosmos and the stars. In particular, she celebrates her oneness with the powerful fire of the Zodiac sign Leo. She feels that she has a roaring lion inside her – a primal and elemental force which she thinks will one day make her 'combust', but which is also likened to a 'storm at sea' (Winterson 1990: 20, 61).

Mrs Munde is cast as an allegory over the experience of oneness between macro- and microcosmos that is central to astrological cosmology. Accordingly, Gloria's description of her mother's way of knowing is in line with Cassirer's definition of mythical realism and the bodily episteme of premodern thought. She notices that her mother makes 'no distinction between thinking things and objects of thought' (ibid.: 48) and, in another parallel with astrological thought, Mrs Munde's life is totally guided by her intuitive responses to the coincidences that seem to imprint macro-cosmic meaning onto her life.

Being too naïve to either fake or lie, Mrs Munde is a counter-image to God, who pretends to be the universal and spiritual father of all things, while being no more than the product of base matter and a simple co-incidence. In contrast to God, Mrs Munde does not hide the fact that she is one with elementary material forces; she is happy and proud to have the fire of Leo inside her and to be a tiny, bodily part of the universe instead of its august creator who demands to be worshipped on the (false) pretext of having been there before everybody else.

As an embodied counter-image to God, Mrs Munde shares many features with the Great Cosmic Mother, whom we traced in different versions in the astrological texts. Interpreted together with Gloria, she comes even closer to exposing a female divine. As an allegory of the female world body and her daughter, the aureole, whom the 'immortal Fathergod' threatens to overthrow with his *Sic transit gloria mundi*, Mrs Munde and Gloria act as an alternative to the Bible's phallogocentric Trinity. Winterson's novel casts them as a down-to-earth version of the divine mother–daughter genealogies of pre-patriarchal religions that appear as the 'overthrown goddesses' of Trivia in Noah's flood film (ibid.: 21).

Insisting on this mother–daughter pair, whose vigour and vitality cannot be totally repressed by the master narrative of the Fathergod, Winterson's novel offers an image of the female divine that meets the need we, together with Irigaray, ascribed to modern women. We traced one version of this female divine in the astrological universe, but in a limited form that *Boating for Beginners* manages to transgress. In line with Irigaray, who criticizes spiritual feminists and astrologers for their reversion to a regressive and non-empowering symbiosis with the Great Cosmic Mother, the novel rewrites the figuration in a carnivalesque, down-to-earth manner that avoids projecting it as an alien, transcendent authority, like Moira, to whom we remain powerless as babies. Mrs Munde radiates macrocosmic and poetic grandeur, but she is also a trivial, everyday woman who lays no claims to transcendency. Moreover, the novel shows that the mother–daughter symbiosis is not a static given. The depictions of Gloria entering a second phase of personal development and becoming a mature, independent subject, who has reached a mental stage that goes beyond Mrs Munde's mythic–realistic world view, are allegoric illustrations of this. In this second developmental phase, Gloria can understand, love, bond and interact with her mother in new and more productive ways than before.

Ocean and Cosmos Revisited: A Feminist Reconfiguration

> She gave up her heart quite willingly. (McIntyre 1983: 1)

> Her suit glowed faintly blue against the formidable blackness. Lacking even a tether, she floated in space as she might float in the sea. (ibid.: 220)

> The great blue whale blinked at him again, embracing Radu in sound. [...] He lay motionless, entranced by the whale's sheer presence. (ibid.: 285)

The last of the three novels, Vonda McIntyre's *Superluminal* (1983), is a part of our conclusion because it questions the gendered and ethnicized hierarchy between cosmos and ocean. It challenges the stereotypes of Father Sky and Mother Sea which we saw revitalized by a post-Second World War science that perceived the trinity Woman–Native–Nature emerging from the ocean, while Cyber-Godfathers and supermen in the guise of astronaut-heroes occupied the cosmos. With this challenge, the novel promotes subversive processes that are in line with the scope of our argument.

However, compared to the texts of Pelevin and Winterson, the critical mode of McIntyre's novel is quite different. In contrast with the carnivalesque and deconstructive styles of *Omon Ra* and *Boating for Beginners*, *Superluminal* is a romantic Utopianist novel. It is grounded in a classic feminist utopianism and constructs counter-images that are as romantically closed on certain standpoints and identities as the master narratives it challenges. Nevertheless, with its alternative approaches to cosmos and ocean, and its discussions of space flight and cetaceans, *Superluminal*'s themes are close to our own, and we find it relevant to our arguments.

McIntyre's novel focuses on three extraterrestrial spaces: the ocean, the cosmos of galaxies and interstellar space, and finally the nothingness on the other side of the 'edge' of the universe's current expansion. Each of the three spaces represents a specific kind of desirable wisdom, all of equal value, but different from one another. Cetaceans, and in particular one old female blue whale, embody the wisdom of the ocean in the novel. The oceanic environment has bestowed on these sea mammals a different and higher intelligence than humans. Instead of a wisdom built primarily from visual experiences, the intelligence of the cetaceans is based on their highly developed intuitive communication skills, and on their sensitivity to sound, touch, scent and heat perception that altogether intensify the 'density of experience' (ibid.: 172) as well as on their capability to see across a broader spectrum than humans (their vision includes ultraviolet and infrared wavelengths that are not perceptible to the human eye).

In the futuristic setting of the novel, a large group of former humans, now 'divers', are in the process of transforming bodily and mentally into cetaceans in order to share their wisdom and conditions of life. The transformation is engendered by bio-engineering processes based on the controlled use of viruses; the divers are cyborgs existing in a state of transition between human and cetacean.

In our context, these human–cetacean cyborgs represent a counter-image to the cyborg-dolphin icon we have previously outlined. Cyborgification as the means to promote an education in humanity is substituted by one that aims at an education in animality. But although this reversal brings to mind the self–other relationship of the noble savage dolphin narrative that imprints the human with a 'purely natural' wisdom, it should be noted that the divers' story is also different from this version of the traditional dolphin master narratives. *Superluminal* does depict the wise blue whale matriarch, the playfulness of cetaceans, their extraordinary wisdom and life in harmony with nature in a way that is close to the pastoral images of the noble savage dolphin story, but the means by which the humans attempt to become one with the cetaceans makes the story-line significantly different. The divers' education in animality is engendered via a relentlessly artificial reinvention of nature that inscribes it in the cyborg world.

Unlike the oceanic intelligence, which is connected to sound, touch, etc., the wisdom of interstellar space is tied to the sense of vision within the spectrum of colours and light and to a mathematical, but also intuitive, perception of seven dimensions that makes it possible to understand and embrace the whole universe beyond Einsteinian space. Those who can reach an understanding of this post-Einsteinian universe are space pilots, who have gone through a scheme of bodily modifications just as drastic as those of the divers. To become a space pilot, whose body can survive superluminal flight without being anaesthetized, it is necessary to sacrifice the human heart in favour of a mechanical one that detaches its bearer from dependency on biorhythms and circadian rhythms, on natural life cycles and ageing processes. But, even so, not every pilot can actually perceive all seven dimensions. The mechanical cyborgification of the body is only a first step. Mathematical skills and in particular intuition, a feeling for and openness towards the experiences encountered during superluminal flights, are important factors too.

While the oceanic wisdom of the cetaceans to which the divers aspire is embodied and multisensorial, the pilots' insight draws on visual and mathematical skills. Moreover, detachment from the demands of the bio-logical body, i.e. total bio-control, is a prerequisite. Such a description directs the attention towards a traditional picture of the masculine subject of Enlightenment *ratio* and the cool, detached superhero that we met in the master narrative of space flight. But the cyborg pilots of *Superluminal* are different. Intuition, feelings and aesthetic perception are also prerequisite in their gaining of universal insight. Their wisdom is inspired by the aesthetics and beauty of mathematics and physics, i.e. by a ratio that is informed by feeling and intuition. Moreover, the pilot who discovers the seventh dimension – the most difficult and decisive of them all – is a woman.

The third space of the novel, the abyss of nothingness beyond the 'edge' of expanding interstellar space, is in the strictest sense not a space at all; it has no dimensions and no past, present or future. It is 'a place that did not yet exist and never would exist', because 'the universe, still expand-ing, would engulf it, and it never would have been' (ibid.: 208). It is a place unable to give sensual clues either; no vision, no sound, a place which is unknowable in the sense that no known means of gaining insight can lead to understanding. It is the sphere of ultimate mystery, and as such it represents a deep meditative wisdom, not unlike the one the novel romantic-ally ascribes to the cetaceans. It is a wisdom that principally evades the enlightened vision to which interstellar space gives rise.

As an antipode to the cosmos of light and Enlightenment, which historic-ally suggests masculinity, the mysterious nothingness could be interpreted as a space of female divine wisdom. But the novel evades this dichotomy, posing the 'space' beyond the 'edge' as one that attracts the most complex and inappropriate figure in the novel, the diver Orca (who shares her name with her cousins, the killer whales or orcas). She is in a process of trans-formation from human to animal and has developed cetacean senses, but she also wants to become a pilot, i.e. begin the transition from a creature embedded in biorhythms to machinic detachment and mechanical bio-control. This desire is aroused by the abyss of nothingness that she, unlike the pilots and due to her cetacean sensuality, can understand as a source of wisdom. In her complex aspirations and desires, she comes to embody a network of interrelations between cosmos and ocean, between human, animal and pilot (posthuman machine) and to transgress the traditional boundaries and hierarchies between them. Through her attraction to it, the abyss of nothingness comes to share this transgression; it is articulated as a space of mediations, where the traditional opposition between Father Sky and Mother Sea is displaced.

In our context, Orca's complexities make her a cousin to the dolphin, whose amazing iconographic polysemy we have displayed. We showed how it performed now as oceanic noble savage, and now as cosmic high-tech cyborg; now as stand-in for Mother Sea, and now for Father Sky. In this way, we exposed the dolphin as a jester capable of carnivalesque acts of blurring boundaries and mocking genderized and ethnicized hierarchies and oppositions whose displacement the Orca-figure of *Superluminal* summarizes.

We have travelled a long way in the writing of this book – from a feminist conference in Dublin to the void beyond the edges of the universe – and traversed some truly amazing landscapes. We hope that our journey has helped to open up the worlds of both space flight and astrology for further feminist investigation. Space flight is important for feminists both because of its technological spin-offs and because it touches on esoteric questions of the nature of cosmos and the divine. As we hope to have shown, it is far more than a nuts-and-bolts, hard science, toys for the boys endeavour. The question of how we should relate to that which we cannot control is still up for grabs, and as this question has become displaced, along with the wilderness, into the ocean deeps and the depths of space, so feminists must follow, or else leave the way open for the twin spectres of sacralizing and cannibalizing that, as we have shown, weave their way through the discourses of the spaceship, the horoscope and the dolphin.

Perhaps the most important thing we have learned from the research for this book is that present-day cultural oscillations between the two illusory positions of self-aggrandizing and self-abandoning, *vis-à-vis* the wild other, are destructive and dangerous, based as they are on complementary denials. While the former tries to deny that, as living beings, we cannot evade our position as objects of cosmic and biological forces beyond our control, the latter, conversely, attempts to ignore the fact that, nevertheless, we do have some opportunities for subjective and socio-technical intervention. In confronting these complementary positions and denials via the configuration of stories about our three icons, we hope to have created a discursive space for the transgression of both.

Note

1. Written in the Cyrillic alphabet of Russian, Omon spells *homo* backwards. However, the name is also an acronym for Soviet military special forces.

Bibliography

Adams, C. J. (1990) *The Sexual Politics of Meat: A Feminist-Vegetarian Critical Theory*, New York: Continuum.

Adams, C. J. and J. Donovan (eds) (1995) *Animals and Women. Feminist Theoretical Explorations*, Durham and London: Duke University Press.

Aitmatov, Ch. (1995) *Tavro Kassandry*, Moscow: Eksmo.

Aldrin, E., Jr. with W. Warga (1973) *Return to Earth*, New York: Random House.

Alpers, A. (1960) *A Book of Dolphins*, London: John Murray.

— (1961) *Dolphins: The Myth and the Mammal*, Cambridge, MA: Riverside Press.

Arrhenius, S. (1907), *Världarnas Utveckling*, Stockholm: Hugo Gebers Förlag (1st edn 1906; translated as *Worlds in the Making*, New York 1908).

Bakhtin, M. (1984) *Rabelais and his World*, Bloomington: Indiana University Press.

Bardach, J. (1968) *Harvest of the Sea*, New York: Harper & Row.

Barker, A. (1993) 'The divided self: Yuri Rytkheu and contemporary Chukchi literature', in D. Diment and Yu. Slezkine (eds) *Between Heaven and Hell: The Myth of Siberia in Russian Culture*, New York: St Martin's Press.

Barnes, R. (1994) *The Blue Dolphin*, Tiburon, CA: H. J. Kramer Inc.

Barr, M. S. (1993) *Lost in Space: Probing Feminist Science Fiction and Beyond*, London and Chapel Hill, NC: University of North Carolina Press.

Belkovich, V., S. Kleinenberg and A. Yablokov (1965) *Zagadka okeana*, Moscow: Molodaya Gvardiya.

— (1967) *Nash drug – delfin*, Moscow: Molodaya Gvardiya.

Benford, T. B. and B. Wilkes (1985) *The Space Program Quiz & Fact Book*, New York: Harper & Row.

Berry, P. and A. Wernick (eds) (1992) *Shadow of Spirit: Postmodernism and Religion*, London and New York: Routledge.

Birke, L. (1994) *Feminism, Animals and Science: The Naming of the Shrew*, Buckingham and Philadelphia: Open University Press.

Bitov, A. (1976) *Dni cheloveka*, Moscow: Molodaya Gvardiya.

— (ed.) (1994) *Nachatki astrologii russkoy literatury*, Moscow: Fortuna.

Borisenko, I. and A. Romanov (1982) *Where All Roads into Space Begin: An Account of the Baikonur Cosmodrome*, Moscow: Progress Publishers.

Bova, B. and B. Preiss (eds) (1991) *First Contact: The Search for Extraterrestrial Intelligence*, New York: Plume Books.

Boym, S. (1996) 'Everyday culture', in D. N. Shalin (ed.) *Russian Culture at the Crossroads: Paradoxes of Postcommunist Consciousness*, Boulder, CO and Oxford: Westview Press, pp. 157–83.

Braidotti, R. (1991) *Patterns of Dissonance*, Cambridge: Polity Press.

— (1994) *Nomadic Subjects: Embodiment and Sexual Difference in Contemporary Feminist Theory*, New York: Columbia University Press.

Brecht, B. (1964) *Brecht on Theatre: The Development of an Aesthetic*, ed. and trans. J. Willett, London: Eyre Methuen.

Brill, R. and W. A. Friedl (1993) *Reintroduction to the Wild as an Option for Managing Navy Marine Mammals*, Technical Report 1549, U.S. Navy, Naval Command, Control and Ocean Surveillance Center, San Diego, October.

Brin, D. (1996) *Startide Rising*, London: Orbit (1st edn 1983).

Brougher, V. G. (1997) 'The occult in Russian literature of the 1990s', *The Russian Review*, Vol. 56, No. 1: 110–24.

Bryld, M. (1998) 'The days of dogs and dolphins: Aesopian metaphors of Soviet science', in M. Bryld and E. Kulavig (eds) *Soviet Civilization between Past and Present*, Odense: Odense University Press, pp. 53–75.

Burke, E. (1990) *A Philosophical Enquiry into the Origin of Our Ideas of the Sublime and Beautiful*, Oxford: Oxford University Press (1st edn 1756).

Cadigan, P. (1991) *Synners*, London: HarperCollins.

Caldecott, L. and S. Leland (eds) (1983) *Reclaim the Earth: Women Speak Out for Life on Earth*, London: Women's Press.

Cameron, A. (ed.) (1963) *Interstellar Communication*, New York and Amsterdam: NASA/ Institute for Space Studies.

Campbell, J. (1968) *The Hero with a Thousand Faces*, Bollingen Series XVII, Princeton, NJ: Princeton University Press (1st edn 1949).

Capra, F. (1991) *The Tao of Physics: An Exploration of the Parallels between Modern Physics and Eastern Mysticism*, Shambhala Publications (3rd edn).

— (1982) *The Turning Point: Science, Society, and the Rising Culture*, New York: Simon and Schuster.

Carpenter, M. S., G. Cooper, Jr, J. Glenn, Jr, V. Grissom, W. Schirra, Jr, A. Shepard, Jr and D. Slayton (1963) *We Seven*, New York: Pocket Books (1st edn 1962).

Carson, R. (1961) *The Sea Around Us*, Oxford and New York: Oxford University Press (1st edn 1951).

Casper, M. J. and L. J. More (1995) 'Inscribing bodies, inscribing the future: gender, sex, and reproduction in outer space', *Sociological Perspectives* (Summer): 311–23.

Cassirer, E. (1922) *Die Begriffsform im mythischen Denken*, Leipzig and Berlin: Teubner.

— (1987) *Das mythische Denken. Philosophie der symbolischen Formen*, 2. Teil, Darmstadt: Wissenschaftliche Buchgesellschaft.

Chaikin, A. (1994) *A Man on the Moon: The Voyages of the Apollo Astronauts*, London: Michael Joseph.

Chapskii, K. K. and V. Sokolov (eds) (1973) *Morphology and Ecology of Marine Mammals*, New York and Toronto: John Wiley & Sons.

Cixous, H. (1985) 'The laugh of the Medusa', trans K. Cohen and P. Cohen, in E. Marks and I. de Courtivron (eds) *New French Feminisms: An Anthology*, Brighton: Harvester Press, pp. 245–65 (1st French edn 1975).

— (1991) *Coming to Writing and Other Essays*, trans. S. Cornell, D. Jenson, A. Liddle and S. Sellers, Cambridge, MA and London: Harvard University Press (1st French edn 1977).

Cixous, H. and C. Clément (1986) *The Newly Born Woman*, trans. B. Wing, Vol. 24 of Theory and History of Literature series, Minneapolis and Oxford: University of Minnesota Press (1st French edn 1975).

Clarke, A. C. (1960) *The Challenge of the Sea*, New York, Chicago and San Francisco: Holt, Rinehart & Winston.

— (1964) *Profiles of the Future*, London: Pan Books (1st edn 1962).

— (1966) *Voices from the Sky: Previews of the Coming Space Age*, London: Gollancz.

— (1988) *The Deep Range*, London: VGSF Classic Series (1st edn 1957).

Clynes, M. E. and N. S. Kline (1960) 'Cyborgs and space', *Astronautics*, September. Reprinted in C. H. Gray, H. J. Figueroa-Sarriera and S. Mentor (eds) (1995) *The Cyborg Handbook*, London and New York: Routledge, pp. 29–33.

Cocconi, G. and P. Morrison (1959) 'Searching for interstellar communication', *Nature* 184: 844. Reproduced in D. Goldsmith (ed.) (1980) *The Quest for Extraterrestrial Life: A Book of Readings*, Mill Valley, CA: University Science Books.

Collins, M. (1974) *Carrying the Fire: An Astronaut's Journey*, New York: Farrar, Strauss & Giroux.

Costlow, J. T., S. Sandler and J. Vowles (eds) (1993) *Sexuality and the Body in Russian Culture*, Stanford, CA: Stanford University Press.

Cousteau, J. Y. and F. Dumas (1953) *The Silent World*, London: Hamish Hamilton.

Cousteau, J. Y. with J. Dugan (1963) *The Living Sea*, New York and Evanston: Harper & Row.

Coward, R. (1989) *The Whole Truth: The Myth of Alternative Health*, London and Boston: Faber & Faber.

Cowen, R. C. (1960) *Frontiers of the Sea: The Story of Oceanographic Exploration*, London: Gollancz.

Crick, F. (1981) *Life Itself: Its Origin and Nature*, New York: Simon & Schuster.

Cullen, M., M. Fine-Davis, E. McCarthy, G. Moane and A. Saunders (eds) (1987) *Book of Abstracts*: Women's Worlds. Visions and Revisions, Third International Interdisciplinary Congress on Women, Trinity College, University of Dublin, Ireland.

Daniloff, N. (1972) *The Kremlin and the Cosmos*, New York: Alfred A. Knopf.

Davis, S. G. (1997) *Spectacular Nature: Corporate Culture and the Sea World Experience*, Berkeley, CA and London: University of California Press.

Dawson, G. (1994) *Soldier Heroes: British Adventure, Empire and the Imagining of Masculinities*, London and New York: Routledge.

Derrida, J. (1979) *Spurs: Nietzsche's Styles*, trans. B. Harlow, Chicago and London: University of Chicago Press (1st French edn 1978).

— (1987) *Positions*, trans. A. Bass, London: The Athlone Press (1st French edn 1972).

Devine, E. and M. Clark (eds) (1967) *The Dolphin Smile: Centuries of Dolphin Lore*, New York and London: Macmillan/Collier-Macmillan.

DeVorkin, D. H. (1992): *Science with a Vengeance: How the Military Created US Space Sciences After World War II*, Berin and New York: Springer-Verlag.

Diamond, I. and G. F. Orenstein (eds) (1990) *Reweaving the World: The Emergence of Ecofeminism*, San Francisco: Sierra Club Books.

Doria, C. (1974) 'The dolphin rider', in J. McIntyre (ed.) *Mind in the Waters: A Book to Celebrate the Consciousness of Whales and Dolphins*, San Francisco: Sierra Club Books, pp. 33–51.

Douglas, G. (1981) *Physics, Astrology and Semiotics*, London: author's own publishing house.

Drake, F. and D. Sobel (1992) *Is Anyone Out There? The Scientific Search for Extra-terrestrial Intelligence*, New York: Delacorte Press.

Dugan, J. and R. Vahan (eds) (1965) *Men Under Water*, Philadelphia and New York: Chilton Books.

Dyson, F. (1979) *Disturbing the Universe*, New York: Harper & Row.

Earle, S. A. (1995) *Sea Change. A Message of the Oceans*, New York: G. P. Putnam's Sons.

Easlea, B. (1983) *Fathering the Unthinkable: Masculinity, Scientists and the Nuclear Arms Race*, London: Pluto.

Edmonds, R. (1994) *Pushkin: The Man and his Age*, London: Macmillan.

Elias, G. H. (1990): *Breakout into Space: Mission for a Generation*, New York: William Morrow.

Engel, L. and the Editors of *Life* (1961) *The Sea*, New York: Life Nature Library, Time Inc.

Fairchild, H. N. (1961) *The Noble Savage: A Study in Romantic Naturalism*, New York: Russell & Russell.

Farrant, S. (1989) *Symbols for Women: A Matrilineal Zodiac*, London and Wellington: Mandala.

Fedorov, A. and I. Izvekov (1998) 'Predstartovaya podgotovka "Altairov"', *Novosti Kosmonavtiki*, No. 17/18: 2–6.

Feuerbach, L. (1957) *The Essence of Christianity*, trans. George Eliot, New York, San Francisco and London: Harper & Row.

Feuerstein, T. Lamb (1998) Bibliography on the Whale-Watching-Web: www.physics. helsinki.fi/whale/

Fogg, M. J. (1995) *Terraforming: Engineering Planetary Environments*, Warrendale, PA: Society of Automotive Engineers.

Foucault, M. (1978) *The History of Sexuality: An Introduction*, Vol. 1, trans. R. Hurley, London: Penguin (1st French edn 1976).

— (1980) *Power/Knowledge: Selected Interviews & Other Writings 1972–1977*, ed. C. Gordon, New York: Pantheon Books.

— (1989) *Madness and Civilization: A History of Insanity in the Age of Reason*, London: Routledge.

Freudenthal, H. (1960) *Lincos: Design of a Language for Cosmic Intercourse*, Part I, Studies in Logic and the Foundations of Mathematics, Amsterdam: North-Holland Publishing Company.

Fuller, R. Buckminster (1981) *Critical Path*, New York: St Martin's Press.

Gaard, G. (ed.) (1993) *Ecofeminism: Women, Animals, Nature*, Philadelphia: Temple University Press.

Gagarin, Yu. (1971) *Est Plamya!*, Moscow: Molodaya Gvardiya (2nd edn).

Galison, P. and B. Hevly (eds) (1992) *Big Science: The Growth of Large-Scale Research*, Stanford, CA: Stanford University Press.

Gareev, Z. (1991) 'Allergiya Aleksandra Petrovicha', *Volga*, No. 4: 86–106.

George, D. (1992) *Mysteries of the Dark Moon: The Healing Power of the Dark Goddess*, San Francisco: HarperSanFrancisco.

Gibson, W. (1995) *Johnny Mnemonic*, New York: Ace Books (1st edn 1981).

Gimbutas, M. (1982) *The Goddesses and Gods of Old Europe*, Berkeley and Los Angeles: University of California Press.

GlobaLearn, Inc. (1998) *The Dolphins of Sevastopol*, www.globalearn.com/expeditions/bsne/

Glueck, N. (1966) *Deities and Dolphins: The Story of the Nebateans*, London: Cassell.

Goldsmith, D. (ed.) (1980) *The Quest for Extraterrestrial Life: A Book Of Readings*, Mill Valley, CA: University Science Books.

Goldsmith, D. and T. Owen (1992) *The Search for Life in the Universe*, Reading, MA, New York and Paris: Addison-Wesley Publishing Company (2nd edn).

Golovanov, Ya. (1994) *Korolev: Fakty i mify*, Moscow: Nauka.

Göttner-Abendroth, H. (1980) *Die Göttin und ihr Heros: Die matriarchalen Religionen in Mythos, Märchen und Dichtung*, Munich: Frauenoffensive.

Graham, L. R. (ed.) (1990) *Science and the Soviet Social Order*, Cambridge, MA and London: Harvard University Press.

Gray, C. H., H. J. Figueroa-Sarriera and S. Mentor (eds) (1995) *The Cyborg Handbook*, London and New York: Routledge.

Green, M. (1990) *The Robinson Crusoe Story*, Pennsylvania: Pennsylvania State University Press.

— (1991) *Seven Types of Adventure Tale: An Etiology of a Major Genre*, Pennsylvania: Pennsylvania State University Press.

— (1993) *The Adventurous Male: Chapters in the History of the White Male Mind*, Pennsylvania: Pennsylvania State University Press.

Greene, L. (1984) *The Astrology of Fate*, London, Boston and Sydney: Allen & Unwin.

Greenleaf, M. (1994) *Pushkin and Romantic Fashion*, Stanford, CA: Stanford University Press.

Greimas, A. J. (1983) *Structural Semantics: An Attempt at a Method*, Lincoln, NE and London: University of Nebraska Press.

Griffin, D. R. (1974) *Listening in the Dark: The Acoustic Orientation in Bats and Men*, New York: Dover Publications (1st edn 1958).

— (1992) *Animal Minds*, Chicago and London: University of Chicago Press.

Grimwood, K. (1996) *Into the Deep*, New York and Auckland: Onyx.

Grossberg, L. and C. Nelson, P. Treichler (eds) (1992) *Cultural Studies*, London and New York: Routledge.

Gunn, J. (1974) *The Listeners*, New York: Signet.

Haraway, D. (1989) *Primate Visions: Gender, Race and Nature in the World of Modern Science*, London and New York: Routledge.

— (1991) *Simians, Cyborgs and Women: The Reinvention of Nature*, London: Free Association Books.

— (1991a) 'The actors are cyborg, nature is coyote, and the geography is elsewhere: postscript to "Cyborgs at large"', in C. Penley and A. Ross (eds), *Technoculture*,

Cultural Politics, Vol. 3, Minneapolis and Oxford: University of Minnesota Press, pp. 21–7.

— (1992) 'The promises of monsters: a regenerative politics for inappropriate/d others', in L. Grossberg, C. Nelson and P. Treichler (eds), *Cultural Studies*, London and New York: Routledge, pp. 295–338.

— (1997) *Modest_Witness@Second_Millennium. FemaleMan©_Meets_OncoMouse™. Feminism and Technoscience*, London and New York: Routledge.

Hartmann, W. K., R. Miller and P. Lee (1984) *Out of the Cradle: Exploring the Frontiers Beyond Earth*, New York: Workman Publishing.

Hastrup, K. (1992) *Det antropologiske projekt: Om forbløffelse*, Copenhagen: Gyldendal.

Heidegger, M. (1979) 'The age of the world view', in W. V. Spanos (ed.) *Martin Heidegger and the Question of Literature. Toward a Postermodern Literary Hermeneutics*, Bloomington and London: Indiana University Press, pp. 1–15 (1st German edn 1938).

Heinlein, R. A. (1950) *Farmer in the Sky*, New York: Charles Scribner's Sons.

Herman, L. (ed.) (1980) *Cetacean Behavior: Mechanisms and Functions*, New York and Toronto: John Wiley & Sons.

Hess, D. J. (1993) *Science in the New Age: The Paranormal, Its Defenders and Debunkers, and American Culture*, Madison: University of Wisconsin Press.

Holmes, D. C. (1967) *The Search for Life on Other Worlds*, Toronto, New York and London: Bantam Books.

Hunter, R. (1980) *The Greenpeace Chronicle*, London: Picador.

Irigaray, L. (1981) 'And the one doesn't stir without the other', trans H. V. Wenzel, *Signs* Vol. 7, No. 1: 60–7 (1st French edn 1979).

— (1985a) *Speculum of the other Woman*, trans. G. C. Gill, Ithaca, NY: Cornell University Press (1st French edn 1974).

— (1985b) *This Sex Which is not One*, trans. C. Porter and C. Burke, Ithaca, NY: Cornell University Press (1st French edn 1977).

— (1993) *Sexes and Genealogies*, New York: Columbia University Press.

Jakobson, R. (1987) 'Marginal notes on the prose of the poet Pasternak', in K. Pomorska and S. Rudy (eds), *Language and Literature*, Cambridge, MA and London: Harvard University Press, pp. 301–18.

Jung, C. G. (1972) *Synchronicity: An Acausal Connecting Principle*, London: Routledge & Kegan Paul (1st German edn 1952).

Keller, E. F. (1983) *A Feeling for the Organism: The Life and Work of Barbara McClintock*, New York: W. H. Freeman and Company.

— (1985) *Reflections on Gender and Science*, New Haven, CT and London: Yale University Press.

— (1989) 'The gender/science system: or, is sex to gender as nature is to science?', in N. Tuana (ed.), *Feminism and Science*, Bloomington: Indiana University Press, pp. 33–45.

— (1992) *Secrets of Life. Secrets of Death. Essays on Language, Gender and Science*, New York London: Routledge.

Keller, O. (1887) *Thiere des Classischen Alterthums in Culturgeschichtlicher Beziehung*, Innsbruck: Verlag der Wagner'schen Universitäts-Buchhandlung.

Kelley, K. W. (ed.) (1988) *The Home Planet*, Reading, MA and Moscow: Addison-Wesley and Mir Publishers.

Kellogg, W. N. (1961) *Porpoises and Sonar*, Chicago and London: University of Chicago Press.

Kesarev, V. (1968) 'A chem delfinu dumat?', *Znanie-sila*, No. 7: 22–4.

— (1971) 'The inferior brain of the dolphin', *Soviet Science Review*, Vol. 2: 52–8.

Kindersley, K. (undated) *Eyes of the Soul*, video trailer, KK films (not for sale or broadcast).

Konstantinov, B. (ed.) (1972) *Naselennniy kosmos*, Moscow: Nauka.

Kopylova, T. and G. Yurkina (eds) (1962) *Pioner iz Pionerov*, Moscow: Molodaya Gvardiya.

Koval, A. and L. Desinov (1987) *Space Flights Serve Life on Earth*, Moscow: Progress Publishers.

Kraus, J. (1995) *Big Ear Two: Listening for Other-Worlds*, Ohio: Cygnus-Quasar Books.

Kristeva, J. (1980): *Desire in Language: A Semiotic Approach to Literature and Art*, trans. T. Gora, A. Jardine and L. S. Roudiez, New York: Columbia University Press (1st French edns 1969 and 1977).

— (1984) *The Revolution in Poetic Language*, trans. M. Waller, New York: Columbia University Press (1st French edn 1974).

— (1986) *The Kristeva Reader*, ed. T. Moi, Oxford: Blackwell.

— (1987) *In the Beginning was Love: Psychoanalysis and Faith*, trans. A. Goldhammer, New York: Columbia University Press (1st French edn 1985).

Kurrels, J. (1992) *Astrology for the Age of Aquarius*, London: Tiger Books International.

Laan, N. v.d. (1997) 'Ukraine trains kamikaze dolphins to heal', *The Electronic Telegraph*, 23 July 1997.

Laird, S. (1999) *Voices of Russian Literature: Interviews with Ten Contemporary Writers*, Oxford: Oxford University Press.

Latour, B. (1993) *We have Never been Modern*, New York and London: Harvester Wheatsheaf.

Lebedev, L., B. Lykyanov and A. Romanov (eds) (1973) *Sons of the Blue Planet* (*Syny Goluboi Planety*), New Delhi: Amerind Publishing (Russian edn 1971).

Le Guin, U. K. (1972) *The Farthest Shore*, New York: Atheneum.

Lewis, J. R. and J. G. Melton (1992) *Perspectives on the New Age*, Albany: State University of New York Press.

Lilly, J. C. (1962a) *Man and Dolphin*, London: Gollancz (1st edn 1961).

— (1962b) 'Kak ya nauchilsya govorit s moimi delfinami', *Nauka i zhizn* , No. 12: 82–6.

— (1967) *The Mind of the Dolphin: A Nonhuman Intelligence*, New York: Doubleday.

— (1973) *The Centre of the Cyclone: An Autobiography of Inner Space*, London: Calder & Boyars.

— (1975) *Lilly on Dolphins: Humans of the Sea*, New York: Anchor Books.

— (1978) *Communication between Man and Dolphin: The Possibilities of Talking to Other Species*, New York: Crown Publishers.

— (1994) *The Emerging Love of Man & Dolphin (ECCO)*, Silent Records CD, USA.

Lovelock, J. (1987) *Gaia: A New Look at Life on Earth*, Oxford and New York: Oxford University Press (1st edn 1979).

Lukina, L. (1996) 'Results of using Afalina dolphins with a purpose of rehabilitation, social adaptation and medical treatment of children in the program called Dolphin

Therapy', paper delivered at a symposium arranged by AquaThought: www. aquathought.com

Lykke, N. (1997) 'To be a cyborg or a goddess?', *Gender, Technology and Development*, Vol. 1, No. 1: 5–22.

Lykke, N. and R. Braidotti (eds) (1996) *Between Monsters, Goddesses and Cyborgs: Feminist Confrontations with Science, Medicine and Cyberspace*, London: Zed Books.

Mailer, N. (1971) *A Fire on the Moon*, London: Pan Books.

Malmgren, C. D. (1991) *Worlds Apart: Narratology of Science Fiction*, Bloomington: Indiana University Press.

Markley, R. (1997) 'Falling into theory: simulation, terraformation, and eco-economics in Kim Stanley Robinson's Martian Trilogy', *Modern Fiction Studies, Technocriticism and Hypernarrative*, Vol. 43, No. 3: 773–99.

Marx, G. (ed.) (1988) *Bioastronomy: The Next Steps*, Dordrecht, Boston and London: Kluwer Academic Publishers.

McCaffrey, A. (1996) *The Dolphins of Pern*, London: Corgi (1st edn 1994).

McIntyre, J. (ed.) (1974) *Mind in the Waters: A Book to Celebrate the Consciousness of Whales and Dolphins*, San Francisco: Sierra Club Books.

McIntyre, V. (1983) *Superluminal*, Boston, MD: Houghton Mifflin.

Merchant, C. (1980) *The Death of Nature: Women, Ecology, and the Scientific Revolution*, San Francisco: Harper & Row.

Merle, R. (1969) *The Day of the Dolphin*, New York: Simon and Schuster (French edn 1967).

Mooney, T. (1983) *Easy Travel to Other Planets*, London: Arrow Books.

Morgan, J. H. and J. Ragusa (1987) 'Women: a key work force in preparation for space flight', in M. Cullen et al. (eds), *Book of Abstracts*, Third International Interdisciplinary Congress on Women, University of Dublin, Ireland, p. 433.

Morrison, P. (1962) 'Interstellar communication', *Bulletin of the Philosophical Society of Washington*, Vol. 16: 58. Reproduced in D. Goldsmith (ed.), *The Quest for Extraterrestrial Life: A Book of Readings*, Mill Valley, CA: University Science Books, 1980, pp. 122–31.

Mowat, F. (1978) *A Whale for the Killing*, Toronto: Seal Books, McClelland-Bantam (2nd edn).

Nash, R. (1982) *Wilderness and the American Mind*, New Haven, CT and London: Yale University Press (3rd edn).

Nye, D. E. (1994) *American Technological Sublime*, Cambridge, MA, London: MIT Press.

O'Barry, R. with K. Coulbourn (1988) *Behind the Dolphin Smile*, Chapel Hill, NC and Dallas: Algonquin Books.

O'Barry, R. (1999) 'Why call it science?', www.dolphinproject.org/Rehab.html

Oberg, J. E. (1981) *New Earths: Transforming Other Planets for Humanity*, New York: Stackpole Books.

Ocean, J. (1997) *Dolphins into the Future*, Hawaii: Dolphin Connection.

O'Neill, G. K. (1978) *The High Frontier: Human Colonies in Space*, London: Corgi (1st edn 1976).

Ong, W. J. (1997) *Orality & Literacy: The Technologizing of the Word*, London and New York: Routledge (1st edn 1982).

Panov, E. N. (1980) *Znaki Simvoly Yazyki*, Moscow: Znanie.

Pelevin, V. (1992) 'Omon Ra', *Znamya*, No. 5: 11–63.

— (1992/1996) *Omon Ra*, trans A. Bromfield, London and Boston: Faber & Faber.

Penley, C. (1997) *NASA/TREK: Popular Science and Sex in America*, London and New York: Verso.

Penley, C. and A. Ross (1991) *Technoculture: Cultural Politics*, Vol. 3, Minneapolis and Oxford: University of Minnesota Press.

Piccard, J. and R. S. Dietz (1961) *Seven Miles Down: The Story of the Bathyscape Trieste*, New York: G. P. Putnam's Sons.

Plant, J. (ed.) (1989) *Healing the Wounds: The Promise of Ecofeminism*, Philadelphia and Santa Cruz: New Society Publishers.

Plato (1973) *The Timaeus of Plato*, ed. R. D. Archer-Hind, New York: Arno Press.

Plumwood, V. (1993) *Feminism and the Mastery of Nature*, London and New York: Routledge.

Polevoi, B. (1970) *A Story about a Real Man*, London: Greenwood Publishing (1st Soviet Russian edn 1946).

Popovich, P. R., E. E. Malakhovskaya and N. G. Polivin (eds) (1989) *Kosmos – moya rabota*, Moscow: Profizdat.

Propp, V. (1975) *Morphology of the Folktale*, trans. L. Scott, Austin, TX: University of Texas Press (2nd edn).

Ragni, G. and J. Rado (1970) *Hair: The American Tribal Love-rock Musical*, New York: Pocket Books.

Redfield, J. (1993) *The Celestine Prophecy: An Adventure*, New York: Warner Books.

— (1996) *The Tenth Insight: Holding the Vision. Further Adventures of the Celestine Prophecy*, London: Bantam.

— (1997) *The Celestine Vision: Living the New Spiritual Awareness*, London: Bantam.

Redfield J. and C. Adrienne (1995) *The Celestine Prophecy: An Experiential Guide*, New York: Warner Books.

Ridgway, S. (1987) *The Dolphin Doctor: A Pioneering Veterinarian Remembers the Extraordinary Dolphin that Inspired his Career*, New York: Ballantine.

Robertson, G., M. Mash, L. Tickner, J. Bird, B. Curtis and T. Putnam (eds) (1996) *FutureNatural: Nature, Science, Culture*, London and New York: Routledge.

Romanyshyn, R. D. (1989) *Technology as Symptom & Dream*, London: Routledge.

Rosenberg, A. (1984) *Zeichen am Himmel: Das Weltbild der Astrologie*, Munich: Kösel-Verlag (1st edn 1949).

Rosenthal, B. G. (ed.) (1997) *The Occult in Russian and Soviet Culture*, Ithaca, NY and London: Cornell University Press.

Ross, A. (1991) *Strange Weather: Culture, Science, and Technology in the Age of Limits*, London and New York: Verso.

Rudhyar, D. (1975) *Occult Preparations for a New Age*, Madras and London: Theosophical Publishing House.

— (1991) *The Astrology of Personality*, Santa Fe, NM: Aurora Press (1st edn 1936).

Rybakov, B. A. (1981) *Yazychestvo drevnikh slavian*, Moscow: Nauka.

Rytkheu, Yu. (1977) 'When the whales leave', *Soviet Literature*, No. 12: 3–73.

Sagan, C. (ed.) (1973) *Communication with Extraterrestrial Intelligence (CETI)*, Cambridge, MA and London: MIT Press.

— (1975) *The Cosmic Connection: An Extraterrestrial Perspective*, New York: Dell Books.

— (1995) *Pale Blue Dot: A Vision of the Human Future in Space*, London: Headline.

— (1997) *Contact*, London: Orbit (1st edn 1985).

Said, E. (1979) *Orientalism*, New York: Pantheon Books.

Saint-Pierre, B. J.-H. de (1989) *Paul and Virginia*, trans. J. Donovan, London and New York: Penguin (1st French edn 1788).

Saussure, F. de (1974) *Course in General Linguistics*, ed. J. Culler, trans. W. Baskin. London: Fontana.

Savinych, V. P. (1983) *Zemlya zhdet i nadeetsya*, Perm: Permskoe knizhnoe Izdatelstvo.

Schiebinger, L. (1993) *Nature's Body: Gender in the Making of Modern Science*, Boston, MD: Beacon Press.

Scholes, R. (1976) 'The roots of science fiction', in M. Rose (ed.) *Science Fiction: A Collection of Critical Essays*, Englewood Cliffs, NJ: Prentice Hall.

Scholes, R. and E. S. Rabkin (1977) *Science Fiction: History, Science, Vision*, Oxford and New York: Oxford University Press.

Schusterman, R. J., J. A. Thomas and F. G. Wood (eds) (1986) *Dolphin Cognition and Behavior: A Comparative Approach*, Hillsdale, NJ and London: Lawrence Erlbaum.

Science (1960) 'Science in the news', *Science*, Vol. 131, No. 3413: 1592.

Sebeok, T. A. (1972) *Perspectives in Zoosemiotics*, The Hague and Paris: Mouton.

Shepard, A. and D. Slayton (1995) *Moon Shot: The Inside Story of America's's Race to the Moon*, London: Virgin Books.

Shklovsky, I. S. (1976) *Vselennaya, Zhizn, Razum*, Moscow: Nauka (1st edn 1962).

— (1990) *Theory of Prose*, Elmwood Park, IL: Dalkey Archive Press (trans B. Sher from 2nd Russian edn 1929).

— (1991) *Five Billion Vodka Bottles to the Moon*, New York London: W. W. Norton & Company.

Shklovsky, I. S. and C. Sagan (1968) *Intelligent Life in the Universe*, New York: Delta (1st edn 1966).

Sjöö, M. (1992) *New Age and Armageddon: The Goddess or the Gurus? Towards a Feminist Vision of the Future*, London: The Women's Press.

Sjöö, M. and B. Mor (1987) *The Great Cosmic Mother: Rediscovering the Religion of the Earth*, San Francisco: Harper & Row.

Slonczewski, J. (1986) *A Door into Ocean*, New York: Arbor House.

Solomko, Yu. M. (1994) *The Memorial Museum of Cosmonautics*, Moscow: Aero-S.

Spangler, D. and W. I. Thompson (1991) *Reimagination of the World: A Critique of the New Age Science, and Popular Culture*, Santa Fe, NM: Bear and Company.

Spretnak, C. (1991) *States of Grace: The Recovery of Meaning in the Postmodern Age*, San Francisco: HarperSanFrancisco.

Springer, H. (ed.) (1995) *America and the Sea: A Literary History*, Athens, OH and London: University of Georgia Press.

Steels, L. and R. Brooks (eds) (1995) *The Artificial Life Route to Artificial Intelligence: Building Embodied, Situated Agents*, Hillsdale, NJ and Hove, UK: Lawrence Erlbaum.

Stenuit, R. (1969) *The Dolphin: Cousin to Man*, Harmondsworth: Penguin.

Stetson, H. T. (1934) *Earth Radio and the Stars*, New York London: McGraw-Hill.

Strathern, M. (1987) 'Out of context: the persuasive fictions of anthropology', *Current Anthropology*, Vol. 28, No. 3, June: 251–81.

Sullivan, W. (1966) *We are not Alone: The Search for Intelligent Life on Other Worlds*, New York and London: McGraw-Hill (rev. edn).

Sullivan, W. T., III (ed.) (1984) *The Early Years of Radio Astronomy*, Cambridge: Cambridge University Press.

Suvin, D. (1979) *Metamorphoses of Science Fiction: On the Poetics and History of a Literary Genre*, New Haven, CT and London: Yale University Press.

Swift, D. W. (1990) *SETI Pioneers: Scientists Talk about their Search for Extraterrestrial Intelligence*, Tucson and London: University of Arizona Press.

Szilard, L. (1992) *The Voice of the Dolphins and Other Stories*, Stanford, CA: Stanford University Press (1st edn 1961).

Tarasov, N. I. (1956) *More zhivet*, Moscow: Sovetskaya Nauka.

— (1960) *Zhivye zvuki morya*, Moscow: Akademiya Nauk SSSR.

Tavolga, W. N. and J. C. Steinberg (1961) 'Marine animal sounds', *Science*, Vol. 134, No. 1: 288.

Tomilin, A. G. (1965) *Istoriya slepogo kachalota*, Moscow: Nauka.

— (1969) *Delfiny sluzhat cheloveku*, Moscow: Nauka.

— (1980) *V mire kitov i delfinov*, Moscow: Znanie.

Tovmasyan, G. M. (ed.) (1965) *Vnezemnye Tsivilizatsii. Trudy Soveshschaniya Byurakan, 20–23 maia 1964 g.* Yerevan: Izd. Akademii Nauk Armyanskoj SSSR (English translation: *Extraterrestrial Civilizations*, Israel Programme for Scientific Translations, IPST 1823, 1967).

Traweek, S. (1988) *Beamtimes and Lifetimes: The World of High Energy Physics*, Cambridge, MA and London: Harvard University Press.

Tsiolkovsky, K. E. (1954) *Sobranie Sochinenii*, Vol. 2, Moscow: Izdatelstvo Akademii Nauk SSSR.

— (1962) *The Call of the Cosmos*, Moscow: Foreign Languages Publishing House.

Turkle, S. (1984): *The Second Self: Computers and the Human Spirit*, London and New York: Granada.

Turner, F. J. (1996) *The Frontier in American History*, New York: Dover Publications (1st edn 1920).

Ulubekov, A. T. (1984) *Bogatstva vnezemnykh resursov*, Moscow: Znanie.

Ursul, A. D. (ed.) (1990) *Osvoenie kosmosa i problemy ekologii*, Kishinev: Shtiintsa.

Vasilchikov, N. V. (1964) *Podelis Neptun!*, Moscow: Sovetskaya Rossiya.

Von Bencke, M. J. (1997) *The Politics of Space: A History of U.S.–Soviet/Russian Competition and Cooperation in Space*, Boulder, CO and Oxford: Westview Press.

Voronin, L. G. (1970) 'Povedenine "primat" morja-delfina afaliny Tursiops Trunchatus Montagu', *Uspekhi sovremennoi biologii*, vyp. 2: 191–207.

Warren, K. J. (1990) 'The power and the promise of ecological feminism', *Environmental Ethics*, Vol. 12, No. 2: 125–46.

WCED (World Commission on Environment and Development) (1987) *Our Common Future* (the Bruntland Report), Oxford and New York: Oxford University Press.

White, F. (1987) *The Overview Effect: Space Exploration and Human Evolution*, Boston, MD: Houghton Mifflin.

Whitford, M. (1991) *Luce Irigaray. Philosophy in the Feminine*, London and New York: Routledge.

Wilford, J. N. (1969) *We Reach the Moon, the New York Times Story of Man's Greatest Adventure*, New York and London: Bantam Books.

Williams, H. (1988) *Whale Nation*, London: Jonathan Cape.

Winterson, J. (1990) *Boating for Beginners*, London: Minerva (1st edn 1985).

Wolfe, T. (1988) *The Right Stuff*, Bantam Books (17th edn).

Wood, F. G. (1973) *Marine Mammals and Man: The Navy's Porpoises and Sea Lions*, Washington, DC and New York: Robert B. Luce.

Wyschogrod, E. (1990) *Saints and Postmodernism. Revisioning Moral Philosophy*, Chicago and London: University of Chicago Press.

Yefremov, I. (1987) *Zvezdnye korabli. Tumannost Andromedy*, Moscow: Khudozhest-vennaya literatura (1st edn 1957).

Young, H., B. Silcock and P. Dunn (1969) *Journey to Tranquility: The History of Man's Assault on the Moon*, London: Jonathan Cape.

Index

Adams, C.J., 32
adventure stories, 10, 11, 72, 76–8, 100,
    122; analysis of, 56–8
Age of Aquarius, 17, 59, 150
Aimatov, Chingiz, *Tavro Kassandry*, 169
Aldrin, Edwin E., 118
Aldrin, Edwin E. Sr., 121
Alpers, A., 170
amazement, 50–71, 69; cultural, 23
Amazing Stories, 44
American Wilderness Society, 80
animals, as feminist issue, 32–3
Aphrodite, as dolphin goddess, 185
Apollo, 64; portrayed as riding dolphin,
    185–6, 197
Apollo 11, 54, 65, 115, 118
Apollo 13, 111; disaster, 16
Apollo 17, 78
Apollo Project, 78, 87, 197; women's
    involvement in, 74
Armstrong, Neil, 118
Arrhenius, Svante, 104; *Worlds in the
    Making*, 103
Askold, a Russian flight technician,
    129, 135–6
astrologers, interviews with, 122–38
astrology, 28, 35, 58, 59–60, 122–38;
    and gender, 130–6; as *écriture
    féminine*, 140–1; attitude of
    conventional science to, 132;
    attraction for women, 130–6;
    cyclicity of, 150; different uses of,
    139; femininity of, 132; place of
    men in, 134; place of women in,
    133–4; traditional patriarchy of, 132
astronauts, 41, 45, 53, 54–5, 56, 84, 88,
    98, 108, 128, 135, 216; as soldier

heroes, 54, 58, 118; women as, 89,
    90, 111–13
atheism, 28, 83, 125

Baikonur launch site, 41; construction
    of, 99
Bailey, Alice, 151
Bakhtin, Mikhail, 23, 143, 148–51
Barnes, R., 167
Barr, Marlene, 40
Bateson, George, 201
Belkovich, V., 205
Berry, P., 38
'big mission' of space flight, 72–91, 95;
    devotion to, 73–6
bio-power, 92, 93–6, 115–16, 140;
    cosmic, 99–100
Birke, L., 28, 32, 33, 37
Bitov, Andrey, 125–6, 170
Blavatskaya, Helena, 151
Bracewell, R.N., 195
Brecht, Bertolt, 50, 51
Brin, David, *Startide Rising*, 68
Brundtland Report, 20

Cadigan, Pat, *Synners*, 170
Calvin, Melvin, 196
Campbell, J., 61
Capra, Fritjof, 63
carnivalesque, spirit of, 12, 18, 23, 217,
    218, 219, 220–2
Carpenter, Scott, 111; et al., *We Seven*,
    109
Cassirer, Ernst, 143, 145–8, 154, 156
Cathy, an American astrologer, 131
Celestine messages, 59–61
Challenger disaster, 85

chora, concept of, 156
Chukchi people, 208, 209
Cixous, Hélène, 37, 39, 140, 141, 153
Clarke, Arthur C., 101; *The Deep Range*, 166, 167
Clynes, Manfred, 31
Cocconi, Giuseppe, 176
coincidences, 123; meaningful, 59–61
Cold War, 85, 160, 171, 187, 188
colonialism, 215; in space, 93
Columbus, Christopher, 76–7, 81, 93
commons, global, 19–21, 71, 95, 161–4; imprinted with human meaning, 71
Communication Research Institute, 48, 189, 190, 192, 199
Communication with Extra Terrestrial Intelligence (CETI), 176, 177
contiguities, inappropriate, 17, 24, 215–26
correspondences, theory of, 143
cosmic exodus, 85
cosmic flashes, 120
cosmodolphins, message of, 159–61
cosmology: gendering of, 18; need for, 34–6
cosmonauts *see* astronauts
cosmos: as 'deserts of space', 98, 100; as commons, 19–21; as living body, 143–4, 145; as mother body, 148–51; as Mother Goddess, 136, 139, 142; boundary with human body, 155; interconnectedness with, 137; perceived as noisy, 172–5; refiguring of, 222–6; viewed as enigma, 81–3
Cousteau, J.Y., 167
Coward, R., 38
Coyote, as trickster, 37
cradle-image of Earth, 107
Crick, Francis, 116; *Life Itself*, 105
critical distance, 69
cultural studies, scope of, 40–2 *see also* feminist cultural studies
Cyber-Godfather, 16, 17, 19, 101–2, 103, 104, 105, 107, 116, 139, 159, 198, 199, 209, 211, 218, 222
cybergods, 104, 114, 122, 151, 177
cyborgs, 6, 34, 36, 55, 69, 92, 101, 106, 113–15, 170, 224; concept of, 30–2; dolphins as, 191–4, 194–7 *see also* dolphins as cyborgs

Dana, Bill, 110
Debbie, a Space Camp teacher, 90
Defoe, Daniel, *Robinson Crusoe*, 57
Delphi, oracle at, 64, 185, 197
delphys, 185; meaning of, 1
demographic problems of space expansion, 80
Denmark, 27
Derrida, Jacques, 18
desire in language, 141, 142, 153–7
Discovery space shuttle, 27
DNA, discovery of, 116
dolphins, 14–19, 26, 33, 51, 66, 68, 159–61; ambiguities of, 184–6 (sexual, 198–9); appearance in advertisements, 18, 211; as boundary figures, 168; as cyborgs, 52, 63–4, 67, 191–4, 194–7; as healers, 169; as icons, 13, 23, 28, 41, 44–9, 52, 63, 183–213, 225; as jester, 225; as mines, 180; as minesweepers, 181; as noble savages, 52, 63–4, 168, 170, 202, 206, 209, 210; connotation of femininity, 192; 'grandmammification' of, 205; inferiority of brains, 203; intelligence of, 13 (superior, 198, 206); linguistic abilities of, 49, 65, 168–71, 192, 195, 200; longing to merge with, 64; mapping of brain of, 48; masturbating of, 200; mythology of, 8; polysemy of sexual appearance of, 184–5; protection of, 203; research into brains of, 191–4; sacralization of, 206; sonar abilities of, 186; within circulating meanings, 209–12
Doris, Noah's charwoman, 218–19
Dr B, a Nasa doctor, 77, 78, 79
Drake, Frank, 195, 196
dyadic mother/child relationship, 3, 136–7, 149, 153, 199
Dyson, Freeman, *Disturbing the Universe*, 96

Earth Dolphins picture *see* McCulloch, Daniel
Earth: as blue planet, 14, 108, 109; as radio star, 174; as spaceship, 54; as womb, 108; recreation of, 96, 108; viewed from space, 2, 95

Earth Mother, 2, 3, 5, 4, 14, 16, 109, 111, 127, 136, 151
écriture féminine, 140–1, 142, 143, 153–7
Eden, Garden of, 64, 65, 96
Eisenhower, Dwight D., Christmas speech, 100
elsewhere, 11, 50, 51, 56, 57, 62, 86, 93, 152; quest for, 7, 8, 16
Enlightenment, 8, 12, 22, 38, 58, 139, 169, 224
estrangement, 50–71
European Particle Research Laboratory (CERN), 35
extraterrestrialism, 39–40, 50, 69, 82, 176

fable, 53; concept of, 51
Fairchild, H.N., 66
fairy tales, theory of, 57, 61
Farida, a Russian astrologer, 129, 130, 133, 134, 137
father sky, refiguring of, 159–79
female body, speaking of, 153–5
female divine, 39, 220–2, 224; reclaiming of, 156–7
feminine libidinal economy, 156
feminine principle, 132
femininity, 131, 133, 136
feminism, 9, 27, 36–7, 39–40, 132, 133, 154; and cosmology, 34–6; animals and, 32–3; attitude to space flight, 10; eco-, 29, 30, 34; liberal, 11; spiritual, 17, 36
feminist cultural studies, 25, 28–30
feminist fabulation, 40
feminist science fiction, 34
feminist science history, 34
feminist science studies, 30, 32
feminization of poverty, 9
Feuerbach, Ludwig, 157, 219
Flipper, 187, 188, 200
Foucault, Michel, 21; analysis of power, 92, 93–6, 109, 115
Freudenthal, H., 176
frontier, myth of, 78, 80, 100 (of Soviet Union, 93; of Wild West, 93)

Gaard, G., 32
gadget-fetishism, 16
Gagarin, Yuri, 13, 55, 75, 77, 80, 111, 197

Gaia, 2, 14, 16, 24
'garbage' hypothesis, 104
Gareev, Zufar, 144; *The Allergy of Aleksandr Petrovich*, 152
gender reversals, 17
gender/nature nexus, 28
Genesis, new, 103–6
genetic code, universality of, 105
George, Demetra, 144, 152–3
Gernsback, Hugo, 44
Gibson, William, *Johnny Mnemonic*, 68
Gimbuta, Marija, 132
Glenn, John, 13
God: Christian, 4, 16, 35, 93, 101, 139, 218, 220, 221; the Father, 106, 155, 157, 163, 220 *see also* Cyber-Godfather
goddess worship, 36, 37, 63
Goodall, Jane, 200
Göttner-Abendroth, H., 61
gravity, 107, 108; escape from, 106
Great Cosmic Mother, 39, 151–3, 154, 157, 159, 185, 218, 221
Great Goddess, 132
Great Year, 150, 158
Green, Martin, 57–8, 115
Greene, Liz, 143–4; *The Astrology of Fate*, 144–5
Greenpeace, 206, 207
Gregory, an American astrologer, 124, 129, 130
Griffin, Donald, 190
Grimwood, Ken, *Into the Deep*, 64–5, 168
grotesque, 154; images of, 148
Gunn, J.E., *The Listeners*, 177

Haraway, Donna, 28, 30, 31, 33, 34, 36, 37, 39; cyborg manifesto, 69
Hastrup, Kirsten, 69
Haun, Jeffrey, 182
Heidegger, Martin, 4, 5
Heinlein, Robert, *Farmer in the Sky*, 92
Heller, Renée, 35
Herman, Louis M., 189
Hess, D.J., 38
homo spaciens, 53, 56, 74
horoscopes, 14–19; as icon, 13, 17, 28, 41, 44–9, 52, 63, 70, reading of, 129, 130, 145, 146, 150

Howe, Margaret, 200–1, 210
human body: as machine, 94, 109–13; of astronauts, monitoring of, 114, 115; redesign of, 31; speech of, 114
human, the, 30–2
human–nature axis, 30–2
Hunter, Robert, 207

imaginary, 21; concept of, 8
imprinting with cosmic meaning, 126–30
Institute of Cosmic Research (IKI), 42, 77, 81, 82, 128; interviews with employees, 72–91; male domination of, 89
Interdisciplinary Congress on Women, 9
International Space Station, 53
intuition, 131
Irene, a Kennedy Space Center doctor, 75–6, 79
Irigaray, Luce, 37–8, 39, 140, 141, 142, 153

Jiménez, José, 110–11, 217
Johnson Space Center, Houston, Texas, 44, 45
jouissance, 37, 155
Jung, C.G., 61, 144, 146

Keller, Evelyn Fox, 30, 32, 36, 115–16
Kennedy Space Center see NASA
Kindersley, Kim, Eyes of the Soul, 207–9
Kleinenberg, S., 205
Kline, Nathan, 31
know, to, 84–7
know-how, to, 84–7
Korolev, Sergei P., 41
Kristeva, Julia, 37, 39, 140, 141, 142, 153

Laan, N., 181
Laika the dog, 100, 217
Latour, B., 28
Le Guin, Ursula, 167
Leary, Timothy, 107
Lederberg, J., 104
Leonov, A., 113
Leopold, Aldo, 80

Lilly, John C., 48–9, 65, 68, 164, 186, 189–94, 191, 196, 198–201, 203; experiments on dolphins, 191–4; Man and Dolphin, 48, 189
lingua cosmica (Lincos), 176–7
Lizzie the dolphin, 48–9
Logos Spermatikos, 151
Lovell, Jim, 4, 8
Lovelock, James, 24
Lukina, Ludmilla, 180

magic helpers, 55, 60
Mailer, Norman, 115, 120
male genius, myth of, 35
A Man on the Moon, 111
Manhattan Project, 187, 195
Marianas Trench, descent in, 21
Martians, 102
Marxism–Leninism, 139, 170, 217
masculine hero, 87–91
masculinity, 54, 56–8, 62, 72
Matyshovna, Svetlana, 180, 181
McAuliffe, Christa, 15
McCaffrey, Anne, The Dolphins of Pern, 68
McCall, Robert, Washington mural, 54–5, 56, 57
McClintock, Barbara, 37
McCulloch, Daniel, 1–8, 14; Earth Dolphins picture, 1–8, 14, 64, 71, 109, 210
McIntyre, Vonda, Superluminal, 15, 216, 222
mechanical men, 110–11
Memorial Museum of Cosmonautics, Moscow, 55
menfish, relationship with sea, 167
menstruation, 152
Merchant, Carolyn, 28, 34, 36, 143, 148–51
methodology, 26
Metzner, Ralph, 202
Mikhail, a Russian astrologer, 123–4, 126, 133, 134–5
Mir, 53
Moon, 21, 27, 128; as female body, 119; as symbol in astrology, 134; dark, 152–3, 154; dark side of, 118–21; imprinting of, 84; landing on, 74, 75, 76, 78, 87, 108; mining of, 80;

oedipal relationship with, 120;
planting of flags on, 84; power of,
135; reconnecting with, 45; rock
samples, 44–5; symbolic in New
Age astrology, 127
Moon, Marion, 121
Mooney, Ted, 167; *Easy Travel to Other
Planets*, 189
Morgan, JoAnn, 9, 10, 74, 79, 84–6, 88
Morrison, Philip, 176, 195
mother sea, refiguring of, 159–79
mother-images, 144
Mowat, Farley, 65–6; *A Whale for the
Killing*, 65
Munde, Mrs, 220–1
mysterious, view of cosmos, 81–3
mysticism, 82
mythical semiosis, 143, 145, 146, 147

NASA, 2, 3, 6, 7, 9, 24, 68, 74, 78, 80,
82, 85, 111, 127, 194; African-
Americans in, 75; as allegedly civil
organization, 73; Astronauts'
Memorial, 53; attitude to sexuality,
12; criticism of, 12; interviews with
employees, 34, 72–91; involvement
with military, 9; Kennedy Space
Center, 11, 78, 107; mask of
openness, 41; Mission to Planet
Earth, 95; rational outlook of
interviewees, 83; skill at contruction
of imageries, 81; women employed
at, 75, 88, 89
National Air and Space Museum,
Washington DC, 54
National Oceanographic Institute of
Ukraine, 180
national parks, underwater, 19
native, as icon, 7, 8, 15
nature, 30; as icon, 7, 15; as primal
mother, 37; death of, 36; in feminist
cultural studies, 28–30; return to,
22, 66; sublime and sacred, 7
naturism, 33; concept of, 8 (coinage of,
29)
New Age, 7, 13, 14, 16, 17, 25, 28, 36,
38, 39, 46, 49, 51, 58–9, 83, 122–38,
139–58, 159, 181, 183, 207, 209,
211; master narrative, 8, 18, 61–3,
140, 152, 160, 210

Nikolai, an IKI astrophysicist, 75, 80,
86
Noah, 218–19, 220
noble savage, 52, 66 *see also* dolphin, as
noble savage
novum, 67, 92; space fable as, 56

O'Barry, Rick, 182
ocean: as commons, 19–21; as deep
frontier, 21, 26; as pastoral source,
166–8; as wilderness, for recreation,
167; farming of, 164; military
expansion in, 164; mining of, 164
Ocean, Joan, 160–1, 210–12; *Dolphins
Into the Future*, 210
Olga, a radio engineer at IKI, 77, 78
O'Neill, Gerard, *The High Frontier*, 79,
107
Ong, W.J., 161–2, 164, 172
Opo, the 'gay dolphin', 170
orality, 161–2; primary, 161, 169, 199;
secondary, 161, 162, 164, 165, 172,
173, 175, 199
Order of the Dolphin, 196
Orgel, L., 105
Others, 21, 25; dialogue with, 215;
treatment of, 29; wild, 32, 48, 71 *see
also* elsewhere
out of the cradle, notion of, 106–9

Pamela dolphin, 200
panspermia, 103–6, 116, 151; directed,
105
parler-femme, 141, 153–7
patriarchy, 40, 63, 89, 131, 134, 152
Pavlov, Ivan, 203, 205
Pelevin, Victor, *Omon Ra*, 15, 41,
216–18, 222
Penley, Constance, 13, 34; *NASA/
TREK*, 12
Peter Dolphin, 200, 210
Petr, a Russian doctor, 128, 133–4, 135,
137
phallagocentrism, 35, 36, 39, 57, 62, 63,
69, 103, 106, 116, 142, 151–3, 185,
219; subverting of, 155
Piccard, Jacques, 21, 165
pioneering spirit, 79
Pioneers organization, 77
Plato, 156

Plumwood, Val, 29
Pluto, 145, 146, 147
pollution of space, 19
population policies, 94
post-human, 30–2, 69, 113–15
poststructuralism, 37, 38
potency, 58
potestas, 58
Propp, Vladimir, 57, 61
Pushkin, 27

quasars, 175
questing hero, fairy tale of, 57, 73, 123
racism, 97
radio waves of the universe, 163
Ralph, a New Age philosopher, 131,
    132
ratio, cult of, 17
reading out of context, 39, 50, 69–71
Reagan, Ronald, 11
Redfield, James: *The Celestine Prophecy*,
    59–61; *The Celestine Vision*, 60; *The
    Tenth Insight*, 60
religion, revival of interest in, 38
Renaissance, 21, 34, 76
Return to Earth, 118
reversals, world of, 61–3
Rick, a New Age philosopher, 127, 132
'right stuff' masculinity, 87–8, 90, 98,
    113, 217; in the Soviet Union, 88
robots, 110
rockets: aesthetics of, 14; as icon, 188
Rodin, Auguste, *Thinker*, 35
Romanticism, 2, 10, 22, 66
Ross, a NASA ecobiologist, 80, 82, 84
Ross, A., 38
Rousseau, J.J., 22
Rudhyar, Dane, 125, 143–4, 148–51,
    152
Rybakov, B.A., 133
Rytkheu, Yuri, *When the Whales Leave*,
    65, 208
sacred, 34, 37; reordering of, 93

Sagan, Carl, 83, 102, 201; *Contact*,
    173–4
Said, Edward, 96
de Saint-Pierre, Bernard, *Paul et
    Virginie*, 66
satellites, 100–1, 102

Saturn V rocket, 11
de Saussure, Ferdinand, 140
Savchenko, Nikolai, 180
Save the Whale campaigns, 207
Schiebinger, L., 28
Scholes, Robert, 40, 50–1, 69
science: as story-telling, 39; objectifying
    gaze of, 5, 6
science fiction, 35, 40, 50, 52, 62, 67
Sea of Tranquillity, 108, 118
sea, refiguring of, 222–6 *see also* ocean
secularism, 8, 34, 116, 139
Sergei, a student at IKI, 76, 82
sexism, 97, 111
sexual difference theory, 34
Shamu, the killer whale, 190, 214
Shannon, a computer science engineer
    at Nasa, 76, 79
Shepard, Al, 108, 110
Shklovsky, I., 175, I.S., 102, 196
Sjöö, Monica, 152; and B. Mor, *The
    Great Cosmic Mother*, 152
slash-writing, 12, 23
space: as high frontier, 20, 21, 26,
    78–80; as panopticon, 100, 108, 109;
    conquest of, 46, 53; humanization
    of, 103; imbued with sounds, 161–4;
    impenetrability of, 20; inner, 24;
    messages from, 175–8; mining of,
    171
Space Camp, Kennedy Space Center, 90
space flight, 3, 8, 13, 35, 127;
    celebration of, 94; critical inquiry
    of, 11; feminist attitude to, 10; in
    feminist cultural studies
    perspective, 34; masculine
    subculture of, 27; master narrative
    of, 12, 15, 16, 53, 62, 72, 122, 215
    (in USSR, 216–17)
space race, 10–11
space-off perspective, 3
spaceship, as icon, 14–19, 28, 41, 44–9,
    52, 63, 70
Spiritual Alliance, 160
spirituality, 28, 32, 36–7, 38, 39, 83, 106
Sputnik, 75, 80, 82, 83, 85, 100, 102,
    175, 188, 197
Star Wars, 11
Stephanie, an American astrologer, 124,
    126–7, 137

Stephens, Holly DeNio, 133
story-telling, 39–40
Struve, Otto, 174
Suvin, Darko, 50–1, 56, 62, 69, 70
Sveta, a Russian astrologer, 128
swimming with dolphins, 27, 180–1,
   210, 211
synchronicity, concept of, 146
Szilard, Leo, 'The Voice of the
   Dolphins', 187

Tavolga, William, 189–90
technoscientific venture, 15, 16, 21, 28,
   29, 54, 84, 85, 86
Tereshkova, Valentina, 88, 111–13, 217;
   wedding of, 113
terraforming, 24, 85, 86, 92–117
toadfish, communication of, 165–6
Tomilin, A.G., *Dolphins Serve Man*,
   204
trickster, figure of, 192, 225
Tsiolkovsky, Konstantin, 8, 106, 128
Turner, Frederick J., 79

UFOs, 160; stories about, 82
Ukraine, dolphin research centre, 180
Ulubekov, A.T., 108
uncontrollability, 15
Union of Soviet Socialist Republics
   (USSR): 1917 Revolution, 97;
   collapse of, 42, 46, 81, 180
Universal Feminine, 62, 63
Universal Man, 31
Universe, as incomprehensible, 82
uplift, 68–9
Ursul, A.D., 96
Utopia, 8, 22; feminist, 222

Vasiliev, Dr, 82, 89
VDNKh exhibition park, 46, 55
Venus, 104

Vera, a Russian astrologer, 46–7, 125,
   126, 136
Verne, Jules, 10
Victoria, an American astrologer, 130
Victoria, an IKI mathematician, 82–3
virility, 55
Vostock space ship, 27

Walsh, Don, 21
Warren, Karen, 29
weightlessness, 113; and gender, 88
Weird Tales, 44
Wernick, A., 38
wet live-in with dolphins, 197–201, 210
Whale Nation, 202
whales, 18, 33, 66
Where All Roads Into Space Begin, 96
White Desert Sun, 96–9
wilderness, 19, 20, 21–3, 40, 78, 79, 87;
   as symbol, 98; as *topos*, 27;
   reinvention of, 23
wildness, 181, 194; of nature, 7;
   reintroduction of dolphins, 182
will, to, 84–7
Winterson, Jeanette, *Boating for
   Beginners*, 15, 216, 218–19, 220–2
Wolfe, Tom, 87
woman, as icon, 7, 8, 15, 18
woman/nature relationship, 19, 28, 29,
   133, 135, 136, 163, 206, 215, 222
women: exiled from divine space, 157;
   role of, in myth, 131
World Commission on Environment
   and Development (WCED), 20, 94
worship, desire for, 21–3

Yablokov, Aleksei, 205
Yefremov, I., *The Andromeda Nebula*, 174

Zhanna, an IKI engineer, 82, 84
Zodiac, 59, 147, 149, 150, 151, 220